T0224927

Information Retrieval Models

Foundations and Relationships

Synthesis Lectures on Information Concepts, Retrieval, and Services

Editor
Gary Machionini, *University of North Carolina, Chapel Hill*

Synthesis Lectures on Information Concepts, Retrieval, and Services is edited by Gary Marchionini of the University of North Carolina. The series will publish 50- to 100-page publications on topics pertaining to information science and applications of technology to information discovery, production, distribution, and management. The scope will largely follow the purview of premier information and computer science conferences, such as ASIST, ACM SIGIR, ACM/IEEE JCDL, and ACM CIKM. Potential topics include, but are not limited to: data models, indexing theory and algorithms, classification, information architecture, information economics, privacy and identity, scholarly communication, bibliometrics and webometrics, personal information management, human information behavior, digital libraries, archives and preservation, cultural informatics, information retrieval evaluation, data fusion, relevance feedback, recommendation systems, question answering, natural language processing for retrieval, text summarization, multimedia retrieval, multilingual retrieval, and exploratory search.

Information Retrieval Models: Foundations and Relationships
Thomas Roelleke
2013

Key Issues Regarding Digital Libraries: Evaluation and Integration
Rao Shen, Marcos André Gonçalves, and Edward A. Fox
2013

Visual Information Retrieval using Java and LIRE
Mathias Lux and Oge Marques
2013

On the Efficient Determination of Most Near Neighbors: Horseshoes, Hand Grenades, Web Search and Other Situations When Close is Close Enough
Mark S. Manasse
2012

Multimedia Information Retrieval
Stefan Rüger
2009

Online Multiplayer Games
William Sims Bainbridge
2009

Information Architecture: The Design and Integration of Information Spaces
Wei Ding and Xia Lin
2009

Reading and Writing the Electronic Book
Catherine C. Marshall
2009

Hypermedia Genes: An Evolutionary Perspective on Concepts, Models, and Architectures
Nuno M. Guimarães and Luís M. Carrico
2009

Understanding User-Web Interactions via Web Analytics
Bernard J. (Jim) Jansen
2009

XML Retrieval
Mounia Lalmas
2009

Faceted Search
Daniel Tunkelang
2009

Introduction to Webometrics: Quantitative Web Research for the Social Sciences
Michael Thelwall
2009

Exploratory Search: Beyond the Query-Response Paradigm
Ryen W. White and Resa A. Roth
2009

New Concepts in Digital Reference
R. David Lankes
2009

Automated Metadata in Multimedia Information Systems: Creation, Refinement, Use in Surrogates, and Evaluation
Michael G. Christel
2009

Information Retrieval Models: Foundations and Relationships
Thomas Roelleke

ISBN: 978-3-031-01200-6   paperback
ISBN: 978-3-031-02328-6   ebook

DOI 10.1007/978-3-031-02328-6

A Publication in Springer series
SYNTHESIS LECTURES ON INFORMATION CONCEPTS, RETRIEVAL, AND SERVICES

Lecture #27
Series Editor: Gary Machionini, *University of North Carolina, Chapel Hill*
Series ISSN
Synthesis Lectures on Information Concepts, Retrieval, and Services
Print 1947-945X   Electronic 1947-9468

Information Retrieval Models

Foundations and Relationships

Thomas Roelleke
Queen Mary University of London

SYNTHESIS LECTURES ON INFORMATION CONCEPTS, RETRIEVAL, AND SERVICES #27

ABSTRACT

Information Retrieval (IR) models are a core component of IR research and IR systems. The past decade brought a consolidation of the family of IR models, which by 2000 consisted of relatively isolated views on TF-IDF (Term-Frequency times Inverse-Document-Frequency) as the weighting scheme in the vector-space model (VSM), the probabilistic relevance framework (PRF), the binary independence retrieval (BIR) model, BM25 (Best-Match Version 25, the main instantiation of the PRF/BIR), and language modelling (LM). Also, the early 2000s saw the arrival of divergence from randomness (DFR).

Regarding intuition and simplicity, though LM is clear from a probabilistic point of view, several people stated: "It is easy to understand TF-IDF and BM25. For LM, however, we understand the math, but we do not fully understand why it works."

This book takes a horizontal approach gathering the foundations of TF-IDF, PRF, BIR, Poisson, BM25, LM, probabilistic inference networks (PIN's), and divergence-based models. The aim is to create a consolidated and balanced view on the main models.

A particular focus of this book is on the "relationships between models." This includes an overview over the main frameworks (PRF, logical IR, VSM, generalized VSM) and a pairing of TF-IDF with other models. It becomes evident that TF-IDF and LM measure the same, namely the dependence (overlap) between document and query. The Poisson probability helps to establish probabilistic, non-heuristic roots for TF-IDF, and the Poisson parameter, average term frequency, is a binding link between several retrieval models and model parameters.

KEYWORDS

Information Retrieval (IR) Models, Foundations & Relationships, TF-IDF, probability of relevance framework (PRF), Poisson, BM25, language modelling (LM), divergence from randomness (DFR), probabilistic roots of IR models

To my father, Anton Roelleke.

"Knowing some basics of math is useful in life."

Contents

List of Figures

Preface

"Why did you never write a book?" "I started one, and even a second one; but I never finished them, because I found it impossible to keep the notation consistent." This reply by Stephen Robertson—in a discussion about why writing books takes long and finishing feels impossible when aiming for perfection—was a main motivation to work on a book about IR models and theory. The material went into this M&C title on "IR Models: Foundations & Relationships."

Over the years, I have witnessed several statements on retrieval models. "TF-IDF is purely heuristic;" "TF-IDF is not a model, it is a weighting scheme in the vector-space model;" "LM is a clean probabilistic approach;" "LM is full of hacks and holes;" "TF-IDF is intuitive; we know why it works; it is still not clear why LM works."

TF-IDF is still the best known model, at least outside of the IR community. Inside of the IR research community, BM25 and LM are gaining ground. BM25 is viewed as being a heuristic composition of PRF-based, and therefore well-defined, parameters. BM25 replaced TF-IDF in the mid 90s, though there is a close connection between the two, and in current literature we often find the BM25 formulation involving the IDF. LM is a clean probabilistic approach, and while surprisingly simple it is a very effective approach to IR. There is an interesting perception of LM. Whereas the mathematical formulation has been described as clean and even "simple," there is the view "it is not clear why LM works." Also, there is the issue regarding the relationship between the PRF/BM25 and LM.

While TF-IDF and BM25 are intuitive but there is the view that they are "heuristic," LM is a clean and probabilistic approach, but there are issues regarding intuition. There is a similar aspect regarding BIR and Poisson. Whereas the BIR model is widely known and understood, its generalization, the Poisson model, and its role in showing the probabilistic roots of TF-IDF may be less known.

Last but not least, there is DFR (divergence from randomness). Several researchers told me: "We will never understand it." My confession is that I thought I had understood DFR, but when consolidating material for this book, I had to revisit several foundations to arrive at an explanatory formulation.

This book brings together on around 100 pages an account of the main formulae that I believe form the mathematical core to describe the foundations of and relationships between models. There are many formulae, but I hope that this account helps to consolidate the state-of-the-art of retrieval models.

The Morgan & Claypool lecture Zhai [2009] on "Statistical Language Models for Information Retrieval," by ChengXiang Zhai, is the M&C title most closely related to this book on

IR Models. With regard to LM, Zhai's book is much more comprehensive than this book, in particular with regard to smoothing techniques and application-domains of LM.

This lecture book takes a horizontal approach pulling together the foundations for the main strands of IR models. Care has been taken to achieve a notation that is consistent across different retrieval models. A particular emphasis of this book is on the relationships between retrieval models.

Special effort went into the index and into hyper referencing in this book. Regarding the paper version, the hyper referencing shows the page number to facilitate navigation. The hyper-links in the electronic version make it quick (and hopefully easy) to tack between models, and to explore equations.

Thomas Roelleke
May 2013

Acknowledgments

I express my thanks to the colleagues who showed to me the ways into IR models and theory: Norbert Fuhr, Gianni Amati, Keith van Rijsbergen, Stephen Robertson, Hugo Zaragoza, Arjen deVries, Djoerd Hiemstra, Fabio Crestani, Mounia Lalmas, Fabrizio Sebastiani, Ingo Frommholz, ChengXiang Zhai, and Riccardo Baeza-Yates. It is thanks to their knowledge, comments, and questions, that I kept being encouraged to refine and rewrite formulae again, and all over again. Also, my students Jun Wang, Hengzhi Wu, Fred Forst, Hany Azzam, Miguel Martinez-Alvarez, and Marco Bonzanini have greatly contributed to shape our view on what constitutes and relates IR models.

This lecture book on "IR Models" overlaps somewhat with another book in preparation: "Probabilistic logical models for DB+IR." While in this lecture, the focus is on the foundations and relationships of IR models, the DB+IR book takes these as prerequisite knowledge to represent knowledge, and to implement retrieval models and retrieval tasks.

Special thanks go to Riccardo Baeza-Yates. While visiting Yahoo Labs at Barcelona Media, I had the peace and inspiration to consolidate research results regarding abstraction and probability theory in IR models. This led to the groundwork for this book. I hope that the collection of material and formulae will help to establish common foundations, including a general notation, for IR.

Many thanks go to Gianni Amati and Stephen Robertson for explaining on several occasions, with their knowledge and views, the hidden but so important details. Also, the comments by Andreas Kaltenbrunner and Norman Fenton on the notation proposed in this book were very helpful when consolidating the final formulation. Thanks to my colleagues Tassos Tombros and Fabrizio Smeraldi for proofreading the final version.

I am indebted to Djoerd Hiemstra, Gianni Amati, Miguel Martinez-Alvarez, Marco Bonzanini, and Ingo Frommholz, who were willing to explore some of the details and formulae of this book. I am also grateful for the suggestions and comments by Norbert Fuhr and Keith van Rijsbergen. Finally, I would like to thank Gary Marchionini and Diane Cerra from Morgan & Claypool for supporting a book on models and theory.

When trying to finish a book, work becomes part of private life. My family has been patient on many occasions, asking only sometimes: "Are you in your math world again? Can you come to our world?"

Thomas Roelleke
May 2013

CHAPTER 1

Introduction

1.1 STRUCTURE AND CONTRIBUTION OF THIS BOOK

This book is structured into two main chapters: Chapter 2, Foundations of IR Models, and Chapter 3, Relationships between IR Models. Many parts of this book are about widely known models. The contribution of this book is to consolidate foundations and to highlight relationships. We view models as members of a family, having one ancestor: probability theory. There is no quest to show that one model is superior to another.

Most of the content of this book is based on published material, however, some insights have not been published previously or are not widely known. These are listed in the summary, 4.1. The outlook, 4.2, arranges retrieval models in a lattice to position TF-IDF, BM25, and LM with respect to each other. This extends toward a lattice positioning retrieval and evaluation. We also look at potential roads ahead that could lead to extensions of existing models or even to new models for IR.

1.2 BACKGROUND: A TIMELINE OF IR MODELS

Figure 1.1 shows a timeline of IR models.

Maron and Kuhns [1960] is viewed as the inspiration for probabilistic IR. Earlier research includes the work of Zipf and Luhn in the 50s, and these studies into the distribution of document frequencies inspired the area of "IR models."

The 70s were dominated by the vector-space model (VSM), Salton [1971], in combination with TF-IDF, Salton et al. [1975], and the relevance feedback model, Rocchio [1971]. The probabilistic model matured, Robertson and Sparck-Jones [1976], and Croft and Harper [1979] showed that the model works for missing relevance information.

In the 80s, Fuzzy retrieval, Bookstein [1980], and extended Boolean, Salton et al. [1983], were proposed, but the models did not surpass the VSM and TF-IDF.

In the late 80s, logical IR, van Rijsbergen [1986], entered the stage, leading to various research branches, one being the endeavour to relate $P(d \rightarrow q)$ to the VSM Wong and Yao [1995] and to TF-IDF.

The mid 90s saw BM25 taking the lead, Robertson and Walker [1994], Robertson et al. [1995], where the pivoted document length, Singhal et al. [1996], became known to be a crucial component.

The late 90s saw language modeling (LM) emerging, Ponte and Croft [1998]. Challenges included to relate LM to the probability of relevance framework (PRF), Lafferty and Zhai [2003],

ICTIR 2009 and ICTIR 2011
Roelleke and Wang [2008]: TF-IDF Uncovered
Luk [2008]: Event Spaces
Roelleke and Wang [2006]: Parallel Derivation of Models
Fang and Zhai [2005]: Axiomatic approach
He and Ounis [2005]: TF in BM25 and DFR
Metzler and Croft [2004]: LM and PIN's
Robertson [2005]: Event Spaces
Robertson [2004]: Understanding IDF
Sparck-Jones et al. [2003]: LM and Relevance
Croft and Lafferty [2003], Lafferty and Zhai [2003]: LM book
Zaragoza et al. [2003]: Bayesian extension to LM
Bruza and Song [2003]: probabilistic dependencies in LM
Amati and van Rijsbergen [2002]: DFR
Lavrenko and Croft [2001]: Relevance-based LM
Hiemstra [2000]: TF-IDF and LM
Sparck-Jones et al. [2000]: probabilistic model: status
Ponte and Croft [1998]: LM
Brin and Page [1998a], Kleinberg [1999]: Pagerank and Hits
Robertson et al. [1994], Singhal et al. [1996]:
Pivoted Document Length Normalization
Wong and Yao [1995]: $P(d \rightarrow q)$
Robertson and Walker [1994], Robertson et al. [1995]: 2-Poisson, BM25
Church and Gale [1995], Margulis [1992]: Poisson
Fuhr [1992b]: Probabilistic Models in IR
Turtle and Croft [1991, 1990]: PIN's
Fuhr [1989]: Models for Probabilistic Indexing
Cooper [1991, 1988, 1994]: Beyond Boole, Probability Theory in IR: An Encumbrance
Deerwester et al. [1990], Dumais et al. [1988]: Latent semantic indexing
van Rijsbergen [1986, 1989]: $P(d \rightarrow q)$
Bookstein [1980], Salton et al. [1983]: Fuzzy, extended Boolean
Croft and Harper [1979]: BIR without relevance
Robertson and Sparck-Jones [1976]: BIR
Salton [1971], Salton et al. [1975]: VSM, TF-IDF
Rocchio [1971]: Relevance feedback
Maron and Kuhns [1960]: On Relevance, Probabilistic Indexing, and IR

Figure 1.1: Timeline of research on IR models.

Lavrenko and Croft [2001], Sparck-Jones et al. [2003]. Moreover, LM was thought to poten-tially bring a probabilistic justification to heuristic TF-IDF, Hiemstra [2000]. Pathbreaking "ap-proaches for using probabilistic dependencies," Bruza and Song [2003], point at capturing de-pendencies, and this is of growing importance, Hou et al. [2011].

Then, Amati and van Rijsbergen [2002], "Divergence from Randomness (DFR)," created a new branch of retrieval models, or, as some will say, a new root of models. This was followed by more meta-work on models, such as Fang and Zhai [2005], "Axiomatic Approach," and Roelleke and Wang [2006], "Parallel Derivation." Similar to the early work in Hiemstra [2000], the motivation was to relate IR models with each other. Robertson [2004] discussed theoretical arguments for IDF, revisiting the BIR-based justification of IDF. Robertson [2005] pointed at the issue regarding "event spaces." Luk [2008] picked this up and questioned the assumptions made in Lafferty and Zhai [2003] when relating LM to the probability of relevance. Roelleke and Wang [2008] presented a study where TF-IDF was derived from $P(d|q)$, and this is related to the way LM is based on $P(q|d)$. Robertson and Zaragoza [2009], "The PRF: BM25 and Beyond," gathered the state-of-the-art foundations and formulation of PRF and BM25.

While the theory underlying TF-IDF, LM and PRF/BM25 evolved, van Rijsbergen [2004] promoted "The Geometry of IR." The approach calls for "back-to-the-roots," and advocates the well-defined combination of concepts of geometry (vectors, matrices) and concepts of probability theory.

The conferences ICTIR 2009 and ICTIR 2011 brought several new insights into the world of IR models. Among others, the topics "relationships," Aly and Demeester [2011], and "dependencies," Hou et al. [2011], point at promising research directions. The recent research is more specific and adventurous than this book about foundations and relationships.

IR models are introduced in several text books such as Baeza-Yates and Ribeiro-Neto [2011]: 2nd edition of "Modern IR;" Zhai [2009]: "Statistical LM for IR;" Manning et al. [2008]: "Introduction to Information Retrieval;" Belew [2000]: "Finding out about;" Grossman and Frieder [2004]: 2nd edition of "IR: Algorithms and Heuristics;" van Rijsbergen [1979]: "Information Retrieval."

1.3   NOTATION

Notation ... it is a tedious start, however, it is a must-have. Whereas the "document frequency of a term" is an intuitive and consistent notion, the "within-document term frequency (of a term)" is familiar, but causes inconsistency in the mathematical world. I was confronted with this issue in the mid 90s when Peter Schaeuble pointed out that the "inverse term frequency of a document" is a useful parameter, however, when defining "itf" in a dual way to the commonly used "inverse document frequency," then there is a clash with the notion "term frequency." In our work over the past decade where we tried to achieve the probabilistic logical modeling of *all* IR models, the notation issue "term frequency" turned out to be a hurdle important to be overcome; *see also* Section 1.3.1 (p. 6), TF Notation Issue; Section 3.5.2 (p. 90), General Matrix Framework: TF Notation Issue.

For achieving a consistent notation which is applicable across different models, we apply a notation that makes explicit the "event space." For example, we apply $n_D(t, c)$ and $n_L(t, c)$ to refer to *Document-based* and *Location-based* counts (frequencies), i.e., the subscript in n_D and n_L is the event space. In traditional IR notation, the symbol n_t is applied, where $n_t := n_D(t, c)$ is the number of *Documents* in which term t occurs. This is also denoted as $df(t, c) := n_D(t, c)$, the document frequency of term t in collection c. Regarding the Location-based frequency, some authors employed capital TF, i.e., $\text{TF} := n_L(t, c)$, to refer to the number of times term t occurs in the collection c.

Figure 1.2 shows step-by-step the basic sets, frequencies, and probabilities.

Special care has been taken to achieve a notation that fits all models, and that underlines the dualities between probabilities. The first block shows the basic variables and sets. The main variables are: term t, document d, query q, collection c, and relevance r. The main types of sets are Documents, Locations, and Terms. For example, D_c is the set of documents in collection c, and so forth. The lines separating groups of rows elicit that for the conditionals, namely document d, query q, collection c, and relevance r, frequencies are denoted in a systematic way.

Below the first block of rows, there is a block regarding the document-related and query-related frequencies (Location-based). For example, $\text{tf}_d := n_L(t, d)$ is the number of *Locations* at which term t occurs in document d.

This is followed by two blocks regarding collection-oriented and relevance-oriented frequencies: Location-based and Document-based frequencies. For example, $\text{tf}_c := \text{lf}(t, c) := n_L(t, c)$ is the number of *Locations* at which term t occurs in collection c, and $N_L(c)$ is the total number of *Locations* in collection c. $\text{df}(t, c) := n_D(t, c)$ is the number of *Documents* in which term t occurs in collection c, and $N_D(c)$ is the total number of *Documents* in collection c. The same formalism applies to the relevant documents, the "collection" r.

To be precise, the counts are defined as follows: $n_L(t, c) := n_{L_c}(t)$, and $N_L(c) := N_{L_c}$. The notation where we avoid the double subscript is preferable for readability.

The next block shows Term-based frequencies: $n_T(d, c)$ is the number of *Terms* in document d in collection c, and $N_T(c)$ is the number of *Terms* in collection c. We will make little use of Term-based frequencies, however, they are included here to emphasize the duality between Documents and Terms, i.e., $\text{df}(t, c) := n_D(t, c)$, the document frequency of term t, is dual to $\text{tf}(d, c) := n_T(d, c)$, the term frequency of document d.

Then, there are averages (for parameter u): $u = c$ is for the set of all documents in the collection; $u = r$ is for the set of relevant documents; $u = \bar{r}$ is for the set of non-relevant documents. These are the most common sets, but the averages can be denoted for any set of documents (e.g., elite sets).

The expression $\text{avgdl}(u)$ denotes the average document length over the documents in set D_u. Then, $\text{pivdl}(d, u) := \text{dl}/\text{avgdl}(u)$ is the pivoted document length of document d; it is greater than 1.0 for long documents, and smaller for short documents.

Moreover, there are several "average term frequencies." Let $\lambda(t, u)$ denote the average frequency over *all* documents in the set D_u. Let $\text{avgtf}(t, u)$ denote the average frequency over *term-elite* documents, i.e., the average value of tf_d over the documents in which the term occurs. Finally, let $\lambda(t, u_q)$ denote the average frequency over all the documents in the *query-elite* set. The query-elite set is the set of documents that contain at least one query term (disjunctive interpretation of query). Note that in the term-elite set, for all documents, $\text{tf}_d \geq 1$, whereas in the

Book's notation	Description of events, sets, and frequencies	Traditional notation
t, d, q, c, r	term t, document d, query q, collection c, relevant r	
D_c, D_r	$D_c = \{d_1,...\}$ set of *Documents* in collection c ; D_r : relevant documents	
T_c, T_r	$T_c = \{t_1,...\}$ set of *Terms* in collection c; T_r : terms that occur in relevant documents	
L_c, L_r	$L_c = \{l_1,...\}$ set of *Locations* in collection c; L_r : locations in relevant documents	
$n_L(t, d)$	number of *Locations* at which term t occurs in document d	tf, tf_d
$N_L(d)$	number of *Locations* in document d (document length)	dl
$n_L(t, q)$	number of *Locations* at which term t occurs in query q	qtf, tf_q
$N_L(q)$	number of *Locations* in query q (query length)	ql
$n_L(t, c)$	number of *Locations* at which term t occurs in collection c	TF, cf(t)
$N_L(c)$	number of *Locations* in collection c	
$n_L(t, r)$	number of *Locations* at which term t occurs in the set L_r	
$N_L(r)$	number of *Locations* in the set L_r	
$n_D(t, c)$	number of *Documents* in which term t occurs in the set D_c of collection c	n_t, df(t)
$N_D(c)$	number of *Documents* in the set D_c of collection c	N
$n_D(t, r)$	number of *Documents* in which term t occurs in the set D_r of relevant documents	r_t
$N_D(r)$	number of *Documents* in the set D_r of relevant documents	R
$n_T(d, c)$	number of *Terms* in document d in collection c	
$N_T(c)$	number of *Terms* in collection c	
Let u denote a collection associated with a set of documents. For example: $u = c$, or $u = r$, or $u = \hat{r}$.		
avgdl(u)	average document length: avgdl(u) = $N_L(u)/N_D(u)$ where the collection is implicit, we use avgdl	avgdl
pivdl(d, u)	pivoted document length: pivdl(d, u) = $N_L(d)/$avgdl(u) = dl$/$avgdl(u) where the collection is implicit, we use pivdl(d)	pivdl
$\lambda(t, u)$	average term frequency over *all* documents in D_u: $n_L(t,u)/N_D(u)$	
avgtf(t,u)	average term frequency over *term-elite* documents: $n_L(t,u)/n_D(t,u)$	
$\lambda(t, u_q)$	average term frequency over *query-elite* documents in D_{u_q}: $n_L(t,u_q)/N_D(u_q)$ D_{u_q} : set of documents that contain at least one query term	

Book's notation	Description of probabilities	Traditional notation
$P_L(t\mid d) := \frac{n_L(t,d)}{N_L(d)}$	Location-based within-document term probability	$P(t\mid d) = \frac{tf_d}{\mid d\mid}, \mid d\mid = \mathrm{dl} = N_L(d)$
$P_L(t\mid q) := \frac{n_L(t,q)}{N_L(q)}$	Location-based within-query term probability	$P(t\mid q) = \frac{tf_q}{\mid q\mid}, \mid q\mid = \mathrm{ql} = N_L(q)$
$P_L(t\mid c) := \frac{n_L(t,c)}{N_L(c)}$	Location-based within-collection term probability	$P(t\mid c) = \frac{tf_c}{\mid c\mid}, \mid c\mid = N_L(c)$
$P_L(t\mid r) := \frac{n_L(t,r)}{N_L(r)}$	Location-based within-relevance term probability	
$P_D(t\mid c) := \frac{n_D(t,c)}{N_D(c)}$	Document-based within-collection term probability	$P(t) = \frac{n_t}{N}, N = N_D(c)$
$P_D(t\mid r) := \frac{n_D(t,r)}{N_D(r)}$	Document-based within-relevance term probability	$P(t) = \frac{r_t}{R}, R = N_D(r)$
$P_T(d\mid c) := \frac{n_T(d,c)}{N_T(c)}$	Term-based document probability	
$P_{avg}(t\mid c) := \frac{avgtf(t,c)}{avgdl(c)}$	probability that t occurs in document with average length; avgtf($t\mid c$) $\leq$ avgdl(c)	

Figure 1.2: Notation: sets, symbols, and probabilities.

query-elite set, $\text{tf}_d = 0$ may occur for some terms. This aspect is important when estimating the probability $P(\text{tf}_d = 0|\text{set of documents})$.

In the lower part of Figure 1.2, the main probabilities are listed. For example, $P_L(t|d)$ is the Location-based term probability in document d, and $P_D(t|c)$ is the Document-based term probability in collection c. The subscripts D and L indicate the respective event space, namely Documents and Locations. The duality between probabilities is in particular evident when considering the Term-based document probability $P_T(d|c)$, a probability we show to underline the duality, but we will not utilize this probability in this book on foundations. Finally, there is the probability $P_{\text{avg}}(t|c) = \text{avgtf}(t,c)/\text{avgdl}(c)$. This is the probability to observe a term in a document with average length. We will refer to this probability frequently when discussing relationships between models.

The notation meets the requirement to capture all parameters of the main IR models. The type of the event space (D, T, or L) is specified as a subscript. The instantiation of a space (c, r, $\bar{r}$) is specified as a subscript of the event space or as a parameter in frequency counts. For example, D_r is the set of relevant documents, and $n_D(t,r) := n_{D_r}(t)$ is the number of documents with term t.

The notation allows us to refer in a non-ambiguous way to document-related and to collection-related parameters, and to document-based and location-based frequencies. This book's notation maintains the traditional notation. For example: $\text{tf}_d := \text{lf}(t,d) := n_L(t,d)$ is the "within-document term frequency," and $\text{tf}_c := \text{lf}(t,d) := n_L(t,c)$ is the "within-collection term frequency," and $\text{df}(t,c) := n_D(t,c)$ is the "document frequency." The notation was developed as part of the general matrix framework for IR, Roelleke et al. [2006]. A summary of the framework is in Section 3.5 (p. 88), General Matrix Framework. Systematically, if we refer to $\text{df}(t,c) := n_D(t,c)$ as the *document frequency of term t*, then $\text{tf}(d,c) := n_T(d,c)$ is the *term frequency of document d*. We look closer at this notation issue.

1.3.1   THE NOTATION ISSUE "TERM FREQUENCY"

In traditional IR terminology, the notion "term frequency" refers to the within-document location frequency of a term, that is: $\text{tf}_d := \text{lf}(t,d) := n_L(t,d)$ is the within-document term frequency. Analogously, $\text{tf}_c := \text{lf}(t,c) := n_L(t,c)$ is the collection-wide term frequency.

The notion "document frequency" refers to the number of documents that contain a term, that is: $\text{df}(t,c) := n_D(t,c)$ is the within-document term frequency. When trying to create the duality between "df" and "tf," then there is an inconsistency, as the following formulation shows.

> $\text{df}(t,c) := n_D(t,c)$: "document frequency of term t in collection c:"
> number of *Documents* in which term t occurs in collection c

In the dual formulation, exchange the roles of document and term:

> $\text{tf}(d,c) := n_T(d,c)$: "term frequency of document d in collection c:"
> number of *Terms* in document d in collection c

This mathematical duality between document and term frequency follows from the Term-Document matrix; see Section 3.5 (p. 88), General-Matrix-Framework.

To overcome this notation issue, we define tf_d and tf_c as follows:

$\text{tf}_d := \text{lf}(t, d) := n_L(t, d)$: "(term) location frequency of term t in document d:" number of *Locations* at which term t occurs in document d

$\text{tf}_c := \text{lf}(t, c) := n_L(t, c)$: "(term) location frequency of term t in collection c:" number of *Locations* at which term t occurs in collection c

We avoid expressions such as $\text{tf}(t, d)$ or $c(t, d)$ ("c" for "count") for within-document counts. Also, we employ tf_c instead of the sometimes used capital TF for the collection-wide term frequency, since TF is the place holder for any TF quantification. The collection-wide term frequency, tf_c, has also been denoted in the literature as "collection frequency $cf(t)$," however, in a dual notation, the collection frequency is the number of collections in which the term occurs. This parameter is for example useful in large-scale distributed IR, for data source selection.

The tedious details of notation are "heavy going," however, a consistent notation will advance IR research. When discussing TF-IDF with a mathematical researcher, he pointed at the TF-issue within minutes, and by resolving it, it became much easier to express IR in matlab. Also, an early review of this section by an expert in Bayesian reasoning immediately asked for clarification on the TF notation.

Dual definitions of basic notions such as IDF (inverse document frequency) and ITF (inverse term frequency) are difficult to achieve in a less formal notation. The event-space-based notation with sets (subscripts) T for Terms, D for Documents, and L for Locations, allows for non-ambiguous definitions. This helps to work out the foundations of and relationships between IR models.

1.3.2   NOTATION: ZHAI'S BOOK AND THIS BOOK

Figure 1.3 shows the notation used in Zhai [2009], "Statistical LM for IR." The figure relates the notations to improve the readability of both books.

Zhai's M&C book on LM	This M&C book on IR Models
page 31: Smoothing Using Collection Language Model	
Let $p(w\|C)$ denote the collection language model.	Let $P_L(t\|c)$ denote the collection language model.
$$p(w\|C) = \frac{\sum_{D\in C} c(w,D)}{\sum_{D\in C}\|D\|}$$	$$P_L(t\|c) = \frac{\sum_{d\in c}\mathrm{tf}_d}{\sum_{d\in c}\mathrm{dl}} = \frac{n_L(t,c)}{\sum_{d\in c}N_L(d)} = \frac{\mathrm{tf}_c}{N_L(c)}$$
w is a word (term), C is the collection (set of documents), D is a document, $c(w,D)$ is the within-document word (term) count, $\|D\|$ is the document length (norm).	t is a term, c is a collection, d is a document, tf_d is the within-document term frequency, dl is the document length.
Alternative estimate based on the contribution of documents:	Estimate via total probability theorem; documents are disjoint events.
$$p(w\|C) = \frac{1}{\|C\|}\sum_{D\in C}\frac{c(w,D)}{\|D\|}$$	$$P(t\|c) = \sum_{d\in D_c} P(t\|d,c)\cdot P(d\|c)$$
$\|C\|$ is the number of documents; each document contributes equally.	Each document contributes with its prior, $P(d\|c)$; can be uniform (equi-probable).
page 49: Translation Model	
Let V be the vocabulary (set of all terms). Let $Q = q_1,\dots,q_m$ be the query; q_i is a query word.	Let $q = t_1,\dots,t_m$ be the query; t_i is a query term.
$$p(Q\|D) = \prod_{i=1}^{m}\sum_{w\in V} p(q_i\|w)\,p(w\|\Theta_D)$$ $$p(w\|\Theta_D) = \sum_{w'\in V} p(w\|w')\,p(w'\|D)$$	$$P(q\|d) = \prod_{i=1}^{m}\sum_{t\in V} P(t_i\|t)\cdot P(t\|d)$$ $$P(t\|d) = \sum_{t'\in V} P(t\|t')\cdot P(t'\|d)$$
page 55, KL-Divergence Retrieval Model	
$$\mathrm{score}(D,Q) = -D(\Theta_Q\|\|\Theta_D)$$	$$\mathrm{score}(d,q) = -D_{\mathrm{KL}}\left(P_q\|\|P_d\right)$$
LM ranking, $\log P(q\|d)$, is the same as ranking based on the negative cross entropy.	In this book, we view the score to be related to the difference between divergences.
	$$\mathrm{score}_{\mathrm{LM}}(d,q) = D_{\mathrm{KL}}\left(P_q\|\|P_c\right) - D_{\mathrm{KL}}\left(P_q\|\|P_d\right)$$ $$\mathrm{score}_{\mathrm{TF\text{-}IDF}}(d,q) = D_{\mathrm{KL}}\left(P_d\|\|P_c\right) - D_{\mathrm{KL}}\left(P_d\|\|P_q\right)$$
page 65, Relevance Model	
$$O(R\|D,Q) \propto \frac{p(D\|Q,R=r)}{p(D\|Q,R=\bar{r})}$$	$$O(r\|d,q) \propto \frac{P(d\|q,r)}{P(d\|q,\bar{r})}$$
R: event and variable; D: document event; Q: query event.	r: event "relevant;" $R = \{r,\bar{r}\}$: set of events; d: document event; q: query event; $D = \{d_1,\dots,d_n\}$: set of documents; $Q = \{q_1,\dots,q_m\}$: set of queries.

Figure 1.3: Notation: Zhai's book on LM and this book on IR models.

CHAPTER 2

Foundations of IR Models

The following list shows the structure of this chapter (the electronic version provides hyperlinks):

Section 2.1: TF-IDF

Section 2.2: PRF: The Probabilistic Relevance Framework

Section 2.3: BIR: Binary Independence Retrieval

Section 2.4: Poisson and 2-Poisson

Section 2.5: BM25: Best-Match Version 25

Section 2.6: LM: Language Modeling

Section 2.7: PIN's: Probabilistic Inference Networks

Section 2.8: Divergence-based Models (including DFR and KL-Divergence Model)

Section 2.9: Relevance-based Models (Rocchio, PRF and Lavrenko's relevance-based LM)

Section 2.10: Precision and Recall

Section 2.11: Summary (Model Overview in Figure 2.10)

This chapter presents and discusses the foundations of each model. We take a relatively isolated view on each model, indicating some relationships. Chapter 3 discusses the relationships in more detail.

2.1 TF-IDF

It may feel strange to get started with the "heuristic" model TF-IDF. The reason for having TF-IDF first is that TF-IDF is still a very popular model, and the best known IR model outside of IR research. This is probably because TF-IDF is very intuitive, and it has been around since the 60s, as a weighting scheme in the vector-space model (VSM).

Another reason to put TF-IDF first is that while being the most popular model, it is also the most criticized one. "TF-IDF is not a model; it is just a weighting scheme in the vector-space model." "TF-IDF is purely heuristic; it has no probabilistic roots." This book emphasizes that TF-IDF and LM are dual models that can be shown to be derived from the same root.

Moreover, TF-IDF is commonly accepted to be a simplified version of BM25. Also, the vector-space "model" is actually a framework in which TF-IDF, LM, and BM25 can be expressed, which is why the VSM is in Chapter 3.

We capture the main aspects of TF-IDF in the following definitions:

1. TF variants: Definition 2.1 and Definition 2.2;

2. DF and IDF variants: Definition 2.3 and Definition 2.4;

3. TF-IDF term weight: Definition 2.5;

4. TF-IDF RSV: Definition 2.6.

2.1.1 TF VARIANTS

Definition 2.1 TF Variants: $TF(t, d)$. $TF(t, d)$ is a quantification of the within-document term frequency, tf_d. The main variants are:

$$tf_d := TF_{\text{total}}(t, d) := lf_{\text{total}}(t, d) := n_L(t, d) \tag{2.1}$$

$$TF_{\text{sum}}(t, d) := lf_{\text{sum}}(t, d) := \frac{n_L(t, d)}{N_L(d)} \quad \left(= \frac{tf_d}{dl}\right) \tag{2.2}$$

$$TF_{\text{max}}(t, d) := lf_{\text{max}}(t, d) := \frac{n_L(t, d)}{n_L(t_{\text{max}}, d)} \tag{2.3}$$

$$TF_{\text{log}}(t, d) := lf_{\text{log}}(t, d) := \log(1 + n_L(t, d)) \quad \left(= \log(1 + tf_d)\right) \tag{2.4}$$

$$TF_{\text{frac}, K}(t, d) := lf_{\text{frac}, K}(t, d) := \frac{n_L(t, d)}{n_L(t, d) + K_d} \quad \left(= \frac{tf_d}{tf_d + K_d}\right) \tag{2.5}$$

$$TF_{\text{BM25}, k_1, b}(t, d) := lf_{\text{BM25}, k_1, b}(t, d) := \frac{n_L(t, d)}{n_L(t, d) + k_1 \cdot (b \cdot \text{pivdl}(d, c) + (1 - b))} \tag{2.6}$$

Here, $tf_d := n_L(t, d)$ captures the traditional notation, the "term frequency of term t in document d."

We include here the BM25-TF, although Section 2.5 is dedicated to BM25. This is to highlight that the BM25-TF is a special form of $TF_{\text{frac}, K}$. The BM25-TF chooses a parameter function K proportional to the pivoted documents length; the parameters k_1 and b adjust the impact of the pivotization. Strictly speaking, the parameter list should include the collection. For example: $TF_{\text{BM25}, k_1, b}(t, d, c)$. This is because the pivoted document length, $\text{pivdl}(d, c)$, depends on the collection. Then, for the parameter function K, the notation is $K(d, c)$ or $K_d(c)$. For simplicity, we often drop the collection where it is implicit, i.e., we use $\text{pivdl}(d)$ and K_d. Overall, the BM25-TF can be applied for TF-IDF, making the TF_{BM25}-IDF variant.

Analogously to $\mathrm{TF}(t,d)$, the next definition defines the variants of $\mathrm{TF}(t,c)$, the collection-wide term frequency.

Definition 2.2   TF Variants: $\mathrm{TF}(t,c)$. $\mathrm{TF}(t,c)$ is a quantification of the within-collection term frequency, tf_c. In analogy to $\mathrm{TF}(t,d)$, for $\mathrm{TF}(t,c)$, the main variants are:

$$\mathrm{tf}_c := \mathrm{TF}_{\mathrm{total}}(t,c) := \mathrm{lf}_{\mathrm{total}}(t,c) \ := \ n_L(t,c) \tag{2.7}$$

$$\mathrm{TF}_{\mathrm{sum}}(t,c) := \mathrm{lf}_{\mathrm{sum}}(t,c) \ := \ \frac{n_L(t,c)}{N_L(c)} \tag{2.8}$$

$$\left(= \frac{\mathrm{tf}_c}{\sum_d \mathrm{dl}} = \frac{\mathrm{tf}_c}{\mathrm{collection\_length}} \right) \tag{2.9}$$

$$\mathrm{TF}_{\mathrm{max}}(t,c) := \mathrm{lf}_{\mathrm{max}}(t,c) \ := \ \frac{n_L(t,c)}{n_L(t_{\mathrm{max}},c)} \tag{2.10}$$

$$\mathrm{TF}_{\mathrm{log}}(t,c) := \mathrm{lf}_{\mathrm{log}}(t,c) \ := \ \log(1 + n_L(t,c)) \quad (= \log(1 + \mathrm{tf}_c)) \tag{2.11}$$

$$\mathrm{TF}_{\mathrm{frac},K}(t,c) := \mathrm{lf}_{\mathrm{frac},K}(t,c) \ := \ \frac{n_L(t,c)}{n_L(t,c) + K_c} \quad \left(= \frac{\mathrm{tf}_c}{\mathrm{tf}_c + K_c} \right) \tag{2.12}$$

$$\mathrm{TF}_{\mathrm{BM25},k_1,b}(t,c) := \mathrm{lf}_{\mathrm{BM25},k_1,b}(t,c) \ := \ \frac{n_L(t,c)}{n_L(t,c) + k_1 \cdot (b \cdot \mathrm{pivcl}(c, \mathrm{collections}) + (1-b))} \tag{2.13}$$

$\mathrm{TF}(t,c)$ would be used to retrieve a "collection." This form of retrieval is required for distributed IR (database selection). Everything said about $\mathrm{TF}(t,d)$ applies to $\mathrm{TF}(t,c)$. Within the context of this book, however, we will not extend on $\mathrm{TF}(t,c)$. We apply only the total TF, $\mathrm{tf}_c := n_L(t,c)$, the "term frequency in the collection."

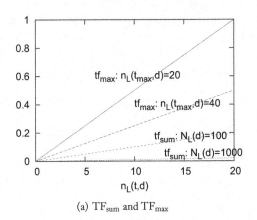

(a) $\mathrm{TF}_{\mathrm{sum}}$ and $\mathrm{TF}_{\mathrm{max}}$

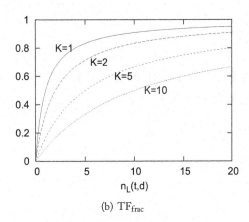

(b) $\mathrm{TF}_{\mathrm{frac}}$

Figure 2.1: TF Variants: $\mathrm{TF}_{\mathrm{sum}}$, $\mathrm{TF}_{\mathrm{max}}$, and $\mathrm{TF}_{\mathrm{frac}}$.

Figure 2.1 shows graphs for some of the main TF variants. These illustrate that $\mathrm{TF}_{\mathrm{max}}$ yields higher TF-values than $\mathrm{TF}_{\mathrm{sum}}$ does. The linear TF variants are not really important anymore, since

TF_{frac} (TF_{BM25}) delivers better and more stable quality. The latter yields relatively high TF-values already for small frequencies, and the curve saturates for large frequencies. The good and stable performance of BM25 indicates that this non-linear nature is key for achieving good retrieval quality. Small values of K lead to a steep rise and early saturation of the TF value, whereas large values of K lead to a smooth rise and delayed saturation.

TF_{total} corresponds to assuming "independence," and TF_{sum} does the same, but normalizes by the document length. TF_{total} and TF_{sum} are two extremes: TF_{total} is steep, too steep. It leads to a bias toward documents with many term occurrences. Therefore, the idea is to lower the curve. TF_{sum} is relatively flat, too flat. For large documents, TF_{sum} values tend to be small, and this disadvantages long documents, or, in other words, leads to a bias toward small documents. The variants TF_{max} and TF_{frac} (TF_{BM25}) mitigate the bias of TF_{total} and TF_{sum}.

The variant TF_{frac} is the general form of the BM25-TF. Whereas in TF_{frac}, the parameter function K can have any form, in TF_{BM25}, K is proportional to the pivoted document length ($pivdl(d, c) = dl/avgdl(c)$) and involves adjustment parameters (k_1, b). The common definition is:

$$K_{BM25, k_1, b}(d, c) := k_1 \cdot (b \cdot pivdl(d, c) + (1 - b)) \qquad (2.14)$$

For $b = 1$, K is equal to k_1 for average documents, less than k_1 for short documents, and greater than k_1 for long documents. Large b and large k_1 lead to a strong variation of K with respect to the document length. A strong variation of K means that the document length has a high impact on the retrieval score, whereby documents shorter than the average documents have an advantage over documents longer than the average.

The good retrieval quality of BM25 indicates that a non-linear form of TF, where TF grows faster for small occurrences than it grows in the linear case, but saturates for large occurrences, is conducive for retrieval quality. Therefore, we discuss in the following two non-linear TF's: TF_{log} and TF_{frac}.

2.1.2 TF_{log}: LOGARITHMIC TF

The logarithmic TF is defined as follows:

$$TF_{log}(t, d) := \log(1 + tf_d)$$

The logarithmic TF assigns less impact to subsequent occurrences than the total TF does. This aspect becomes clear when reconsidering that the logarithm is an approximation of the harmonic sum:

$$\ln(1 + n) \approx 1 + \frac{1}{2} + \ldots + \frac{1}{n} \qquad n > 0 \qquad (2.15)$$

To understand this approximation, we recall the following integral:

$$\int_1^{n+1} \frac{1}{z}\, dz = [\ln(z)]_1^{n+1} = \ln(n + 1)$$

With respect to $\mathrm{TF_{log}}$, the base of the logarithm is ranking invariant, since it is a constant:

$$\mathrm{TF_{log,base}}(t, d) := \frac{\ln(1 + \mathrm{tf}_d)}{\ln(\mathrm{base})}$$

Expressing the logarithm as the harmonic sum shows the type of dependence assumption underlying $\mathrm{TF_{log}}$. The first occurrence of a term counts in full, the second counts $1/2$, the third counts $1/3$, and so forth. This gives a particular insight into the type of dependence that is reflected by "bending" the total TF into a saturating curve.

Given this consideration of the logarithmic TF, the question is which dependence assumptions explain $\mathrm{TF_{frac}}$ and $\mathrm{TF_{BM25}}$?

2.1.3 $\mathrm{TF_{frac}}$: FRACTIONAL (RATIO-BASED) TF

What we refer to as "fractional TF" is a ratio:

$$\mathrm{ratio}(x, y) = \frac{x}{x + y} = \frac{\mathrm{tf}_d}{\mathrm{tf}_d + K_d} = \mathrm{TF_{frac}}, K(t, d)$$

Viewing TF as a ratio connects the TF and the probability mixtures commonly used in LM and Bayesian estimates, but this aspect is beyond the scope of this book.

Moreover, the ratio is related to the harmonic sum of squares.

$$\frac{n}{n + 1} \approx 1 + \frac{1}{2^2} + \ldots + \frac{1}{n^2} \qquad\qquad n > 0 \qquad\qquad (2.16)$$

This approximation is based on the following integral:

$$\int_1^{n+1} \frac{1}{z^2} \, dz = \left[-\frac{1}{z} \right]_1^{n+1} = 1 - \frac{1}{n + 1} = \frac{n}{n + 1}$$

The integral is smaller than the sum, since the curve $1/z^2$ cuts through the rectangles.

The main difference between the logarithmic TF and the fractional TF (BM25-TF) is that the fractional TF corresponds to a stronger dependence assumption than the logarithmic TF. Expressing it via the harmonic sum nicely illustrates the type and strength of the assumption. The fractional TF gives the k-th occurrence of a term an impact of $1/k^2$, whereas for the logarithmic TF, it is $1/k$. Also interesting from a theoretical point of view is that the basic harmonic sum is divergent, whereas the harmonic sum of squares is convergent. We will discuss in Section 2.1.7 (p. 17), Semi-subsumed Event Occurrences, more aspects regarding the probabilistic interpretation of TF quantifications.

Overall, this section showed different TF quantifications. The quantification is crucial for the performance of TF-IDF. Bending the TF like the logarithmic TF does or shaping it into a saturating curve like the BM25-TF, means to model the dependence between subsequent occurrences of an event, giving more importance to the first than to the subsequent occurrences.

We finalize the discussion of TF with a useful rewriting. The fractional (ratio-based) TF can be expressed based on the within-document term probability $P(t|d) = \text{tf}_d/\text{dl}$:

$$\text{TF}_{\text{frac},K}(t,d) = \frac{\text{tf}_d}{\text{tf}_d + K_d} = \frac{P(t|d)}{P(t|d) + K_d/\text{dl}} \left(= \frac{P(t|d)}{P(t|d) + 1/\text{avgdl}}, \text{ if } K_d = \text{dl}/\text{avgdl} \right)$$

(2.17)

This formulation of the fractional TF is of advantage in probabilistic frameworks, since all components, including $1/\text{avgdl}$, are probabilities.

2.1.4   IDF VARIANTS

The IDF (inverse document frequency) is the negative logarithm of the DF (document frequency). The two definitions to follow capture DF and IDF variants.

Definition 2.3   DF Variants. $\text{DF}(t,c)$ is a quantification of the document frequency, $\text{df}(t,c)$. The main variants are:

$$
\begin{aligned}
\text{df}(t,c) := \text{df}_{\text{total}}(t,c) \;\; &:= \;\; n_D(t,c) & (2.18)\\
\text{df}_{\text{sum}}(t,c) \;\; &:= \;\; \frac{n_D(t,c)}{N_D(c)} \quad \left(= \frac{\text{df}(t,c)}{N_D(c)} \right) & (2.19)\\
\text{df}_{\text{sum,smooth}}(t,c) \;\; &:= \;\; \frac{n_D(t,c) + 0.5}{N_D(c) + 1} & (2.20)\\
\text{df}_{\text{BIR}}(t,c) \;\; &:= \;\; \frac{n_D(t,c)}{N_D(c) - n_D(t,c)} & (2.21)\\
\text{df}_{\text{BIR,smooth}}(t,c) \;\; &:= \;\; \frac{n_D(t,c) + 0.5}{N_D(c) - n_D(t,c) + 0.5} & (2.22)
\end{aligned}
$$

Definition 2.4   IDF Variants. $\text{IDF}(t,c)$ is the negative logarithm of a DF quantification. The main variants are:

$$
\begin{aligned}
\text{idf}_{\text{total}}(t,c) \;\; &:= \;\; -\log \text{df}_{\text{total}}(t,c) & (2.23)\\
\text{idf}(t,c) := \text{idf}_{\text{sum}}(t,c) \;\; &:= \;\; -\log \text{df}_{\text{sum}}(t,c) & (2.24)\\
\text{idf}_{\text{sum,smooth}}(t,c) \;\; &:= \;\; -\log \text{df}_{\text{sum,smooth}}(t,c) & (2.25)\\
\text{idf}_{\text{BIR}}(t,c) \;\; &:= \;\; -\log \text{df}_{\text{BIR}}(t,c) & (2.26)\\
\text{idf}_{\text{BIR,smooth}}(t,c) \;\; &:= \;\; -\log \text{df}_{\text{BIR,smooth}}(t,c) & (2.27)
\end{aligned}
$$

Note the defaults: $\text{df}(t,c) := \text{df}_{\text{total}}(t,c)$, and $\text{idf}(t,c) := -\log \text{df}_{\text{sum}}(t,c)$. Whereas $\text{df}(t,c)$ is usually the *total* count, $\text{idf}(t,c)$ is based on the normalized DF, df_{sum}. The latter is equal to the Document-based term probability: $P_D(t|c) = \text{df}_{\text{sum}}(t,c)$.

Figure 2.2 shows the nature of the IDF. The figure also illustrates the notion of burstiness (graphics from Roelleke and Wang [2006]).

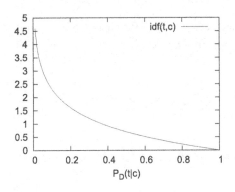 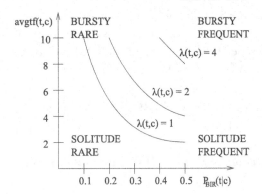

Figure 2.2: IDF and Burstiness.

IDF$(t, c) = -\log P_D(t|c)$, is high for rare terms, and low for frequent terms. Here, $P_D(t|c)$ is the Document-based term probability. IDF is based on rareness among documents, independent of the distribution of term occurrences.

A term is "bursty" if it occurs often in the documents in which it occurs. Burstiness is measured by the average term frequency in the elite set, i.e., avgtf$(t, c) = $ tf$_c$/df(t, c). Here, tf$_c = $ lf$(t, c) = n_L(t, c)$ is the number of Locations at which t occurs, and df$(t, c) = n_D(t, c)$ is the number of Documents in which t occurs.

Interestingly, burstiness is not an explicit component in neither TF-IDF nor LM. The product of burstiness and term probability is equal to the average term frequency over all documents:

$$\lambda(t, c) = \text{avgtf}(t, c) \cdot P_D(t|c) = \frac{n_L(t, c)}{N_D(c)} \qquad \left(= \frac{\text{tf}_c}{N_D(c)} \right)$$

The negative logarithm yields:

$$-\log \lambda(t, c) = -\log\left(\text{avgtf}(t, c) \cdot P_D(t|c)\right) = \text{IDF}(t, c) - \log \text{avgtf}(t, c)$$

We take a closer look at this equation in Section 2.4 (p. 35), Poisson. The intuition is that a good term is rare (not frequent) and solitude (not bursty) in all documents (in all of the non-relevant documents). For the set of relevant documents, the sign changes:

$$\log \lambda(t, r) = \log\left(\text{avgtf}(t, r) \cdot P_D(t|r)\right) = -\text{IDF}(t, r) + \log \text{avgtf}(t, r)$$

Among relevant documents, a good term is frequent (low IDF) and bursty (high avgtf). The IDF in TF-IDF can be interpreted as assuming IDF$(t, r) = 0$ (term occurs in every relevant document, which is also true for the empty set), and avgtf$(t, r) = $ avgtf$(t, \bar{r})$. Then, the approximation is as follows:

$$\text{IDF}(t, c) \approx \text{IDF}(t, \bar{r}) - \text{IDF}(t, r) + \left(\log(\text{avgtf}(t, r)) - \log(\text{avgtf}(t, \bar{r}))\right)$$

see also Section 2.4 (p. 35), Poisson.

Generalizations and issues regarding IDF are manifested in the literature. For example: "Generalised IDF," Metzler [2008] and "Inverse Document Frequency: A Measure of Deviations from Poisson," Church and Gale [1995].

2.1.5 TERM WEIGHT AND RSV

The TF-IDF term weight can be formally defined as follows.

Definition 2.5 TF-IDF term weight $w_{\text{TF-IDF}}$.   Let t be a term, d a document, q a query, and c a collection.

$$w_{\text{TF-IDF}}(t,d,q,c) := \text{TF}(t,d) \cdot \text{TF}(t,q) \cdot \text{IDF}(t,c) \tag{2.28}$$

Here, TF and IDF are placeholders for the different estimates listed in the definitions for TF and IDF. The TF-IDF RSV is defined as the sum of TF-IDF term weights.

Definition 2.6 TF-IDF retrieval status value $\text{RSV}_{\text{TF-IDF}}$.

$$\text{RSV}_{\text{TF-IDF}}(d,q,c) := \sum_t w_{\text{TF-IDF}}(t,d,q,c) \tag{2.29}$$

Inserting $w_{\text{TF-IDF}}$ yields the RSV in decomposed form.

$$\text{RSV}_{\text{TF-IDF}}(d,q,c) = \sum_t \text{TF}(t,d) \cdot \text{TF}(t,q) \cdot \text{IDF}(t,c) \tag{2.30}$$

The sum can be $\sum_t$ or $\sum_{t \in d \cap q}$; this is because $\text{TF}(t,d)=0$ for $t \notin d$, and $\text{TF}(t,q)=0$ for $t \notin q$.

In the remainder of this section on TF-IDF, we reconsider "other TF variants," "semi-subsumed event occurrences: a semantics of the BM25-TF," and "the probabilistic interpretation of $\text{idf}(t,c)/\text{maxidf}(c)$."

2.1.6 OTHER TF VARIANTS: LIFTED TF AND PIVOTED TF

In addition to the previously discussed TF variants, even more TF variants have been proposed. Two representatives are the *lifted* TF and the *pivoted* TF.

$$\text{TF}_{\text{lifted},a}(t,d) \quad := \quad a + (1-a) \cdot \text{TF}(t,d) \tag{2.31}$$

$$\text{TF}_{\text{piv},K}(t,d) \quad := \quad \frac{\text{TF}_{\text{total}}(t,d)}{K_d} \tag{2.32}$$

For $\text{TF}_{\text{lifted}}$, let $0 \le a \le 1$ be the parameter. For TF_{piv}, let K be the parameter function, where $K_d(c) = \text{pivdl}(d,c) = \text{dl}/\text{avgdl}(c)$ is a special setting.

The lifted variant yields TF values greater than the parameter "a;" this guarantees high values already for small frequencies.

The pivoted variant normalizes the total count by a pivotization parameter. The pivoted TF value of large documents is smaller than the non-pivoted value (non-pivoted value divided by denominator greater than 1), whereas the TF value of small documents is greater than the non-pivoted value (denominator less than 1).

The graphs in Figure 2.3 illustrate the nature of lifted and pivoted TF variants.

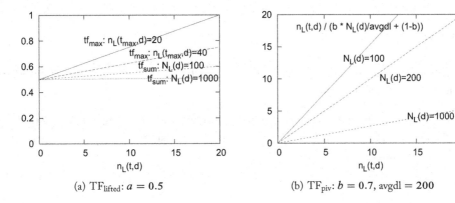

(a) TF_{lifted}: $a = 0.5$ (b) TF_{piv}: $b = 0.7$, avgdl $= 200$

Figure 2.3: Other TF Variants: Lifted TF and Pivoted TF.

Lifted TF yields larger TF values than the respective non-lifted TF; TF_{lifted} can be viewed as the *linear* approximation of TF_{frac}.

Pivoted TF lowers the respective non-pivoted TF value for large documents, and increases the value for small documents. $TF_{piv,K}(t, d) = tf_d / K_d$ can be used conveniently for expressing $TF_{frac,K}$:

$$TF_{frac,K}(t, d) = \frac{tf_d}{tf_d + K_d} = \frac{tf_d / K_d}{tf_d / K_d + 1} = \frac{TF_{piv,K}(t, d)}{TF_{piv,K}(t, d) + 1} \qquad (2.33)$$

See also equation 2.17 where we used $P(t|d)$ to express TF_{frac}. The formulation as a ratio is convenient and useful in several contexts, for example when discussing a probabilistic semantics of the BM25-TF.

2.1.7   SEMI-SUBSUMED EVENT OCCURRENCES: A SEMANTICS OF THE BM25-TF

Figure 2.4 shows the overall idea of semi-subsumed event occurrences, Wu and Roelleke [2009]: in the set-based illustration, the overlap of semi-subsumed event occurrences is greater than for independent event occurrences, and smaller than for subsumed event occurrences.

semi-
umed
event
ences

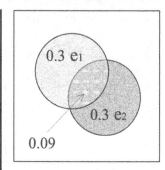 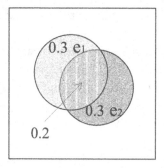 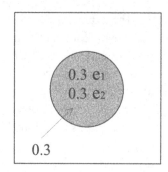

Figure 2.4: Independent, Semi-subsumed, and Subsumed Event Occurrences.

The notion "semi-subsumed" was created to establish a relationship between the BM25-TF quantification and probability theory.

Example 2.7 Semi-subsumed event occurrences.   For example, consider an event e that occurs twice. The two events e_1 and e_2 reflect the two occurrences. The single event probability is $P(e_1) = P(e_2) = 0.3$. The conjunctive probability is:

$$P(e_1 \wedge e_2) = \begin{cases} 0.3^2 = 0.09 & \text{independent: } p^n \\ 0.3^{\left(2 \cdot \frac{2}{2+1}\right)} \approx 0.2008 & \text{semi-subsumed: } p^{2 \cdot \frac{n}{n+1}} \\ 0.3^1 & \text{subsumed: } p^1 \end{cases}$$

Definition 2.8 Semi-subsumed Event (Term) Occurrences.   Let $L_1, \ldots, L_n$ be random variables over the same event space. For IR, let the set of terms be the event space. With respect to IR, a variable L_i corresponds to the i-th *Location* (position) in a document.

Given the term probability $P(L_i = t) = P(t)$, the conjunctive probability of n *independent* occurrences of t is:

$$P(L_1 = t \wedge L_2 = t \wedge \ldots \wedge L_n = t) = P(t)^n$$

In contrast, the conjunctive probability of n *semi-subsumed* occurrences of t is:

$$P(L_1 = t \wedge L_2 = t \wedge \ldots \wedge L_n = t) = P(t)^{\left(2 \cdot \frac{n}{n+1}\right)}$$

When interpreting a document d as a conjunction of term events at locations, for independent event occurrences, the document probability is:

$$P(d) = \prod_{t \text{ IN } d} P(t) = \prod_{t \in d} P(t)^{n_L(t,d)} \qquad \left(= \prod_{t \in d} P(t)^{\text{tf}_d} \right)$$

The notation "t IN d" views d as a sequence, whereas "$t \in d$" views d as a set; $n_L(t, d) = \text{tf}_d$ is the number of occurrences of event t in sequence d. The subscript L denotes the type of random variable.

For semi-subsumed event occurrences, the document probability is:

$$P(d) = \prod_{t \in d} P(t)^{\left(2 \cdot \frac{n_L(t,d)}{n_L(t,d)+1}\right)} = \prod_{t \in d} P(t)^{2 \cdot \text{TF}_{\text{frac}, K=1}(t,d)}$$

The equation underlines that the notion of semi-subsumed explains the meaning of the fractional TF.

Figure 2.5 shows a graphical illustration, the independence-subsumption triangle (IST).

The IST illustrates that semi-subsumed, i.e., the exponent $2 \cdot n/(n + 1)$, is the mid-point between independent (exponent n) and subsumed (exponent 1). This mid-point is the harmonic mean of 1 and n, which is $h(\{1, n\}) = 2 \cdot (1 \cdot n)/(n + 1)$, and equivalently, $h(\{1, n\}) = 2 \cdot 1/(1/1 + 1/n)$.

The left slope of the triangle shows the case for independent event occurrences: the exponent is n, the number of times the event occurs. The right slope shows the case for subsumed event occurrences: the exponent is 1, since the multiple occurrences of the same event coincide. For the altitude, i.e., the middle between independence and subsumption, the exponent is $2 \cdot n/(n + 1)$. Similarly, there is semi-disjoint between independent and disjoint, a notion not further discussed here.

The final example underlines that different terms are independent, whereas the occurrences of the same term are semi-subsumed.

Example 2.9 Independent terms, semi-subsumed term occurrences.   Given a term sequence where t_1 occurs twice, t_2 occurs three times, and t_3 occurs once. The probability of the sequence is:

$$P(t_1, t_1, t_2, t_2, t_2, t_3) = P(t_1)^{\frac{4}{3}} \cdot P(t_2)^{\frac{6}{4}} \cdot P(t_3)^{\frac{2}{2}}$$

We have discussed that the notion "semi-subsumed event occurrences" assigns a probabilistic semantics to the fractional (BM25) TF. The next section looks at IDF: a max-based normalization is sometimes convenient, and does not affect the ranking. From a probabilistic point of view, the question is: which probabilistic semantics can be assigned to the value $\text{idf}(t, c)/\text{maxidf}(c)$?

2.1.8   PROBABILISTIC IDF: THE PROBABILITY OF BEING INFORMATIVE

In probabilistic scenarios, a normalized IDF value such as $0 \leq \text{idf}(t, c)/\text{maxidf}(c) \leq 1$ can be useful, Here, $\text{maxidf}(c) := -\log \frac{1}{N_D(c)}$ is the maximal value of $\text{idf}(t, c)$. We refer to the normalized

	independent			semi-subsumed	subsumed		
1				$\frac{1}{2/2}$			
2			$\frac{2}{1}$	$\frac{2}{3/2}$	$\frac{2}{2}$		
3		$\frac{3}{1}$		$\frac{3}{4/2}$	$\frac{3}{3}$		
4		$\frac{4}{1}$	$\frac{4}{2}$	$\frac{4}{5/2}$	$\frac{4}{3}$	$\frac{4}{4}$	
5	$\frac{5}{1}$		$\frac{5}{2}$	$\frac{5}{6/2}$	$\frac{5}{4}$	$\frac{5}{5}$	
...		...		...		...	
n	$\frac{n}{1}$	$\frac{n}{2}$	$\frac{n}{3}$	$\frac{n}{(n+1)/2}$	$\frac{n}{n-2}$	$\frac{n}{n-1}$	$\frac{n}{n}$

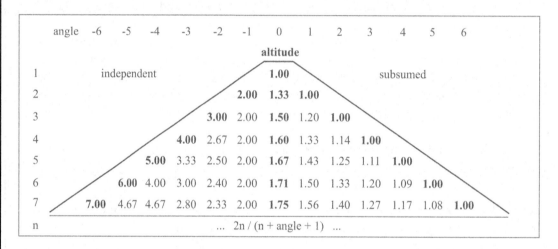

Figure 2.5: IST: Independence-Subsumption-Triangle.

IDF as "probabilistic IDF" (PIDF), and we discuss in this section the relationship between the normalized IDF and probability theory.

A probabilistic semantics of a max-normalized IDF can be achieved by introducing an "informativeness-based" probability, Roelleke [2003], as opposed to the normal notion of "occurrence-based" probability, and we denote the probability as $P(t \text{ informs}|c)$, to contrast it from the usual $P(t|c) := P(t \text{ occurs}|c)$. The next definition captures this approach formally.

Definition 2.10   Probability of being informative (probabilistic idf).

$$\text{maxidf}(c) := -\log \frac{1}{N_D(c)} = \log N_D(c) \qquad (2.34)$$

$$P(t \text{ informs}|c) := \text{pidf}(t, c) := \frac{\text{idf}(t, c)}{\text{maxidf}(c)} \tag{2.35}$$

The normalization corresponds to setting the base of the logarithm, as the following definitions and equations recall. The logarithm to base b is defined as the fraction of the logarithm of the argument x and the logarithm of the base b.

$$\log_b(x) := \frac{\log(x)}{\log(b)} = \frac{\ln(x)}{\ln(b)}$$

Therefore, the PIDF can be formulated as follows:

$$P(t \text{ informs}|c) = \frac{\text{idf}(t, c)}{\text{maxidf}(c)} = \frac{-\log P(t \text{ occurs}|c)}{\log N_D(c)} = -\log_{N_D(c)} \frac{n_D(t, c)}{N_D(c)} \tag{2.36}$$

Continuing with the equation from above leads to the complement probability:

$$P(t \text{ informs}|c) = 1 - \log_{N_D(c)} n_D(t, c) = 1 - \frac{\log n_D(t, c)}{\log N_D(c)} = 1 - P(\neg t \text{ informs}|c) \tag{2.37}$$

In an alternative formulation, we start from the complement probability:

$$P(\neg t \text{ informs}|c) = \frac{\text{maxidf}(c) - \text{idf}(t, c)}{\text{maxidf}(c)} = \frac{\log n_D(t, c)}{\log N_D(c)} \tag{2.38}$$

For the occurrence probability $P_D(t \text{ occurs}|c) = \frac{n_D(t,c)}{N_D(c)}$, if we apply the logarithm to numerator and denominator, then we obtain the complement of the probability of being informative: $P_D(\neg t \text{ informs}|c) = \frac{\log n_D(t,c)}{\log N_D(c)}$.

Though the above shows how we can interpret the value $\text{pidf}(t, c) = \text{idf}(t, c)/\text{maxidf}(c)$, as a probability of being informative, the theoretically inclined researcher will still ask: Is there a better way?

The convergence equation (limit definition) for the exponent function, see Bronstein [1987] or other math text books, leads to a probabilistic semantics. The convergence equation is:

$$\lim_{N \to \infty} \left(1 - \frac{\lambda}{N}\right)^N = e^{-\lambda} \tag{2.39}$$

Here, λ/N is the probability that an event occurs, and the convergence shows that $e^{-\lambda}$ is the probability that the event does not occur in N trials.

The Euler convergence can be related to idf, and this establishes a probabilistic semantics of $P(t \text{ informs}|c)$.

Set $\lambda(t, c) := \text{idf}(t, c)$. Then, $e^{-\text{idf}(t,c)}$ is the probability that the event t which occurs in average $\text{idf}(t, c)$ times, does not occur in $N = \text{maxidf}(c)$ trials.

This assigns a semantics to idf(t, c), and to $P(t \text{ informs}|c)$. Because of idf$(t, c) :=$ $-\log P(t \text{ occurs}|c)$, the occurrence probability is equal to the probability that t is not informative in maxidf(c) trials. The following theorem formalizes this relationship.

Theorem 2.11   Occurrence-Informativeness-Theorem..   *The probability that a term t occurs is equal to the probability that the term is not informative in maxidf trials.*

$$P(t \text{ occurs}|c) = \left(1 - P(t \text{ informs}|c)\right)^{maxidf(c)} \tag{2.40}$$

Proof. Step 1: Insert the definition of $P(t \text{ informs}|c)$ (Definition 2.10 (p. 20), pidf).

$$P(t \text{ occurs}|c) = \left(1 - \frac{\text{idf}(t, c)}{\text{maxidf}(c)}\right)^{maxidf(c)} \tag{2.41}$$

Step 2: Approximate expression by exponent function (Euler convergence).

$$P(t \text{ occurs}|c) = e^{-\text{idf}(t,c)} \tag{2.42}$$

Step 3: Insert definition of idf.

$$P(t \text{ occurs}|c) = e^{\log P(t \text{ occurs}|c)} = P(t \text{ occurs}|c) \tag{2.43}$$

□

After this excursus regarding the probabilistic interpretation of pidf, we show how to formally prove the ranking equivalence between $\text{RSV}_{\text{TF-IDF}}$ and $\text{RSV}_{\text{TF-PIDF}}$. For this proof, we define the notion rank-equivalent and score-equivalent.

Definition 2.12   Rank-equivalent and Score-equivalent.   Two scoring functions A and B are *rank-equivalent* iff for all retrieved objects x and y: if $\text{RSV}_A(x) > \text{RSV}_A(y)$, then $\text{RSV}_B(x) > \text{RSV}_B(y)$.

Two scoring functions A and B are *score-equivalent* iff for all retrieved objects: $\text{RSV}_A(x) = \gamma \cdot \text{RSV}_B(x)$, where γ is a constant.

Theorem 2.13   TF-IDF Ranking Equivalence..   *$RSV_{TF\text{-}IDF}$ and $RSV_{TF\text{-}PIDF}$ are score-equivalent.*

$$RSV_{TF\text{-}IDF}(d, q, c) \stackrel{\text{score}}{=} \sum_{t} TF(t, d) \cdot TF(t, q) \cdot P(t \text{ informs}|c) \tag{2.44}$$

Proof. Insert definition of $\text{RSV}_{\text{TF-IDF}}$ and definition of $P(t \text{ informs}|c)$:

$$\sum_t \text{TF}(t, d) \cdot \text{TF}(t, q) \cdot \text{idf}(t, c) \;\overset{\text{score}}{=}\; \sum_t \text{TF}(t, d) \cdot \text{TF}(t, q) \cdot \frac{\text{idf}(t, c)}{\text{maxidf}(c)} \qquad (2.45)$$

Since $\text{maxidf}(c)$ is a constant, the scoring equivalence holds. $\qquad\qquad\square$

2.1.9   SUMMARY

We have discussed the foundations of TF-IDF. We have considered the different variants of TF and IDF. For TF, we have elaborated that the TF quantifications correspond to dependence assumptions. In particular, the logarithmic TF and fractional TF (BM25-TF) can be expressed as harmonic sums, and this shows the type of dependence assumption that is inherent to TF quantifications. Also, a TF of the form $\frac{tf_d}{tf_d+1}$ corresponds to a particular assumption referred to as "semi-subsumption," an assumption that forms the altitude in the independence-subsumption-triangle. For IDF, we have discussed what a max-based normalization of the form $\text{idf}(t, c)/\text{maxidf}(c)$ means. Overall, we have looked at foundations that assign a meaning to TF and IDF.

2.2   PRF: THE PROBABILITY OF RELEVANCE FRAMEWORK

The PRF is based on the probability of relevance:

$$P(r|d, q)$$

Here, "r" denotes relevant, d stands for a document, and q stands for a query. When I started studying probabilistic IR and first encountered this expression, this probability seemed rather abstract to me. Also, in the literature, it is often denoted as $P(R|d, q)$, and since R is also viewed as a random variable or the set of relevant documents, understanding the probability of relevance does not become easier. In this book, we use lower case letters for events, and view $R = \{r, \bar{r}\}$ as the random variable (set of events). To make the probability less abstract, consider an example.

Example 2.14   Probability of relevance.   Let three users $u1, u2, u3$ have judged document-query pairs. The result is recorded as follows:

User	Doc	Query	Judgement R
$u1$	$d1$	$q1$	r
$u1$	$d2$	$q1$	r
$u1$	$d3$	$q1$	$\bar{r}$
$u2$	$d1$	$q1$	r
$u2$	$d2$	$q1$	$\bar{r}$
$u2$	$d3$	$q1$	$\bar{r}$
$u3$	$d1$	$q1$	r
$u3$	$d2$	$q1$	$\bar{r}$
$u4$	$d1$	$q1$	$\bar{r}$
$u4$	$d2$	$q1$	$\bar{r}$

Then, for example, $P_U(r|d1, q1) = 3/4$, and $P_U(r|d2, q1) = 1/4$, and $P_U(r|d3, q1) = 0/2$. The subscript in P_U denotes the "event space," a set of users. With respect to the theorem of total probability, we can notate:

$$P_U(r|d, q) = \sum_{u \in U} P(r|d, q, u) \cdot P(u)$$

The example indicates that judgments can be incomplete, and the different ways to fill-up the incomplete judgements affects the probability that can be observed.

In any case, for a new query, we do not have judgements. (We leave out approaches that exploit similarities between new and past queries to deduce judgements for a new query.) The probability is estimated via Bayes's theorem:

$$P(r|d, q) = \frac{P(d, q|r) \cdot P(r)}{P(d, q)} = \frac{P(d, q, r)}{P(d, q)} \qquad (2.46)$$

The decision whether or not to retrieve a document is based on the so-called "Bayesian decision rule:" retrieve document d, if the probability of relevance is greater than the probability of non-relevance:

$$\text{retrieve } d \text{ for } q \text{ if } P(r|d, q) > P(\bar{r}|d, q)$$

This can be expressed via probabilistic odds of relevance.

$$O(r|d, q) := \frac{P(r|d, q)}{P(\bar{r}|d, q)} = \frac{P(r|d, q)}{1 - P(r|d, q)} \qquad (2.47)$$

Then, the decision rule is:

$$\text{retrieve } d \text{ for } q \text{ if } O(r|d, q) > 1 \qquad (2.48)$$

To compute the value of the probabilistic odds, the application of Bayes's theorem yields:

$$O(r|d, q) = \frac{P(r|d, q)}{P(\bar{r}|d, q)} = \frac{P(d, q, r)}{P(d, q, \bar{r})} = \frac{P(d, q|r)}{P(d, q|\bar{r})} \cdot \frac{P(r)}{P(\bar{r})} \qquad (2.49)$$

Since $P(r)/P(\bar{r})$ is a constant, the following rank equivalence holds:

$$O(r|d, q) \stackrel{\text{rank}}{=} \frac{P(d, q|r)}{P(d, q|\bar{r})} \qquad (2.50)$$

The document-pair probabilities can be decomposed in two ways:

$$
\begin{aligned}
\frac{P(d, q|r)}{P(d, q|\bar{r})} &= \frac{P(d|q, r) \cdot P(q|r)}{P(d|q, \bar{r}) \cdot P(q|\bar{r})} \qquad (\Rightarrow \text{BM25}) \qquad &(2.51) \\
&= \frac{P(q|d, r) \cdot P(d|r)}{P(q|d, \bar{r}) \cdot P(d|\bar{r})} \qquad (\Rightarrow \text{LM?}) \qquad &(2.52)
\end{aligned}
$$

Equation 2.51, where d depends on q, is the basis of BIR, Poisson and BM25. Those models view d as a vector in the term space of all terms, and decompose the document likelihood $P(d|q, r)$ accordingly.

Equation 2.52 has been related to LM, $P(q|d)$, Lafferty and Zhai [2003], "Probabilistic Relevance Models Based on Document and Query Generation." This relationship and the assumptions required to establish it, are controversial, Luk [2008], since at least one of the assumptions used to establish that $P(q|d)$ is proportional to the odds of relevance, $O(r|d, q)$, is questionable. Azzopardi and Roelleke [2007], "Relevance in LM," discusses several approaches to add relevance into LM. One of the milestones regarding the combination of relevance and LM, Lavrenko and Croft [2001], "Relevance-based Language Models," proposed a relevance-based LM, but this model is actually a query expansion technique, as the authors describe it themselves.

For the purpose of this section, we continue with the decomposition of the document event. In equation 2.51, the factor $P(q|r)/P(q|\bar{r})$ is constant for a set of documents. This justifies the following ranking equivalence:

$$O(r|d, q) \stackrel{\text{rank}}{=} \frac{P(d|q, r)}{P(d|q, \bar{r})} \tag{2.53}$$

The next step represents document d as a vector $\vec{d} = (f_1, \ldots, f_n)$ in a space of features $\vec{f_i}$:

$$P(d|q, r) = P(\vec{d}|q, r) \tag{2.54}$$

A feature could be, for example, the frequency of a word (term), the document length, document creation time, time of last update, document owner, number of in-links, or number of out-links. Often, the PRF model is formulated for a vector of term frequencies only; Fuhr [1992a] extended the model using other features as well.

2.2.1   FEATURE INDEPENDENCE ASSUMPTION

Assumption 1 (PRF feature independence assumption.) *The features are independent events.*

$$\textit{PRF independence assumption:} \quad P(\vec{d}|q, r) \approx \prod_i P(f_i|q, r) \tag{2.55}$$

Often, the term features (term frequencies) constitute the feature space.

Note that this formulation of the independence assumption is stronger than the formulation for the fraction of feature probabilities:

$$\frac{P(d|q, r)}{P(d|q, \bar{r})} \approx \prod_i \frac{P(f_i|q, r)}{P(f_i|q, \bar{r})} \tag{2.56}$$

For the purpose of this book, it is not required to distinguish between these two assumptions.

The next assumption reduces the number of elements in the product. The document vector has a component for each term of the term space. The idea is that the non-query terms can be ignored for retrieval (ranking).

2.2.2 NON-QUERY TERM ASSUMPTION

Assumption 2 (PRF non-query term assumption.) *For non-query terms, the feature probability is the same in relevant documents and non-relevant documents.*

$$\text{PRF non-query term assumption:} \quad \text{for all non-query terms: } P(f_i|q,r) = P(f_i|q,\bar{r}) \quad (2.57)$$

This reduces the product over all the features to the product over the query features, i.e., the features of the query terms:

$$\frac{P(d|q,r)}{P(d|q,\bar{r})} \approx \prod_{i|t_i \in q} \frac{P(f_i|q,r)}{P(f_i|q,\bar{r})} \quad (2.58)$$

A less strict assumption could be based on viewing the product of $P(f_i|q,r)/P(f_i|q,\bar{r})$ of the non-query terms as a constant, but it is sufficient to apply $1 = P(f_i|q,r)/P(f_i|q,\bar{r})$.

2.2.3 TERM FREQUENCY SPLIT

Finally, the product over query terms is split into two parts. The first part captures the $f_i > 0$ features, i.e., the document terms. The second part captures the $f_i = 0$ features, i.e., the non-document terms.

$$\text{PRF term frequency split:} \quad \prod_{i|t_i \in q} \frac{P(f_i|q,r)}{P(f_i|q,\bar{r})} = \left[\prod_{i|t_i \in d \cap q} \frac{P(f_i|q,r)}{P(f_i|q,\bar{r})} \right] \cdot \left[\prod_{i|t_i \in q \backslash d} \frac{P(0|q,r)}{P(0|q,\bar{r})} \right]$$
$$(2.59)$$

The first product is over the terms that occur in both, document *and* query; the second product is over the terms that occur in the query only.

2.2.4 PROBABILITY RANKING PRINCIPLE (PRP)

Robertson [1977], "The Probability Ranking Principle (PRP) in IR," describes the PRP as a framework to discuss formally "what is a good ranking?" Robertson [1977] quotes Cooper's formal statement of the PRP:

> "If a reference retrieval system's response to each request is a ranking of the documents in the collections in order of decreasing probability of usefulness to the user who submitted the request, ..., then the overall effectiveness of the system ... will be the best that is obtainable on the basis of that data."

Then, the paper devises an informal definition of an alternative principle. The key sentences characterizing this alternative principle are:

"Documents should be ranked in such a way that the probability of the user being satisfied by any given rank position is a maximum. This alternative principle deals successfully with some of the situations in which the [original] PRP fails, but there are many problems with it."

Formally, we can capture the principle as follows. Let A and B be rankings. Then, a ranking A is better than a ranking B if at every rank, the probability of satisfaction in A is higher than for B, i.e.:

$$\forall \text{rank} : P(\text{satisfactory}|\text{rank}, A) > P(\text{satisfactory}|\text{rank}, B)$$

Obviously, the notion "at every rank" needs to be softer to compare rankings. For example, one could base the comparison on the area under the probability curve. Also, being satisfactory at early ranks might need to be reflected.

The discussion shows that the implementation of the PRP is difficult.

"Unfortunately, the dilemma is not resolvable: in some circumstances an optimal ranking under one criterion cannot be optimal under another criterion."

For a discussion of the optimality, see Gordon and Lenk [1992], "When is the Probability Ranking Principle Suboptimal?".

To illustrate the role of the PRP, we look next at an example from Fuhr [1989], "Models for Retrieval with Probabilistic Indexing."

The idea is to express the PRP via the expectation value of gain (or costs). Let $g(d)$ be a gain function. With respect to the probability of relevance framework (PRF), let the gain function be defined as the logarithm of the odds of relevance:

$$g(d) := \log O(r|d) = \log \frac{P(r|d)}{P(\bar{r}|d)}$$

The function can be interpreted as "gain," i.e., the gain in relevant information when reading document d. We could view the negative value of gain as costs, i.e., $\text{costs}(d) = -\text{gain}(d)$. This leads to the dual formulation of the PRP based on minimizing the costs. For the purpose of this section, we continue with the gain function.

Let D be a random variable (set of documents). The expected gain is as follows:

$$E_g[D] := \sum_{d \in D} P(d) \cdot g(d) \quad \left(= \sum_{g(d) \in \{g(d_1),...\}} P(g(d)) \cdot g(d) \right)$$

The equation makes explicit the transformation step between the random variable of gains and the random variable of documents.

Now, the idea is that with respect to the PRP, for two sets D_1 and D_2, the expected gain is greater for the set in which the probability of relevance is greater:

$$P(r|D_1) > P(r|D_2) \implies E_g[D_1] > E_g[D_2]$$

One of the main messages in Fuhr [1989] is that this implication does not hold, and we review in the following the example demonstrating this aspect.

Let D_1 and D_2 be two disjoint sets of documents. D_1 contains 80 documents, 40 of which are relevant. D_2 contains 79 documents, 39 of which are relevant. Then, the probability of relevance is greater in D_1 than in D_2.

$$\forall d \in D_1 : P_{D_1}(r|d) = 40/80 = 0.5$$
$$\forall d \in D_2 : P_{D_2}(r|d) = 39/79 < 0.5$$

Therefore, we expect $E_g[D_1] > E_g[D_2]$.

Split set D_1 into two subsets. One subset contains 39 relevant documents, the other contains one relevant document. In a similar way, split set D_2. One subset contains 30 relevant documents, the other contains 10 relevant documents.

This leads to the following subsets:

D_1	D_{11}	D_{12}	Σ
relevant	39	1	40
not relevant	31	9	40
Σ	70	10	80

D_2	D_{21}	D_{22}	Σ
relevant	30	9	39
not relevant	39	1	40
Σ	69	10	79

The motivation underlying the splits is to create extreme cases, where in D_1, the set with more relevant documents, we make the second subset contain mainly non-relevant documents, whereas in D_2, the less good set, we make the second subset contain mainly relevant documents.

The expectation value of D_1 is as follows:

$$E_g[D_1] = P_{D_{11}}(d) \cdot \log \frac{P_{D_{11}}(r|d)}{P_{D_{11}}(\bar{r}|d)} + P_{D_{12}}(d) \cdot \log \frac{P_{D_{12}}(r|d)}{P_{D_{12}}(\bar{r}|d)}$$

When inserting the statistics of the example[1], we obtain for the two sets D_1 and D_2 the following expectation values:

$$E_g[D_1] = 70/80 \cdot \log \frac{39/70}{31/70} + 10/80 \cdot \log \frac{1/10}{9/10} \approx -0.07$$

$$E_g[D_2] = 69/79 \cdot \log \frac{30/69}{39/69} + 10/79 \cdot \log \frac{9/10}{1/10} \approx 0.05$$

The expectation value of D_2 is greater than the one of D_1. Therefore, Fuhr [1989] states: "The ranking function $E_g[D]$ does not yield a ranking according to the PRP."

---

[1] I am grateful to Norbert who cross-checked this example, and this clarified a typo in his original paper; replace $(39/79)/(31/80)$ by $(39/70)/(31/70)$, etc.

2.2.5   SUMMARY

We have discussed the foundations of the PRF. The PRF is based on the probabilistic odds of relevance, $O(r|d,q) = P(r|d,q)/P(\bar{r}|d,q)$. It basically corresponds to the Bayesian decision rule to retrieve a document if its probability of relevance is greater than its probability of non-relevance. The PRF is usually expanded for the document event, $P(d|r,q)$, leading to the BIR and Poisson model.

2.3   BIR: BINARY INDEPENDENCE RETRIEVAL

The BIR instantiation of the PRF assumes the vector components to be binary term features, i.e., $\vec{d} = (x_1, x_2, \ldots, x_n)$, where $x_i \in \{0, 1\}$.

Starting with a conjunction of terms in document d, the occurrences of terms is represented in a binary feature vector $\vec{d}$ in the term space. For example, for a vocabulary (space) of five terms, the term-based probability $P(t_2, t_3, t_2)$ corresponds to the binary feature-based probability $P(0, 1, 1, 0, 0)$.

The product over all features can be reduced to query features, $t \in q$, because for non-query terms, $P(x_t|q,r) = P(x_t|q,\bar{r})$ is assumed. More generally, the assumption is that the product of non-query term feature probabilities does not affect the ranking.

Moreover, instead of the conjunct "q, r," just "r" is used, which is justified by the implication $r \rightarrow q$, the set of relevant documents implies the query. Also, the event $x_t = 1$ is expressed as t, and $x_t = 0$ as $\bar{t}$.

Then, $q = (d \cap q) \cup (q \setminus d)$ is applied to split the product (see Equation 2.59 (p. 26), Term Frequency Split).

$$O(r|d,q) \propto \prod_{t \in q} \frac{P(x_t|r)}{P(x_t|\bar{r})} = \prod_{t \in q} \frac{P(t|r)}{P(t|\bar{r})} = \left[\prod_{t \in d \cap q} \frac{P(t|r)}{P(t|\bar{r})} \right] \cdot \left[\prod_{t \in q \setminus d} \frac{P(\bar{t}|r)}{P(\bar{t}|\bar{r})} \right] \qquad (2.60)$$

Next, we apply a transformation to make the second product (the product over non-document terms) to be independent of the document. Essentially, we multiply the equation by 1.0:

$$1.0 = \prod_{t \in d \cap q} \left[\frac{P(\bar{t}|\bar{r})}{P(\bar{t}|r)} \cdot \frac{P(\bar{t}|r)}{P(\bar{t}|\bar{r})} \right]$$

Then, we obtain for the probabilistic odds:

$$O(r|d,q) \propto \left(\prod_{t \in d \cap q} \left[\frac{P(t|r)}{P(t|\bar{r})} \cdot \frac{P(\bar{t}|\bar{r})}{P(\bar{t}|r)} \right] \right) \cdot \left(\prod_{t \in q} \frac{P(\bar{t}|r)}{P(\bar{t}|\bar{r})} \right) \qquad (2.61)$$

The second product is document-independent, which means it is ranking invariant, and therefore can be dropped.

Alternatively, the BIR weight can be derived using the binomial probability. For this formulation, let $a_t := P(t|r)$ and $b_t := P(t|\bar{r})$ be abbreviations of the respective probabilities.

$$\prod_t \frac{P_{\text{binomial},1,a_t}(x_t)}{P_{\text{binomial},1,b_t}(x_t)} = \prod_t \frac{a_t^{x_t}}{b_t^{x_t}} \cdot \frac{(1-a_t)^{(1-x_t)}}{(1-b_t)^{(1-x_t)}}$$

In the literature, Robertson and Sparck-Jones [1976], van Rijsbergen [1979], the symbols p_i and q_i are used, whereas this book employs a_t and b_t. This is to avoid confusion between p_i and probabilities, and q_i and queries.

The next step is based on inserting the x_t's. $\forall t \in d : x_t = 1$ and $\forall t \notin d : x_t = 0$.

$$O(r|d,q) \propto \prod_{t \in d} \frac{a_t}{b_t} \cdot \prod_{t \notin d} \frac{1-a_t}{1-b_t}$$

By applying the non-query term assumption, Equation 2.57 (p. 26), non-query term assumption, the products reduce to terms that are in the query:

$$O(r|d,q) \propto \prod_{t \in d \cap q} \frac{a_t}{b_t} \cdot \prod_{t \in q \setminus d} \frac{1-a_t}{1-b_t} \tag{2.62}$$

Finally, after multiplying with 1.0 (see above), we obtain the expression equivalent to equation 2.61.

$$O(r|d,q) \propto \prod_{t \in d \cap q} \frac{a_t \cdot (1-b_t)}{b_t \cdot (1-a_t)} \cdot \prod_{t \in q} \frac{1-a_t}{1-b_t} \tag{2.63}$$

2.3.1   TERM WEIGHT AND RSV

The BIR term weight can be formally defined as follows.

Definition 2.15   BIR term weight w_{BIR}.

$$w_{\text{BIR}}(t,r,\bar{r}) := \log\left(\frac{P_D(t|r)}{P_D(t|\bar{r})} \cdot \frac{P_D(\bar{t}|\bar{r})}{P_D(\bar{t}|r)}\right) \tag{2.64}$$

A simplified form, referred to as F1, considers term presence only and uses the collection to approximate term frequencies and probabilities in the set of non-relevant documents.

$$w_{\text{BIR,F1}}(t,r,c) := \log \frac{P_D(t|r)}{P_D(t|c)} \tag{2.65}$$

The term weight reflects the discriminative power of the term to distinguish between relevant and non-relevant documents.

The BIR RSV is defined as the sum of BIR term weights.

Definition 2.16   BIR retrieval status value RSV_{BIR}.

$$\text{RSV}_{\text{BIR}}(d, q, r, \bar{r}) := \sum_{t \in d \cap q} w_{\text{BIR}}(t, r, \bar{r}) \tag{2.66}$$

Inserting w_{BIR} yields the RSV in decomposed form.

$$\text{RSV}_{\text{BIR}}(d, q, r, \bar{r}) = \sum_{t \in d \cap q} \log \frac{P(t|r) \cdot P(\bar{t}|\bar{r})}{P(t|\bar{r}) \cdot P(\bar{t}|r)} \tag{2.67}$$

There are problems for missing relevance information (empty sets). For example, if $N_D(r) = 0$ or $N_D(\bar{r}) = 0$, then the probabilities are not defined (division by zero). Moreover, for $P(t|\bar{r}) = 0$ leads to division-by-zero, and for $P(t|r) = 0$ or $P(\bar{t}|\bar{r}) = 0$, the logarithm is not defined. These problems can be solved conceptually by viewing the query as a relevant and a non-relevant document, i.e., by adding two documents that contain all query terms.

2.3.2   MISSING RELEVANCE INFORMATION

Usually, non-relevance is not explicit, i.e., the set of non-relevant documents is derived from positive relevance judgements. This is in contrast to approaches where we would consider non-relevance to be specified explicitly, for example, by an explicit, negative judgement. For the estimation of non-relevant documents, there are two main approaches:

1. $P(t|\bar{r}) \approx P(t|c)$, where $P(t|c) = \frac{n_D(t,c)}{N_D(c)}$: Assume that the collection-wide term probability is a good approximation of the term probability in non-relevant documents. We will use $\bar{r} \equiv c$ for referring to this approach.

2. $P(t|\bar{r}) \approx \frac{n_D(t,c) - n_D(t,r)}{N_D(c) - N_D(r)}$: Use the set of all documents minus the set of relevant documents to estimate the term probability in non-relevant documents. We will use $\bar{r} \equiv c \setminus r$ for referring to this approach.

The second problem is the "empty" set problem. For $N_D(r) = 0$, the probability $P(t|r)$ is not defined. The same mathematical issue occurs for $N_D(c) = 0$, though an empty set of documents is somewhat artificial. Smoothing deals with the empty set problem:

1. Add the query virtually to the set of relevant documents, and to the set of non-relevant documents (to the collection, respectively). This guarantees that the term probabilities are defined for each query term. This smoothing means, for example, $P(t|r) = \frac{n_D(t,r)+1}{N_D(r)+1}$.

2. Other forms of smoothing. For example, $P(t|r) = \frac{n_D(t,r)+0.5}{N_D(r)+1}$.

Going back to the BIR term weight, for missing relevance information, $P(t|r)$ is not defined, and $P(t|\bar{r}) = P(t|c)$ is assumed. Croft and Harper [1979], Using Probabilistic Models of Document Retrieval without Relevance Information, proposed to define a constant C_r if $P(t|r)$ is not defined:

$$C_r = \frac{P(t|r)}{1 - P(t|r)} \tag{2.68}$$

Then, the BIR term weight is:

$$w_{\mathrm{BIR}}(t, r, c) = C_r \cdot \frac{1 - P(t|c)}{P(t|c)}, \qquad \text{if } D_r = \{\} \tag{2.69}$$

The assumption $C_r = 1$ is a special assumption, and in general, the constant C_r should be considered when formulating the BIR for missing relevance information; *see also* Section 3.9.1 (p. 96), TF-IDF and BIR.

2.3.3   VARIANTS OF THE BIR TERM WEIGHT

This section uses the event-space-based and the conventional notation. Figure 2.6 shows the notations side-by-side.

		conventional	event-based
	$P_D(t|r)$	r_t/R	$n_D(t,r)/N_D(r)$
$\bar{r} := c$	$P_D(t|\bar{r})$	n_t/N	$n_D(t,c)/N_D(c)$
$\bar{r} := c \setminus r$	$P_D(t|\bar{r})$	$(n_t - r_t)/(N - R)$	$(n_D(t,c) - n_D(t,r))/(N_D(c) - N_D(r))$

Figure 2.6: BIR: Conventional and Event-based Notation.

Definition 2.17   Variants of the BIR term weight: estimation of $\bar{r}$.   The four main variants of the BIR term weight reflect the combinations of whether only term presence or presence and absence, and which approximation is applied for the set of non-relevant documents.

The following lattice displays the four variants (before smoothing):

	$\bar{r} \equiv c$	$\bar{r} \equiv c \setminus r$
Presence only	$\dfrac{r_t/R}{n_t/N}$	$\dfrac{r_t/R}{(n_t - r_t)/(N - R)}$
Presence and absence	$\dfrac{r_t \cdot (N - n_t)}{n_t \cdot (R - r_t)}$	$\dfrac{r_t \cdot ((N - R) - (n_t - r_t))}{(n_t - r_t) \cdot (R - r_t)}$

2.3.4   SMOOTH VARIANTS OF THE BIR TERM WEIGHT

Definition 2.18   Smooth variants of the BIR term weight.   The smooth variants are safe for the case where the set of relevant documents is empty. The smoothing shown here can be viewed as assuming two virtual documents, therefore $N + 2$. One of the virtual documents is relevant, therefore $R + 1$.

	$\bar{r} \equiv c$	$\bar{r} \equiv c \setminus r$
Presence only	$\dfrac{(r_t + 0.5)/(R + 1)}{(n_t + 1)/(N + 2)}$	$\dfrac{(r_t + 0.5)/(R + 1)}{(n_t - r_t + 0.5)/(N - R + 1)}$
Presence and absence	$\dfrac{(r_t + 0.5) \cdot (N - n_t + 1)}{(n_t + 1) \cdot (R - r_t + 0.5)}$	$\dfrac{(r_t + 0.5) \cdot ((N - R) - (n_t - r_t) + 0.5)}{(n_t - r_t + 0.5) \cdot (R - r_t + 0.5)}$

2.3.5   RSJ TERM WEIGHT

We refer to the smooth variant of the BIR term weight as RSJ (Robertson-SparckJones) weight.

Definition 2.19   RSJ term weight w_{RSJ}.   The RSJ term weight is a smooth BIR term weight.
The probability estimation is as follows:
$P(t|r) := (\text{df}(t, r) + 0.5)/(N_D(r) + 1);$
$P(t|\bar{r}) := ((\text{df}(t, c) + 1) - (\text{df}(t, r) + 0.5))/((N_D(c) + 2) - (N_D(r) + 1)).$
Inserting these estimates into the BIR term weight yields the RSJ term weight:

$$w_{\text{RSJ,F4}}(t, r, \bar{r}, c) := \frac{(\text{df}(t, r) + 0.5)/(N_D(r) - \text{df}(t, r) + 0.5)}{(\text{df}(t, c) - \text{df}(t, r) + 0.5)/((N_D(c) - N_D(r)) - (\text{df}(t, c) - \text{df}(t, r)) + 0.5)}$$

The traditional notation is: $r_t := \text{df}(t, r)$; $n_t := \text{df}(t, c)$; $N := N_D(c)$; $R := N_D(r)$.

2.3.6   ON THEORETICAL ARGUMENTS FOR 0.5 IN THE RSJ TERM WEIGHT

Norbert Fuhr mentioned on several occasions that the 0.5 in the smooth variant of the BIR term weight requires a justification. When discussing this with Stephen Robertson, he replied: "There is a justification; how was it again?"

Laplace's law of succession offers a justification. Given an event that occurred m_t times in M past trials, then the probability is $P(t) = m_t/M$. After k_t occurrences in K new trials, the probability is:

$$P(t) := \frac{m_t + k_t}{M + K}$$

To improve readability of formulae, we use m_t and M rather than the common notation n_t and N, since for the BIR, $n_t = \mathrm{df}(t, c)$ is the document frequency, and $N = N_D(c)$ is the number of documents.

The frequency-based aggregation of evidence is obviously different from combining the probabilities, where we have lost the information about the cardinalities of the sets involved. For example, combine $P(t) = m_t/M = 5,000/10,000 = 0.5$ with $P(t) = k_t/K = 1/2 = 0.5$.

The law of succession can be expressed as a mixture. For demonstrating this, we form an equation to search for the mixture parameter λ.

$$\frac{m_t + k_t}{M + K} = \lambda \cdot \frac{m_t}{M} + (1 - \lambda) \cdot \frac{k_t}{K} = \lambda \cdot P_M(t) + (1 - \lambda) \cdot P_K(t)$$

Set $\lambda = \frac{M}{M+K}$. This leads to:

$$\frac{m_t + k_t}{M + K} = \frac{M}{M + K} \cdot \frac{m_t}{M} + \frac{K}{K + M} \cdot \frac{k_t}{K} = \frac{m_t}{M + K} + \frac{k_t}{M + K}$$

It is evident that the Laplace smoothing is equivalent to a probability mixture where the mixture parameter is the ratio $\lambda = \frac{M}{M+K}$, i.e., the number of past trials divided by the sum of past trials and new trials; *see also* Section 2.6.1 (p. 49), Probability Mixtures.

For the smoothing of the probabilities in the RSJ weight, this means:

$$P(t|r) = \frac{0.5 + r_t}{1 + R} = \frac{1}{1 + R} \cdot \frac{0.5}{1} + \frac{R}{R + 1} \cdot \frac{r_t}{R} = \frac{0.5}{1 + R} + \frac{r_t}{1 + R}$$

$$P(t|c) = \frac{1 + n_t}{2 + N} = \frac{1}{2 + N} \cdot \frac{2}{1} + \frac{N}{N + 2} \cdot \frac{n_t}{N} = \frac{1}{2 + N} + \frac{n_t}{2 + N}$$

Whereas the smoothing of $P(t|c)$ is based on full integer counts, $m_t = 1$ and $M = 2$, that are intuitive, the smoothing for $P(t|r)$ is based on $m_t = 0.5$, and this lacks intuition. The following transformation helps to discuss the inside of the smoothing.

$$P(t|r) = \frac{0.5 + r_t}{1 + R} = \frac{1/2 + 2 \cdot r_t/2}{2/2 + 2 \cdot R/2} = \frac{1 + 2 \cdot r_t}{2 + 2 \cdot R} \tag{2.70}$$

Now it is evident that the smoothing of $P(t|r)$ means to double the impact of counts in relevant documents. This means we can view fractional values of past occurrences as stretching out the new occurrences. An alternative smoothing based on four virtual documents, two of which are relevant and two are non-relevant, has been discussed in Amati [2009], de Vries and Roelleke [2005]. Each term occurs in one relevant and one non-relevant document. Then, the smoothing is as follows:

$$P(t|r) = \frac{1 + r_t}{2 + R} \qquad P(t|c) = \frac{2 + n_t}{4 + N}$$

Whatever the smoothing, $P(t|r)$ and $P(t|c)$ need to be well-defined for missing evidence. The 0.5 in the RSJ weight makes the weight safe for missing relevance information (empty sets). We have reviewed options to explain where the 0.5 comes from. Thereby, we discussed the relationship between the Laplace law of succession and probability mixtures.

2.3.7 SUMMARY

We have discussed the foundations of BIR. We have made explicit the assumptions that make BIR an instance of the PRF. We defined the term weight w_{BIR} and the score RSV_{BIR}.

Then, we reviewed the variants of the BIR term weight, the variants reflecting missing relevance information, and term presence only. We considered the smooth variants of the BIR term weights, and we discussed theoretical arguments to explain the "0.5-smoothing" applied in the RSJ weight.

The BIR can be viewed as a special case of the next model, the Poisson model.

2.4   POISSON AND 2-POISSON

The Poisson instantiation of the PRF assumes the vector components to be term frequencies, i.e., $\vec{d} = (f_1, \ldots, f_n)$, where $f_i \in \{0, 1, 2, \ldots\}$.

The Poisson model seems to be less known and popular than the BIR and the BM25 model, though the scientific literature offers deep insights into using Poison for IR: e.g., Margulis [1992], N-Poisson Document Modeling, Church and Gale [1995], Inverse Document Frequency: A Measure of Deviations from Poisson.

The main purpose for dedicating a section to the Poisson model is to consolidate the role of Poisson for IR. Also, there is the aim to demystify the Poisson probability; some research students resign when hearing "Poisson." Engaging with the foundations of the Poisson probability is useful:

1. The Poisson model is next to the BIR model the natural instantiation of a PRF model; the BIR model is a special case of the Poisson model.

2. The 2-Poisson probability is arguably the foundation of the BM25-TF quantification Robertson and Walker [1994], "Some Simple Effective Approximations to the 2-Poisson Model."

3. The Poisson probability is a model of randomness. Divergence from randomness (DFR), Section 2.8.1 (p. 63), is based on the probability $P(t \in d | \text{collection}) = P(\text{tf}_d > 0 | \text{collection})$. The probability $P(\text{tf}_d | \text{collection})$ can be estimated by a Poisson probability.

4. The Poisson parameter $\lambda(t, c) = \text{tf}_c / \text{df}(t, c)$, i.e., the average number of term occurrences, relates Document-based and Location-based probabilities.

$$\text{avgtf}(t, c) \cdot P_D(t|c) = \lambda(t, c) = \text{avgdl}(c) \cdot P_L(t|c)$$

We refer to this relationship as Poisson bridge since the average term frequency is the parameter of the Poisson probability; Section 3.7 (p. 93), Poisson Bridge.

5. The Poisson model yields a foundation of TF-IDF; Section 3.9.2 (p. 98), TF-IDF and Poisson.

6. The Poisson bridge helps to relate TF-IDF and LM; Section 3.9.4 (p. 101), TF-IDF and LM.

2.4.1 POISSON PROBABILITY

Definition 2.20 Poisson Probability. Let t an event that occurs in average λ_t times. The Poisson probability is:

$$P_{\text{Poisson},\lambda_t}(k) := \frac{\lambda_t^k}{k!} \cdot e^{-\lambda_t} \tag{2.71}$$

Example 2.21 Poisson Probability. For example, the probability that $k = 4$ sunny days occur in a week, given the average $\lambda = p \cdot n = 180/360 \cdot 7 = 3.5$ sunny days per week, is:

$$P_{\text{Poisson},\lambda=3.5}(k = 4) = \frac{(3.5)^4}{4!} \cdot e^{-3.5} \approx 0.1888 \tag{2.72}$$

For small n, the Poisson probability is quite different from the binomial probability (example p. 39). For $n >> k_t$, and $\lambda_t = n \cdot p_t$, the Poisson probability approximates the binomial probability:

$$P_{\text{Poisson},\lambda_t}(k_t) \approx P_{\text{binomial},n,p_t}(k_t)$$

Details regarding this approximation are discussed in Section 2.4.6 (p. 40), Relationship between Poisson and Binomial Probability.

2.4.2 POISSON ANALOGY: SUNNY DAYS AND TERM OCCURRENCES

To further make Poisson familiar, we underline the parallel between sunny days and term occurrences.

- k_{sunny} *days* correspond to k_t *locations*.

- A *holiday* h of length $N_{\text{Days}}(h)$ corresponds to a *document d* of length $N_{\text{Locations}}(d)$.

- The single event probability p_{sunny} corresponds to the single event probability p_t.

Figure 2.7 shows a table to illustrate the analogy between the scenario "sunny days in a holiday," and the scenario "term occurrences in a document." The analogy helps to relate to the single event probabilities and averages involved. The last row indicates other event spaces.

	Event space	
	Days	Locations
k_e: occurrences of event e	k_{sunny}: number of days that are sunny	k_t: number of locations that show term t
foreground model	sequence of days e.g., holiday h	sequence of locations e.g., document d
background model	sequence of days year y	sequence of locations collection u
N: number of trials, i.e., length of sequence	Days in holiday h $N_{Days}(h)$	Locations in document d $N_{Locations}(d)$
single event probability	$P_{Days}(sunny \mid y) := \dfrac{n_{Days}(sunny, y)}{N_{Days}(y)}$	$P_{Locations}(t \mid u) := \dfrac{n_{Locations}(t, u)}{N_{Locations}(u)}$
average	average number of sunny days in holiday with $N_{Days}(h)$ days $\lambda_{Days}(sunny, h) =$ $P_{Days}(sunny \mid y) \cdot N_{Days}(h)$	average number of t-locations in document with $N_{Locations}(d)$ locations $\lambda_{Locations}(t, d) =$ $P_{Locations}(t \mid u) \cdot N_{Locations}(d)$
probability $P_{p,N}(k)$	probability of k sunny days in a week ($N_{Days} = 7$): $P_{p,N=7}(k)$	probability of k_t locations that show term t in a document with 1,000 words ($N_L = 1{,}000$): $P_{p,N=1{,}000}(k)$
other event spaces	holiday-based statistics $n_{Holidays}(sunny, y)$: number of holidays with a sunny day	document-based statistics $n_{Documents}(t, u)$: number of documents with a t-location

Figure 2.7: "Sunny Days in a Holiday" and "Term Locations in a Document".

2.4.3 POISSON EXAMPLE: TOY DATA

Example 2.22 Poisson: Synthetic Data.   Let u be a collection, and let D_u be the respective set of documents. Let t be a term, and let it occur in $n_D(t, u) = 1{,}000$ documents. Let $n_D(t, u, k_t)$ denote the number of documents in which t occurs k_t times. Let the within-document term frequencies be distributed as follows:

k_t	0	1	2	3	4	5	6	7	8	9	10	$\sum$
$n_D(t, u, k_t)$	4,000	600	200	100	50	30	10	7	1	1	1	5,000
$n_L = k_t \cdot n_D$	0	600	400	300	200	150	60	49	8	9	10	1,786

The term occurs once in 600 documents, twice in 200 documents, etc. The total occurrence is $tf_u = n_L(t, u) = 1{,}786$. The average frequency over t-documents is $avgtf(t, u) = n_L(t, u)/n_D(t, u) = 1{,}786/1{,}000 = 1.786$.

The average frequency over *all* documents is $\lambda(t, u) = n_L(t, u)/N_D(u) = 1{,}786/5{,}000 = 0.3572$.

The following table shows the observed probabilities and the Poisson probabilities.

k_t	0	1	2	3	4	5	6	7	8	9	10	
elite documents												
$n_D(t, u, k_t)$		600	200	100	50	30	10	7	1	1	1	1,000
$P_{\mathrm{obs}}(k_t)$	0	0.600	0.200	0.100	0.050	0.030	0.010	0.007				
n_L		600	400	300	200	150	60	49	8	9	10	1,786
$P_{\mathrm{Poisson}}(k_t)$	0.168	0.299	0.267	0.159	0.071	0.025	0.008	0.002				1.786
all documents												
$n_D(t, u, k_t)$	4,000	600	200	100	50	30	10	7	1	1	1	5,000
$P_{\mathrm{obs}}(k_t)$	0.800	0.120	0.040	0.020	0.010	0.006	0.002	0.0014				
n_L	0	600	400	300	200	150	60	49	8	9	10	1,786
$P_{\mathrm{Poisson}}(k_t)$	0.700	0.250	0.045	$5e-03$	$5e-04$	$3e-05$	$2e-06$	$1e-07$				0.3572

The first Poisson probability is based on avgtf$(t, u) = 1,786/1,000$, i.e., this estimate excludes the documents in which the term does not occur. The second Poisson probability is based on $\lambda(t, u) = 1,786/5,000 = 0.3572$, the average over all documents.

For the second Poisson probability, the main characteristics is that $P_{\mathrm{Poisson},\lambda}(k_t = 1)$ is greater than the observed probability, whereas for $k_t > 1$, the Poisson probability decreases faster than the observed probability. The tail of the Poisson probability is "too thin."

2.4.4   POISSON EXAMPLE: TREC-2

To showcase observed versus Poisson probabilities for real data, consider the statistics for "spy," "africa," and "control" taken from collection TREC-2:

Example 2.23   Poisson: TREC-2.

k_t	0	1	2	3	4	5	6	7	8	9	10	$\frac{n_D}{n_L}$
spy									avgtf $\approx 3,551/1,997 = 1.79$			
n_D	740,614	1,309	320	137	107	54	32	17	12	4	5	1,997
n_L	0	1,309	640	411	428	270	192	119	96	36	50	3,551
$P_{\mathrm{obs}}(k)$	0.9973	0.0018	0.0004	0.0002	0.0001	0.0001	0.0001	$\vdots$				
$P_{\mathrm{Poisson}}\,k/$	0.9952	0.0048	0.0000	0.0000	0.0000	0.0000	0.0000	$\vdots$				
africa									avgtf $= 19,681/8,533 = 2.31$			
n_D	734,078	4,584	1,462	809	550	345	271	182	137	105	88	8,533
n_L	0	4,584	2,924	2,427	2,200	1,725	1,626	1,274	1,096	945	880	19,681
$P_{\mathrm{obs}}(k)$	0.9885	0.0062	0.0020	0.0011	0.0007	0.0005	$\vdots$					
$P_{\mathrm{Poisson}}(k)$	0.9738	0.0258	0.0003	0.0000								
control									avgtf $= 204,888/111,830 = 1.82$			
n_D	630,781	69,990	21,259	8,836	4,444	2,747	1,625	1,113	795	550	471	111,830
n_L	0	69,990	42,518	26,508	17,776	13,735	9,750	7,791	6,360	4,950	4,710	204,088
$P_{\mathrm{obs}}(k)$	0.8494	0.0942	0.0286	0.0119	0.0060	0.0037	0.0022	0.0015	$\vdots$			
$P_{\mathrm{Poisson}}(k)$	0.7597	0.2088	0.0287	0.0026	0.0002	0.0000	$\vdots$					

The statistics for the three terms illustrate the same effect demonstrated for toy data. The Poisson probability spends its mass on small k, whereas the observed probability assigns more mass to larger k. The effect is observable for rare ("spy" is a rare term), medium frequent ("africa"), and relatively frequent ("control") terms. The numerical example underlines that the Poisson probability fails to reflect the burstiness of terms, i.e., there are more documents in which term occurrences co-occur, than the Poisson probability tells.

The Poisson model could be used to estimate the document probability $P(d|q,r)$ as the product of the probabilities of the within-document term frequencies k_t. Let $k_t := \text{tf}_d := n_L(t,d)$ be the total count of locations at which term t occurs. Then, the starting point of the Poisson model is:

$$P(d|q,r) = P(\vec{d}|q,r) = \prod_t P(k_t|q,r) \tag{2.73}$$

Note that the product is over all terms, not just over the document terms. For non-document terms, $k_t = 0$.

The Poisson probability is an approximation of the binomial probability. We review the justification of this approximation in the following section. Readers familiar with Poisson may want to continue at Definition 2.20 (p. 36), Poisson Probability.

2.4.5 BINOMIAL PROBABILITY

Assume we draw balls (events) from an urn u. The set of events is non-distinct, i.e., some events occur several times. The probability to draw the event t is $P(t|u) = \frac{n(t,u)}{N(u)}$, where $n(t,u)$ is the number of occurrences of event t in urn u, and $N(u)$ is the number of elements (balls).

For example, the probability of a sunny day at the east coast of England is $p_{\text{sunny}} := P(\text{sunny}|\text{east-coast}) = 0.5$. We keep in mind that this probability could be based on the statistics over the past 10 years, i.e., $p_{\text{sunny}} = 1{,}800/3{,}600$, or on the statistics over just a fortnight, $p_{\text{sunny}} = 7/14$. In a more general fashion, we may write $P(\text{sunny}|M)$ or $P_M(\text{sunny})$, where M indicates the model (and space) used to estimate the probability.

Given the single event probability p_t, what is the probability that in N trials the event t occurs k_t times? This probability is denoted as $P_{N,p_t}(k_t)$, and the binomial probability $P_{\text{binomial},N,p_t}(k_t)$ is the standard estimate.

Definition 2.24 Binomial Probability. Let t be an event that occurs with probability p_t. Let N be the number of trials. The binomial probability is:

$$P_{\text{binomial},N,p_t}(k_t) := \binom{N}{k_t} \cdot p_t^{k_t} \cdot (1 - p_t)^{(N-k_t)} \tag{2.74}$$

Example 2.25 Binomial Probability. For example, the probability that $k = 4$ sunny days occur in $N = 7$ days, given the single event probability $p = \frac{180}{360} = 0.5$, is:

$$P_{\text{binomial},N=7,p=0.5}(k = 4) = \binom{7}{4} \cdot 0.5^4 \cdot (1 - 0.5)^{(7-4)} \approx 0.2734 \tag{2.75}$$

2.4.6 RELATIONSHIP BETWEEN POISSON AND BINOMIAL PROBABILITY

The Poisson probability is an approximation of the binomial probability.

After setting the single event probability as $p = \lambda/n$, the binomial probability becomes:

$$P_{\text{binomial},n,p}(k) = \binom{n}{k} \cdot \left(\frac{\lambda}{n}\right)^k \cdot \left(1 - \frac{\lambda}{n}\right)^{(n-k)} \approx \frac{\lambda^k}{k!} \cdot e^{-\lambda}$$

The next expression illustrates details of the approximation:

$$\frac{n \cdot (n-1) \cdot \ldots \cdot (n-k+1)}{k!} \cdot \left(\frac{\lambda^k}{n^k}\right) \cdot \left(\frac{n-\lambda}{n}\right)^{-k} \cdot \left(1 - \frac{\lambda}{n}\right)^n$$

The approximation involves the Euler convergence.

$$\lim_{n \to \infty} \left(1 - \frac{\lambda}{n}\right)^n = e^{-\lambda} \tag{2.76}$$

Moreover, the approximation assumes the following:

$$\frac{n \cdot (n-1) \cdot \ldots \cdot (n-k+1)}{(n-\lambda)^k} \approx 1$$

The relationship between binomial and Poisson probability can be viewed differently. Instead of decomposing $(1 - \lambda/n)^{(n-k)}$, we could approximate the whole expression to be $e^{-\lambda}$.

$$\left(1 - \frac{\lambda}{n}\right)^{(n-k)} \approx e^{-\lambda} \qquad n >> k$$

Then, the second approximation is as follows:

$$\frac{n \cdot (n-1) \cdot \ldots \cdot (n-k+1)}{n^k} \approx 1$$

The main fact is that Poisson approximates the binomial probability. Which inner approximation is employed to explain the overall approximation is a secondary issue, but it is useful to reflect the details, in particular when deriving new probability functions that capture the dependence of events.

2.4.7 POISSON PRF

Back to the PRF, we review the derivation steps leading from the odds of relevance, $O(r|d,q)$, toward the Poisson term weight, w_{Poisson}, and the retrieval status value, $\text{RSV}_{\text{Poisson}}$.

After assuming that the product over non-query feature probabilities does not affect the ranking, see Equation 2.57 (p. 26), non-query term assumption, the probabilistic odds of relevance are rank-equivalent (proportional) to the product of the fractions of the frequency probabilities of the query terms:

$$O(r|d,q) \overset{\text{rank}}{=} \prod_{t \in q} \frac{P(k_t|r)}{P(k_t|\bar{r})}, \qquad k_t := \text{tf}_d := n_L(t,d) \qquad (2.77)$$

Splitting the product into document and non-document terms (Equation 2.59 (p. 26), PRF term frequency split) yields:

$$O(r|d,q) \overset{\text{rank}}{=} \prod_{t \in d \cap q} \frac{P(k_t|r)}{P(k_t|\bar{r})} \cdot \prod_{t \in q \setminus d} \frac{P(0|r)}{P(0|\bar{r})} \qquad (2.78)$$

Compare this equation to Equation 2.60 (p. 29), BIR Term Frequency Split.

Next, we insert the Poisson probability, $P_{\text{Poisson},\lambda}(k|u) = \frac{\lambda^k}{k!} \cdot e^{-\lambda}$.

$$O(r|d,q) \overset{\text{rank}}{=} \prod_{t \in d \cap q} \left[\frac{\lambda(t,d,r)^{k_t}}{\lambda(t,d,\bar{r})^{k_t}} \cdot \frac{e^{-\lambda(t,d,r)}}{e^{-\lambda(t,d,\bar{r})}} \right] \cdot \prod_{t \in q \setminus d} \frac{e^{-\lambda(t,d,r)}}{e^{-\lambda(t,d,\bar{r})}} \qquad (2.79)$$

The meaning of the Poisson probability is as follows:

$P_{\text{Poisson},\lambda(t,d,u)}(k_t)$: probability to observe k_t occurrences of term t in dl trials.

$\lambda(t,d,u) = \text{dl} \cdot P_L(t|u)$ is the number of occurrences expected in a document with length dl.

From the relationship between the binomial and Poisson probability, $n \cdot p_t = \lambda_t$ is the Poisson parameter. Therefore, for the PRF, the Poisson parameter is $\text{dl} \cdot P_L(t|u) = \lambda(t,d,u)$.

It remains to rewrite equation 2.79 to group the expressions to obtain a product over query terms.

$$O(r|d,q) \overset{\text{rank}}{=} \prod_{t \in d \cap q} \left[\frac{\lambda(t,d,r)^{k_t}}{\lambda(t,d,\bar{r})^{k_t}} \right] \cdot \prod_{t \in q} \frac{e^{-\lambda(t,d,r)}}{e^{-\lambda(t,d,\bar{r})}} \qquad (2.80)$$

This transformation is reminiscent of the derivation of BIR, Equation 2.61 (p. 29), BIR $O(r|d,q)$. The main difference is that for BIR, the product over query terms was independent of the document, whereas for Poisson, the document length is in a parameter in the product over query terms; for example, for relevant documents, $\lambda(t,d,r) = \text{dl} \cdot P_L(t|r)$. Only if we assume $\lambda(t,d,r) = \lambda(t,d,\bar{r})$, then the second product drops out (as it did for the BIR case).

Finally, we apply the natural logarithm.

$$\log O(r|d,q) \overset{\text{rank}}{=} \left[\sum_{t \in d \cap q} k_t \cdot \log\left(\frac{\lambda(t,d,r)}{\lambda(t,d,\bar{r})} \right) \right] + \sum_{t \in q} (\lambda(t,d,\bar{r}) - \lambda(t,d,r)) \qquad (2.81)$$

Inserting the Poisson parameters, $\lambda(t, d, r) = \mathrm{dl} \cdot P_L(t|r)$, and $\lambda(t, d, \bar{r}) = \mathrm{dl} \cdot P_L(t|\bar{r})$, yields:

$$\log O(r|d, q) \stackrel{\text{rank}}{=} \left[\sum_{t \in d \cap q} k_t \cdot \log \left(\frac{P_L(t|r)}{P_L(t|\bar{r})} \right) \right] + \mathrm{dl} \cdot \sum_{t \in q} (P_L(t|\bar{r}) - P_L(t|r)) \qquad (2.82)$$

By inserting the Poisson bridge, Section 3.7 (p. 93), the Document-based term probability becomes explicit:

$$P_L(t|u) = \frac{\mathrm{avgtf}(t, u)}{\mathrm{avgdl}(u)} \cdot P_D(t|u) \qquad \text{where } u = r \text{ or } u = \bar{r} \qquad (2.83)$$

This will be exploited in Section 3.9.2 (p. 98), TF-IDF and Poisson.

2.4.8   TERM WEIGHT AND RSV

The Poisson term weight can be formally defined as follows.

Definition 2.26   Poisson term weight w_{Poisson}.

$$w_{\text{Poisson}}(t, d, q, r, \bar{r}) := \mathrm{TF}(t, d) \cdot \log \frac{\lambda(t, d, r)}{\lambda(t, d, \bar{r})} \quad \left(= \mathrm{TF}(t, d) \cdot \log \frac{P_L(t|r)}{P_L(t|\bar{r})} \right) \qquad (2.84)$$

The weight is based on the averages in relevant and non-relevant documents; the statistics in non-relevant documents are often approximated by the average in all documents (the collection).

Also, the weight is shown using $\mathrm{TF}(t, d)$; this is to emphasize that we allow for different quantifications of the event occurrences. For the Poisson model which assumes independence, the setting is $\mathrm{TF}(t, d) = \mathrm{tf}_d$, i.e., TF is the total term frequency. However, from TF-IDF and BM25, we know that this independence assumption leads to relatively poor retrieval quality. Therefore, we make the Poisson model less naive by allowing for a smarter TF quantification, smarter in the sense that it reflects the dependence between multiple term occurrences.

The Poisson RSV is defined as the sum of Poisson term weights plus the length normalization.

Definition 2.27   Poisson retrieval status value $\mathrm{RSV}_{\text{Poisson}}$.

$$\mathrm{RSV}_{\text{Poisson}}(d, q, r, \bar{r}) := \left[\sum_{t \in d \cap q} w_{\text{Poisson}}(t, d, q, r, \bar{r}) \right] + \mathrm{len\_norm}_{\text{Poisson}} \qquad (2.85)$$

Inserting w_{Poisson} yields the RSV in decomposed form.

$$\text{RSV}_{\text{Poisson}}(d,q,r,\bar{r}) = \left[\sum_{t \in d \cap q} \text{TF}(t,d) \cdot \log \frac{P_L(t|r)}{P_L(t|\bar{r})} \right] + \text{dl} \cdot \sum_t (P_L(t|\bar{r}) - P_L(t|r)) \quad (2.86)$$

The Poisson bridge can be used to replace the Location-based term probability $P_L(t|u)$ by an expression that involves the Document-based term probability $P_D(t|u)$.

$$\text{avgtf}(t,u) \cdot P_D(t|u) = \lambda(t,u) = \text{avgdl}(u) \cdot P_L(t|u) \quad (2.87)$$

This leads to:

$$\text{RSV}_{\text{Poisson}}(d,q,r,\bar{r}) = \left[\sum_{t \in d \cap q} \text{TF}(t,d) \cdot \log \frac{\text{avgtf}(t,r) \cdot \text{avgdl}(\bar{r}) \cdot P_D(t|r)}{\text{avgtf}(t,\bar{r}) \cdot \text{avgdl}(r) \cdot P_D(t|\bar{r})} \right] + \text{len\_norm}_{\text{Poisson}}$$
$$(2.88)$$

Because of $\text{avgtf}(t,u) \cdot P_D(t|u) = \lambda(t,u)$, the RSV can be formulated as follows:

$$\text{RSV}_{\text{Poisson}}(d,q,r,\bar{r}) = \left[\sum_{t \in d \cap q} \text{TF}(t,d) \cdot \log \frac{\text{avgdl}(\bar{r}) \cdot \lambda(t,r)}{\text{avgdl}(r) \cdot \lambda(t,\bar{r})} \right] + \text{len\_norm}_{\text{Poisson}} \quad (2.89)$$

This equation concludes the discussion of the Poisson model. We focused in this section mainly on Poisson as an instance of the PRF, however, it is evident that the Poisson model has TF-IDF ingredients; *see also* Section 3.9.2 (p. 98), TF-IDF and Poisson.

2.4.9   2-POISSON

The main motivation for a multi-dimensional Poisson probability is to mix the probabilities for different averages. The following example illustrates this.

Example 2.28   2-Poisson: How many cars to expect?

How many cars are expected on a given commuter car park?

Approach 1: In average, there are 700 cars per week. The daily average is: $\lambda = 700/7 = 100$ cars/day.

Then, $P_{\lambda=100}(k)$ is the probability that there are k cars wanting to park on a given day.

This estimation is less accurate than an estimation based on a 2-dimensional model. This is because Mo-Fr are the busy days, and on weekends, the car park is nearly empty. This means that a distribution such as (130, 130, 130, 130, 130, 25, 25) is more likely than 100 each day.

Approach 2: In a more detailed analysis, we observe 650 cars Mon–Fri (work days) and 50 cars Sat–Sun (weekend days). The averages are: $\lambda_1 = 650/5 = 130$ cars/work-day, $\lambda_2 = 50/2 = 25$ cars/we-day.

Then, $P_{\mu_1=5/7,\lambda_1=130,\mu_2=2/7,\lambda_2=25}(k)$ is the 2-dimensional Poisson probability that there are k cars looking for a car park.

The main reason to include in this book the 2-Poisson probability is that it is viewed as a motivation for the BM25-TF quantification, Robertson and Walker [1994], "Simple Approximations to the 2-Poisson Model." In an exchange with Stephen Robertson, he explained:

> "The investigation into the 2-Poisson probability motivated the BM25-TF quantification. Regarding the combination of TF and RSJ weight in BM25, TF can be viewed as a factor to reflect the uncertainty about whether the RSJ weight w_{RSJ} is correct; for terms with a relatively high within-document TF, the weight is correct; for terms with a relatively low within-document TF, there is uncertainty about the correctness. In other words, the TF factor can be viewed as a weight to adjust the impact of the RSJ weight."

Regarding the interpretation of TF quantification ranging between 1 and tf_d, the setting $\mathrm{TF}(t, d) = 1$ reflects *subsumption* of event occurrences, and $\mathrm{TF}(t, d) = \mathrm{tf}_d$ reflects *independence*. The BM25-TF setting, $\mathrm{TF}_{BM25}(t, d) = \mathrm{tf}_d/(\mathrm{tf}_d + K_d)$ is related to assuming *semi-subsumption*; *see also* Section 2.1.7 (p. 17).

Given the effect of 2-Poisson probabilities and the notion of semi-subsumed events, there is an interesting relationship to explore as part of future research. For the scope of this book, we briefly look at the 2-Poisson probability.

The main idea of the 2-Poisson probability is to combine (interpolate) two Poisson probabilities. The following equation shows the combination:

$$P_{2\text{-Poisson},\lambda_1,\lambda_2,\mu}(k_t) := \mu \cdot \frac{\lambda_1^{k_t}}{k_t!} \cdot e^{-\lambda_1} + (1 - \mu) \cdot \frac{\lambda_2^{k_t}}{k_t!} \cdot e^{-\lambda_2} \qquad (2.90)$$

The 2-Poisson probability function peaks at λ_1 and λ_2. Therefore, the distribution function has a plateau. For values $k < \lambda_1$, the probability is small. Then, near $k \approx \lambda_1$, the distribution function steps up to the plateau. The next step is at λ_2, from where the plateau is approximately $\mu \cdot P_{\lambda_1}(\lambda_1) + (1 - \mu) \cdot P_{\lambda_2}(\lambda_2)$.

Regarding the averages λ_1 and λ_2, for example, one average could be over all documents, and the other average could be over an elite set of documents (e.g., the documents that contain at least one query term).

2.4.10 SUMMARY

We have discussed the foundations of the Poisson Model. The main aspect is that the Poisson model interprets the document event as a sequence of *term frequencies*: $P(d|q,c) = \prod_t P_{\text{Poisson},\lambda(t,d,c)}(k_t|q,c)$. Here, $k_t = \mathrm{tf}_d$ is the term frequency of term t in document d, and $\lambda(t, d, c)$ is the average term frequency, the term frequency expected for the document length dl.

Stepwise, we derived the $\text{RSV}_{\text{Poisson}}$, and made explicit the components that relate to IDF, burstiness ($\text{avgtf}(t, c)$), and document length normalization. The Poisson model and its main parameter, $\lambda(t, d, c) = \text{dl} \cdot P_L(t|c)$, is a binding link between IR models.

We also briefly touched on N-Poisson and 2-Poisson, and the latter is viewed as a motivation for the BM25-TF quantification we meet again in the next section.

2.5   BM25

The ingredients of BM25 have been prepared in Section 2.1 (p. 9), TF-IDF, and in Section 2.3 (p. 29), BIR. Central to BM25 (see Robertson et al. [1994], Robertson and Walker [1994], Robertson et al. [1995, 1998], Robertson and Zaragoza [2009] and related publications) is the BM25-TF quantification.

2.5.1   BM25-TF

Definition 2.29   BM25-TF.

$$\text{TF}_{\text{BM25},K}(t, d) := \frac{\text{tf}_d}{\text{tf}_d + K_d} \tag{2.91}$$

K_d adjusts the shape of the quantification. It is proportional to the pivoted document length: $\text{pivdl}(d) := \text{dl}/\text{avgdl}$.

$$K_d := k_1 \cdot \big(b \cdot \text{pivdl}(d) + (1 - b)\big) \tag{2.92}$$

The parameters k_1 and b adjust the effect of the pivotization.

More generally, we require to make explicit the collection (set of documents) for which the pivotization and parametrization shall apply. Let u be a collection. Then, the BM25-TF is as follows;

$$\text{TF}_{\text{BM25},K}(t, d, u) := \frac{\text{tf}_d}{\text{tf}_d + K_d(u)} \tag{2.93}$$

Then, the parameters are collection-specific, i.e., $\text{avgdl}(u)$, $\text{pivdl}(d, u)$, $k_1(u)$ and $b(u)$.

2.5.2   BM25-TF AND PIVOTED TF

In Section 2.1.6 (p. 16), Other TF Variants, we related the fractional TF, TF_{frac}, to the pivoted TF, TF_{piv}. We formalize the relationship in the next definition.

Definition 2.30   TF pivoted.

Pivotization with respect to parameter K_d:

$$\text{TF}_{\text{piv},K}(t, d) := \frac{\text{tf}_d}{K_d} \tag{2.94}$$

Pivotization with respect to the pivoted document length, i.e., $K_d = \text{pivdl}$:

$$\text{TF}_{\text{piv}}(t, d) := \text{TF}_{\text{piv,pivdl}}(t, d) = \frac{\text{tf}_d}{\text{pivdl}} \tag{2.95}$$

Relationships between $\text{TF}_{\text{frac},K}$ and $\text{TF}_{\text{piv},K}$:

$$\text{TF}_{\text{frac},K}(t, d) = \frac{\text{TF}_{\text{piv},K}(t, d)}{\text{TF}_{\text{piv},K}(t, d) + 1} \tag{2.96}$$

Relationship between $\text{TF}_{\text{frac},K}$ and TF_{piv}:

$$\text{TF}_{\text{frac},K}(t, d) = \frac{\text{TF}_{\text{piv}}(t, d)}{\text{TF}_{\text{piv}}(t, d) + K_d/\text{pivdl}} \tag{2.97}$$

(In BM25 SIGIR tutorials, pivoted TF's were denoted as tf'_d).
It is evident that the BM25-TF is an instantiation of the fractional TF.

$$\text{TF}_{\text{BM25},k_1,b}(t, d) = \text{TF}_{\text{frac},K}(t, d) = \frac{\text{tf}_d}{\text{tf}_d + K_d} = \frac{\text{TF}_{\text{piv},K}(t, d)}{\text{TF}_{\text{piv},K}(t, d) + 1} \tag{2.98}$$

This formulation is helpful to relate the BM25-TF to probability theory; *see also* Section 2.1.7 (p. 17), Semi-subsumed Events Occurrences.

2.5.3   BM25: LITERATURE AND WIKIPEDIA END 2012

Since there are many formulations and interpretations of what is BM25, it is worthwhile to briefly document here what we find at the end of 2012 on Wikipedia, http://en.wikipedia.org/wiki/Okapi_BM25.

Given a query Q, containing keywords $q_1, \ldots, q_n$, the BM25 score of a document D is:

$$\text{score}(D, Q) = \sum_{i=1}^{n} \text{IDF}(q_i) \cdot \frac{f(q_i, D) \cdot (k_1 + 1)}{f(q_i, D) + k_1 \cdot (1 - b + b \cdot \frac{|D|}{\text{avgdl}})},$$

where $f(q_i, D)$ is q_i's term frequency in the document D, $|D|$ is the length of the document D in words, and avgdl is the average document length in the text collection from which documents are drawn. k_1 and b are free parameters, usually chosen, in absence of an advanced optimisation, as $k_1 \in [1.2, 2.0]$ and $b = 0.75$. $\text{IDF}(q_i)$ is the IDF (inverse document frequency) weight of the query term q_i. It is usually computed as:

$$\text{IDF}(q_i) = \log \frac{N - n(q_i) + 0.5}{n(q_i) + 0.5},$$

where N is the total number of documents in the collection, and $n(q_i)$ is the number of documents containing q_i.

There are several interpretations for IDF and slight variations on its formula. In the original BM25 derivation, the IDF component is derived from the Binary Independence Model.

This formulation of BM25 is also given in Li [2011], page 16, as a foundation of learning to rank.

There are two differences between this formulation and the formulation given in this book.

1. Instead of IDF, we employ the RSJ weight, w_{RSJ}. For missing relevance information, $w_{RSV}(t) \approx IDF(t)$.

2. The factor $(k_1 + 1)$ is omitted (mostly). As long as k_1 is a constant, independent of term and document, the factor in the numerator is ranking invariant.

2.5.4   TERM WEIGHT AND RSV

The BM25 term weight can be formally defined as follows.

Definition 2.31   BM25 term weight w_{BM25}.

$$w_{BM25,k_1,b,k_3}(t,d,q,r,\bar{r}) := \sum_{t \in d \cap q} TF_{BM25,k_1,b}(t,d) \cdot TF_{BM25,k_3}(t,q) \cdot w_{RSJ}(t,r,\bar{r}) \quad (2.99)$$

The parameters k_1, b, and k_3 allow for adjusting the effect of the pivotization.

For the RSJ term weight, see Definition 2.19 (p. 33), w_{RSJ}.
The BM25 RSV is defined as the sum of BM25 term weights plus the length normalization.

Definition 2.32   BM25 retrieval status value RSV_{BM25}.

$$RSV_{BM25,k_1,b,k_2,k_3}(d,q,r,\bar{r},c) := \left[\sum_{t \in d \cap q} w_{BM25,k_1,b,k_3}(t,d,q,r,\bar{r}) \right] + len\_norm_{BM25,k_2}$$

$$(2.100)$$

Though the BM25-TF normalizes with respect to the document length, BM25 has in addition a length normalization component separate of the term-match component; Robertson et al. [1998]. This is:

$$len\_norm_{BM25,k_2}(d,q,c) := k_2 \cdot ql \cdot \frac{avgdl(c) - dl}{avgdl(c) + dl} \quad (2.101)$$

Long documents are suppressed (value of length norm is negative, this decreases the score), whereas short documents are lifted (value is positive, this increases the score). This separate normalization component reinforces the effect of the normalization as in the BM25-TF, where the TF component is smaller for long and greater for short documents.

Figure 2.8 shows an overview over the symbols used.

traditional notation	book notation	description
tf or tf_d	tf_d or $n_L(t,d)$	within-document term frequency, i.e., number of Locations at which t occurs in d
K	K_d	parameter to adjust impact of tf_d: $K_d = k_1 \cdot (b \cdot \mathrm{pivdl}(d) + (1-b))$
b	b	parameter to adjust impact of pivoted document length normalization
k_1	k_1	parameter to adjust impact of tf_d
tf'_d	$\mathrm{TF}_{\mathrm{piv},K}(t,d)$	normalized (pivoted) within-document term frequency
qtf or tf_q	tf_q or $n_L(t,q)$	within-query term frequency
k_3	k_3	parameter to adjust impact of tf_q
$w_t^{(1)}$	$w_{\mathrm{RSJ}}(t,r,\bar{r})$	RSJ term weight (Section 2.3.5 (p. 33), RSJ term weight)
ql	ql or $N_L(q)$	query length: number of locations in query q
dl	dl or $N_L(d)$	document length: number of locations in document d
avgdl	avgdl(c)	average document length
k_2	k_2	parameter to adjust impact of document length normalization

Figure 2.8: BM25 Notation.

There were variations of BM25 that show a constant used as an exponent: $\frac{\mathrm{tf}_d^a}{\mathrm{tf}_d^a + K_d^a}$. According to Stephen Robertson, the parameter did not stand the test of time.

2.5.5   SUMMARY

We have discussed the foundations of BM25, an instance of the PRF. The main ingredients are:

1. The TF quantification, Definition 2.29 (p. 45), $\mathrm{TF}_{\mathrm{BM25}}$: contains the pivoted document length.

   see also Definition 2.1 (p. 10), TF_d Variants.

2. The RSJ term weight, Definition 2.19 (p. 33), w_{RSJ}: smooth variant of the BIR term weight.

3. A document length normalization separate from the term-based match of document and query.

The BM25-TF quantification is a fractional TF, and the latter can be expressed using the pivoted TF. The RSJ term weight is a smooth variant of the BIR term weight, where the "0.5-smoothing" can be explained through Laplace's law of succession. The document length normalization, can be related to the derivation of the Poisson RSV, Definition 2.27 (p. 42), RSV$_{\text{Poisson}}$. A long document receives a penalty, whereas a short document receives a reward.

We are now leaving the world of document-likelihood models and move toward LM, the query-likelihood model.

2.6   LM: LANGUAGE MODELING

2.6.1   PROBABILITY MIXTURES

Since the late 90s, language modeling (LM), Croft and Lafferty [2003], Hiemstra [2000], Ponte and Croft [1998], is a popular retrieval model. The starting point of LM is to mix the within-document term probability $P(t|d)$ and the collection-wide term probability $P(t|c)$. This mixture resolves the so-called zero-probability problem when computing the probability $P(q|d)$ where q is a conjunction of term events, and there exists a term t where $P(t|d) = 0$. A probabilistic mixture is not specific to LM; it is a general concept of probability theory. We give in the following the general definition and an example where we compute the probability $P(\text{sunny, warm, ...}|\text{glasgow})$.

Definition 2.33   Probability Mixture (General).   Let three events "x, y, z," and two conditional probabilities $P(z|x)$ and $P(z|y)$ be given.

Then, $P(z|x, y)$ can be estimated as a linear combination/mixture of $P(z|x)$ and $P(z|y)$.

$$P(z|x, y) \approx \delta_x \cdot P(z|x) + (1 - \delta_x) \cdot P(z|y) \qquad (2.102)$$

Here, $0 < \delta_x < 1$ is the mixture parameter.

The mixture parameters can be constant (Jelinek-Mercer mixture), or can be set proportional to the total probabilities. This weighs the conditional probabilities according to the total probabilities. Assume that the norm $|x|$ tells how often x occurs, among N trials in total. Then: $P(x) = |x|/N$ and $P(y) = |y|/N$. This estimation transforms the mixture parameter into a norm-based expression: $\delta_x := \frac{|x|}{|x|+|y|}$.

For a conditional with n evidence events, the mixture is:

$$P(z|x_1, x_2, \ldots, x_n) = \sum_i \delta_i \cdot P(z|x_i)$$

The mixture parameter is:

$$\delta_j := \frac{P(x_j)}{\sum_i P(x_i)}$$

Example   2.34   Probability   Mixture   (General).   For   example,   let $P(\text{sunny, warm, rainy, dry, windy}|\text{glasgow})$ describe the probability that a day in Glasgow is sunny, the next day is warm, the next rainy, and so forth. If for one event (e.g., sunny), the probability were zero, then the probability of the conjunction is zero. A mixture solves the problem. For example, mix $P(x|\text{glasgow})$ with $P(x|\text{uk})$ where $P(x|\text{uk}) > 0$ for each event x. Then, in a week in winter, when $P(\text{sunny}|\text{glasgow}) = 0$, and for the whole of the UK, the weather office reports 2 of 7 days as sunny, the mixed probability is:

$$P(\text{sunny}|\text{glasgow}, \text{uk}) = \delta \cdot \frac{0}{7} + (1 - \delta) \cdot \frac{2}{7}$$

The LM term weight is a mixture (interpolation) of the term probabilities $P(t|d)$ and $P(t|c)$.

Definition 2.35   Probability Mixture (LM).   Let $P(t|d)$ and $P(t|c)$ be two term probabilities; $P(t|d)$ is the within-document probability (foreground model), and $P(t|c)$ is the collection-wide probability (background model). Then, $P(t|d,c)$ can be estimated as follows:

$$P(t|d,c) = \delta \cdot P(t|d) + (1 - \delta) \cdot P(t|c)$$

Example 2.36   Probability Mixture (LM).   For example, let $P(\text{sailing}|d) = 2/100$ and $P(\text{sailing}|c) = 100/10^6$ be given.

$$P(\text{sailing}|d, c) = \delta \cdot \frac{2}{100} + (1 - \delta) \cdot \frac{100}{10^6}$$

One of the beauty of LM is that the probability mixture can be easily formulated for several models. Given a set M of models, the term (event) probability is estimated as follows:

$$P(t|m_1, m_2, \ldots, m_n) = \sum_i \delta_i \cdot P(t|m_i) \tag{2.103}$$

We could call this a "weighted sum" approach where the weighted sum is based on the model weights δ_i and the term probabilities $P(t|m_i)$. Xue et al. [2008], "Retrieval models for question and answer archives," showed how an approach with three models (sentence model, document model, collection model) helps solving question-answering tasks (sentence retrieval).

For the purpose of this book, the formulation of LM term weights and RSV's is for the special case where we mix one foreground model with one background model. We introduce in the following sections several variants of LM-based term weights and RSV's. In one overview, the respective term weights are as follows:

Section 2.6.2: LM1: Basic mixture:

$$w_{\text{LM1},\delta_d}(t,d,q,c) := \text{TF}(t,q) \cdot \log\left(\delta_d \cdot P(t|d) + (1-\delta_d) \cdot P(t|c)\right)$$

Section 2.6.3: LM: LM1 normalized: Mixture divided by background probability $P(t|c)$:

$$w_{\text{LM},\delta_d}(t,d,q,c) := \text{TF}(t,q) \cdot \log\left(\frac{\delta_d \cdot P(t|d) + (1-\delta_d) \cdot P(t|c)}{P(t|c)}\right)$$

Section 2.6.4: JM-LM: LM where $\delta := \delta_d$ is a constant, independent of a document.

$$w_{\text{JM-LM},\delta}(t,d,q,c) := \text{TF}(t,q) \cdot \log\left(1 + \frac{\delta}{1-\delta} \cdot \frac{P(t|d)}{P(t|c)}\right)$$

Section 2.6.5: Dirich-LM: LM where δ_d is proportional to the document.

$$\delta_d = \frac{|d|}{|d| + \mu}$$

Section 2.6.6 LM2: A formulation equivalent to w_{LM}:

$$w_{\text{LM2},\delta_d}(t,d,q,c) := \text{TF}(t,q) \cdot -\log\left(\frac{P(t|c)}{(1-\delta_d) \cdot P(t|c) + \delta_d \cdot P(t|d)}\right)$$

2.6.2   TERM WEIGHT AND RSV: LM1

The LM1 term weight can be formally defined as follows.

Definition 2.37   LM1 term weight w_{LM1}**.**   Let $P(t|d)$ be the within-document term probability (foreground probability). Let $P(t|c)$ is the within-collection term probability (background probability). The parameter δ_d is the mixture parameter; this can be proportional to the foreground model (Dirichlet mixture) or a constant (JM mixture).

The probability $P(t|d,c)$ is estimated via a mixture:

$$P(t|d,c) := \delta_d \cdot P(t|d) + (1-\delta_d) \cdot P(t|c) \tag{2.104}$$

Then, the term weight is:

$$w_{\text{LM1},\delta_d}(t,d,q,c) := \text{TF}(t,q) \cdot \log\left(\delta_d \cdot P(t|d) + (1-\delta_d) \cdot P(t|c)\right) \tag{2.105}$$

Regarding the notation, we employ δ rather than λ as the mixture parameter. This is because λ is the parameter reserved for the Poisson probability (λ is the average occurrence of the event).

The LM1 term weight is based on

$$w_{LM1}(t, d, q, c) = TF(t, q) \cdot \log P(t|d, c)$$

$P(t|d, c)$ is greater for document terms than for non-document terms, since $P(t|d) > 0$ for document terms, and $P(t|d) = 0$ for non-document terms. Thus, the product over the mixed probabilities of the query terms is greater for documents that contain the query terms than for documents that do not contain the query terms. Assuming independence of term events, the product over the term probabilities $P(t|d)$ is equal to $P(q|d)$. Formally, the term independence assumption of LM is:

Assumption 3 *Language Modeling Independence (Dependence) Assumption:*

$$P(q|d, c) \approx \prod_{t \text{ IN } q} P(t|d, c) \approx \prod_{t \in q} P(t|d, c)^{TF(t,q)} \qquad (2.106)$$

The notation t IN q views q is a *sequence* of terms (multiple occurrences of the same term), whereas "$t \in q$" views q as a *set*, and the multiple occurrences are reflected in the exponent $TF(t, q)$. Similarly to the discussion regarding the meaning of $TF(t, d)$, Section 2.1.1 (p. 10), TF-Variants, namely that certain TF variants reflect a dependence assumption, $TF(t, q)$ can be interpreted as the dependence between the term occurrences in a document.

Documents that do not contain the rare query terms are penalized strongly, since for rare terms, $P(t|c)$ is small, and thus, $P(q|d, c)$ is small. RSV_{LM1} is the logarithm of $P(q|d, c)$.

The LM1 RSV is defined as the sum of LM1 term weights.

Definition 2.38 LM1 retrieval status value RSV_{LM1}.

$$RSV_{LM1, \delta_d}(d, q, c) := \sum_{t \in q} w_{LM1, \delta_d}(t, d, q, c) \qquad (2.107)$$

Inserting w_{LM1} yields the RSV in decomposed form.

$$RSV_{LM1, \delta_d}(d, q, c) = \sum_{t \in q} TF(t, q) \cdot \log(\delta_d \cdot P(t|d) + (1 - \delta_d) \cdot P(t|c)) \qquad (2.108)$$

For the set-based decomposition, $TF(t, q)$ reflects the multiple occurrences of t in q.

2.6.3 TERM WEIGHT AND RSV: LM (NORMALIZED)

The subscript LM1 is used to refer to the non-normalized term weight and RSV. RSV_{LM} is the normalized RSV, where RSV_{JM-LM} is the normalization of the JM mixture, and $RSV_{Dirich-LM}$ is the normalization of the Dirichlet mixture.

The normalization of LM1 is based on dividing $P(q|d, c)$ by the document-independent constant $P(q|c)$, where $P(q|c) = \prod_{t \ \mathrm{IN} \ q} P(t|c)$ is the query probability.

The LM term weight can be formally defined as follows.

Definition 2.39   LM term weight w_{LM}.

$$w_{\mathrm{LM},\delta_d}(t, d, q, c) := \mathrm{TF}(t, q) \cdot \log\left(\frac{(1 - \delta_d) \cdot P(t|c) + \delta_d \cdot P(t|d)}{P(t|c)} \right) \tag{2.109}$$

The LM RSV is defined as the sum of LM term weights.

Definition 2.40   LM retrieval status value $\mathrm{RSV}_{\mathrm{LM}}$.

$$\mathrm{RSV}_{\mathrm{LM},\delta_d}(d, q, c) := \sum_{t \in q} w_{\mathrm{LM},\delta_d}(t, d, q, c) \tag{2.110}$$

Inserting w_{LM} yields the RSV in decomposed form.

$$\mathrm{RSV}_{\mathrm{LM},\delta_d}(d, q, c) = \sum_{t \in q} \mathrm{TF}(t, q) \cdot \log\left(\frac{(1 - \delta_d) \cdot P(t|c) + \delta_d \cdot P(t|d)}{P(t|c)} \right) \tag{2.111}$$

The relationship between LM and LM1 is based on dividing $P(q|d, c)$ by $P(q|c)$, a constant, document-independent factor.

$$\log \frac{P(q|d, c)}{P(q|c)} = \log P(q|d, c) - \log P(q|c)$$

This leads to the following equation:

$$\mathrm{RSV}_{\mathrm{LM}}(d, q, c) = \mathrm{RSV}_{\mathrm{LM1}}(d, q, c) - \sum_{t \in q} \mathrm{TF}(t, q) \cdot \log P(t|c) \tag{2.112}$$

$\mathrm{RSV}_{\mathrm{LM}}$ is equal to the difference between $\mathrm{RSV}_{\mathrm{LM1}}$ and the document-independent factor $\sum_{t \in q} \log P(t|c)$.

2.6.4 TERM WEIGHT AND RSV: JM-LM

In addition, for constant δ, the score can be divided by $\prod_{t \text{ IN } q}(1 - \delta)$. This leads to the following equation, Hiemstra [2000]:

$$\frac{P(q|d,c)}{P(q|c) \cdot \prod_{t \text{ IN } q}(1 - \delta)} = \frac{\prod_{t \text{ IN } q} P(t|d,c)}{\prod_{t \text{ IN } q}[(1 - \delta) \cdot P(t|c)]} = \prod_{t \in d \cap q}\left(1 + \frac{\delta}{1 - \delta} \cdot \frac{P(t|d)}{P(t|c)}\right)^{\text{TF}(t,q)}$$

$$(2.113)$$

This transformation is helpful since the product over query terms is reduced to the product over terms that occur in document and query.

The JM-LM term weight can be formally defined as follows.

Definition 2.41 JM-LM term weight $w_{\text{JM-LM}}$.

$$w_{\text{JM-LM},\delta}(t,d,q,c) := \text{TF}(t,q) \cdot \log\left(1 + \frac{\delta}{1 - \delta} \cdot \frac{P(t|d)}{P(t|c)}\right) \qquad (2.114)$$

The JM-LM RSV is defined as the sum of JM-LM term weights.

Definition 2.42 JM-LM retrieval status value $\text{RSV}_{\text{JM-LM}}$.

$$\text{RSV}_{\text{JM-LM},\delta}(d,q,c) := \sum_{t \in d \cap q} w_{\text{JM-LM},\delta}(t,d,q,c) \qquad (2.115)$$

Inserting $w_{\text{JM-LM}}$ yields the RSV in decomposed form.

$$\text{RSV}_{\text{JM-LM},\delta}(d,q,c) := \sum_{t \in q} \text{TF}(t,q) \cdot \log\left(1 + \frac{\delta}{1 - \delta} \cdot \frac{P(t|d)}{P(t|c)}\right) \qquad (2.116)$$

2.6.5 TERM WEIGHT AND RSV: DIRICH-LM

The Dirichlet-based LM applies a document-dependent (foreground-dependent) mixture parameter such as $\delta_d = \text{dl}/(\text{dl} + \mu)$. The RSV is based on $P(q|d)/P(q)$.

The Dirich-LM term weight can be formally defined as follows.

Definition 2.43 Dirich-LM term weight $w_{\text{Dirich-LM}}$.

$$w_{\text{Dirich-LM},\mu}(t,d,q,c) := \text{TF}(t,q) \cdot \log\left(\frac{\mu}{\mu + |d|} + \frac{|d|}{|d| + \mu} \cdot \frac{P(t|d)}{P(t|c)}\right) \qquad (2.117)$$

The usage of $|d|$ underlines that any normalization of the document d could be used to parametrize the mixture. Often, the normalization is $|d| = \mathrm{dl} = N_L(d)$, i.e., the normalization is with respect to the document length.

The Dirich-LM RSV is defined as the sum of Dirich-LM term weights.

Definition 2.44   Dirich-LM retrieval status value $\mathrm{RSV}_{\text{Dirich-LM}}$.

$$\mathrm{RSV}_{\text{Dirich-LM},\mu}(d,q,c) := \sum_{t \in q} w_{\text{Dirich-LM},\mu}(t,d,q,c) \tag{2.118}$$

Inserting $w_{\text{Dirich-LM}}$ yields the RSV in decomposed form.

$$\mathrm{RSV}_{\text{Dirich-LM}}(d,q,c,\mu) := \sum_{t \in q} \mathrm{TF}(t,q) \cdot \log\left(\frac{\mu}{\mu + |d|} + \frac{|d|}{|d| + \mu} \cdot \frac{P(t|d)}{P(t|c)}\right) \tag{2.119}$$

Finally, we show some transformations that make the length component explicit. For $\mathrm{TF}(t,q) = \mathrm{tf}_q$, and by isolating $\mu/(\mu + |d|)$, for the RSV, we obtain:

$$\mathrm{RSV}_{\text{Dirich-LM},\mu}(d,q,c) = \sum_{t \in q} \mathrm{tf}_q \cdot \log\left(\frac{\mu}{\mu + |d|} \cdot \left(1 + \frac{|d|}{\mu} \cdot \frac{P(t|d)}{P(t|c)}\right)\right) \tag{2.120}$$

Next, we make use of $\mathrm{ql} = \sum_t \mathrm{tf}_q$. Also, we choose $|d| = \mathrm{dl}$. Moreover, $P(t|d) = \mathrm{tf}_d/\mathrm{dl}$ is the common estimate for the within-document term probability.

$$\mathrm{RSV}_{\text{Dirich-LM},\mu}(d,q,c) = \left[\sum_{t \in d \cap q} \mathrm{tf}_q \cdot \log\left(1 + \frac{\mathrm{tf}_d}{\mu} \cdot \frac{1}{P(t|c)}\right)\right] + \mathrm{ql} \cdot \log\frac{\mu}{\mu + \mathrm{dl}} \tag{2.121}$$

What is the setting of μ? One option is: $\mu = \mathrm{avgdl}$, i.e., the Dirichlet parameter is equal to the average document length. Then $\mathrm{RSV}_{\text{Dirich-LM}}$ becomes:

$$\mathrm{RSV}_{\text{Dirich-LM},\mu=\mathrm{avgdl}}(d,q,c) = \left[\sum_{t \in d \cap q} \mathrm{tf}_q \cdot \log\left(1 + \frac{\mathrm{tf}_d}{\mathrm{tf}_c} \cdot N_D(c)\right)\right] + \mathrm{ql} \cdot \log\frac{\mathrm{avgdl}(c)}{\mathrm{avgdl}(c) + \mathrm{dl}}$$

In the term matching component, $\mathrm{avgdl} \cdot P(t|c) = \mathrm{tf}_c/N_D(c) = \lambda(t,c)$ is the average term frequency (the expected term frequency in a document of average length), the parameter we know from Section 2.4 (p. 35), Poisson. In the length normalization component, $\mathrm{avgdl}/(\mathrm{avgdl}+\mathrm{dl})$ is reminiscent of the document length normalization component of BM25; Equation 2.101 (p. 47), $\mathrm{len\_norm}_{\text{BM25}}$.

2.6.6 TERM WEIGHT AND RSV: LM2

In Section 3.9.4 (p. 101), TF-IDF and LM, we discuss that TF-IDF is based on the negative logarithm of $P_D(t|c)^{\mathrm{TF}(t,d)}$, and that this is an approximation of an expression dual to the LM term weight.

$$- \log P_D(t|c)^{\mathrm{TF}(t,d)} \approx - \log \left(\frac{P_L(t|c)}{P_L(t|q,c)} \right)^{\mathrm{TF}(t,d)} = - \log \left(\frac{P_L(t|c)}{P_L(t|c)/P_D(t|c)} \right)^{\mathrm{TF}(t,d)}$$

This relationship between TF-IDF and LM, and also the modeling of LM in a probabilistic logical framework, motivated the definition of an LM variant referred to as LM2. Essentially, LM2 is the same as LM, we just swap numerator and denominator in the normalization, i.e., we apply

$$\log \frac{P(t|d,c)}{P(t|c)} = - \log \frac{P(t|c)}{P(t|d,c)}$$

The LM2 term weight can be formally defined as follows.

Definition 2.45 LM2 term weight w_{LM2}.

$$w_{\mathrm{LM2},\delta_d}(t,d,q,c) := \mathrm{TF}(t,q) \cdot - \log \left(\frac{P(t|c)}{(1-\delta_d) \cdot P(t|c) + \delta_d \cdot P(t|d)} \right) \tag{2.122}$$

The LM2 RSV is defined as the sum of LM2 term weights.

Definition 2.46 LM2 retrieval status value $\mathrm{RSV}_{\mathrm{LM2}}$.

$$\mathrm{RSV}_{\mathrm{LM2},\delta_d}(d,q,c) := \sum_{t \in q} w_{\mathrm{LM2},\delta_d}(t,d,q,c) \tag{2.123}$$

Inserting w_{LM2} yields the RSV in decomposed form.

$$\mathrm{RSV}_{\mathrm{LM2},\delta_d}(d,q,c) = \sum_{t \in q} \mathrm{TF}(t,q) \cdot - \log \left(\frac{P(t|c)}{(1-\delta_d) \cdot P(t|c) + \delta_d \cdot P(t|d)} \right) \tag{2.124}$$

The relationship between LM2 and LM1 is expressed similarly to Equation 2.112 (p. 53), LM and LM1.

$$\mathrm{RSV}_{\mathrm{LM2}}(d,q,c) = \left[\sum_{t \in q} \mathrm{TF}(t,q) \cdot - \log P(t|c) \right] + \mathrm{RSV}_{\mathrm{LM1}}(d,q,c) \tag{2.125}$$

Next, we consider the JM-LM2 term weight, and this is followed by the Dirich-LM2 term weight.

The JM-LM2 term weight can be formally defined as follows.

Definition 2.47 JM-LM2 term weight $w_{\text{JM-LM2}}$.

$$w_{\text{JM-LM2},\delta}(t,d,q,c) := \text{TF}(t,q) \cdot -\log\left(\frac{(1-\delta) \cdot P(t|c)}{(1-\delta) \cdot P(t|c) + \delta \cdot P(t|d)}\right) \qquad (2.126)$$

The Dirichlet-based term weight can be obtained by inserting $\delta_d = \frac{\text{dl}}{\text{dl}+\mu}$ into the general LM term weight, equation 2.122.

$$w_{\text{Dirich-LM2},\mu}(t,d,q,c) = \text{TF}(t,q) \cdot -\log\frac{(\mu + \text{dl}) \cdot P(t|c)}{\mu \cdot P(t|c) + \text{dl} \cdot P(t|d)}$$

The Dirich-LM2 term weight can be formally defined as follows.

Definition 2.48 Dirich-LM2 term weight $w_{\text{Dirich-LM2}}$.

$$w_{\text{Dirich-LM2},\mu}(t,d,q,c) := \text{TF}(t,q) \cdot -\log\left(\frac{\mu \cdot P(t|c) + \text{dl} \cdot P(t|c)}{\mu \cdot P(t|c) + \text{dl} \cdot P(t|d)}\right) \qquad (2.127)$$

In this formulation, in the numerator, the expression $\text{dl} \cdot P(t|c) = E[\text{tf}_d]$, is the expected within-document term frequency; *see also* Section 2.4 (p. 35), Poisson. In the denominator, the expression $\text{dl} \cdot P(t|d) = \text{tf}_d$, is the actual within-document term frequency. This shows that Dirichlet-based LM measures the difference between the expected term frequency, $\text{dl} \cdot P_L(t|c)$, and the actual term frequency, tf_d.

2.6.7 SUMMARY

We have discussed the foundations of LM. We referred to the basic mixture as LM1, to distinguish it from three normalizations: the general normalization $P(q|d)/P(q)$, and the specific normalizations JM-LM and Dirich-LM. JM-LM is based on $P(q|d)/P(q)/\prod_{t \text{ IN } q}(1-\delta)$, where δ is a constant. Dirich-LM is based on $P(q|d)/P(q)$, where $\delta_d = \frac{|d|}{|d|+\mu}$ is the mixture parameter proportional to the document length.

There are several research issues regarding LM:

1. Estimation of $P(t|d)$ and $P(t|c)$:

   The intuitive estimates are: $P_L(t|d):=n_L(t,d)/N_L(d) = \text{tf}_d/\text{dl}$ and $P_L(t|c):= n_L(t,c)/N_L(c) = \text{tf}_c/(\sum_d \text{dl})$.

   For $P(t|c)$, another estimate is the Document-based estimate: $P_D(t|c):= n_D(t,c)/N_D(c) = \text{df}(t,c)/N_D(c)$. This needs careful consideration since then, $P(t|d)$ and $P(t|c)$ are based on different event spaces.

Since the Document-based estimate is the one used in IDF, $-\log P_D(t|c)$, this estimate motivates one to view LM as a probabilistic interpretation of TF-IDF; *see also* Section 3.9.4 (p. 101), TF-IDF and LM.

2. Setting of the mixture parameter δ:

In JM-LM, δ is constant. For example $\delta := 0.8$, means to assign a higher impact to the document-based probability $P(t|d)$ than to the collection-based probability $P(t|c)$.

Alternatively, and conducive for retrieval performance, is the proportional setting in Dirich-LM. This is $\delta_d := \frac{|d|}{|d|+\mu}$, where a norm (e.g., $|d|$ could be the document length) is applied to balance $P(t|d)$ and $P(t|c)$. This reflects that there is more trust in probabilities estimated from large (long) documents than small (short) documents. The choices for $|d|$ and μ open up several pathways.

3. Relationship between LM and the probability of relevance?

Azzopardi and Roelleke [2007], Lafferty and Zhai [2003], Lavrenko and Croft [2001], Sparck-Jones et al. [2003] discuss the relationship between the odds of relevance, $O(r|d,q)$, and LM, $P(q|d)$.

In addition to the common formulations here denoted LM1, LM, JM-LM and Dirich-LM, this book introduces a formulation referred to as LM2. LM2 is based on the negative logarithm, namely $\log \frac{P(t|d,c)}{P(t|c)} = -\log \frac{P(t|c)}{P(t|d,c)}$. This formulation is of advantage in the probabilistic logical modeling of LM, and can be also used to describe relationships between LM and TF-IDF.

LM is the model based on the *conjunctive* decomposition of $P(q|d)$. Twenty years before LM became popular, Turtle and Croft [1990] proposed a PIN-based modeling of retrieval, which explains IR as being based on the *disjunctive* decomposition of $P(q|d)$.

2.7 PIN'S: PROBABILISTIC INFERENCE NETWORKS

Figure 2.9 shows two PIN's, one for modeling document retrieval, and another one for modeling "Find Mr. X." The side-by-side arrangement underlines the duality between document retrieval and "Find Mr. X." For document retrieval, the PIN models the relationships (inference) between documents, terms, and queries. The purpose is to estimate the probability that document d is relevant to query q, i.e., that query q is inferred from document d, or in other words, that d implies q. For "Find Mr. X," the PIN models the inference between cities, activities, and Mr. X. The purpose is to estimate the probability that Mr. X is inferred from a given city. The parallels between the two scenarios helps to compare PIN's in IR against the general role of PIN's for modeling knowledge and reasoning.

The documents (cities) are the *source* events, and the query (Mr. X) is the *target* event. Note that the detective wants $P(\text{london}|\text{mrx})$ to make a decision about the city to travel to. Transferring this to the IR case means that a search engine wants $P(d|q)$ to make a decision

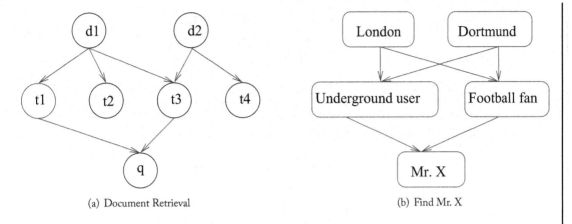

(a) Document Retrieval   (b) Find Mr. X

Figure 2.9: Two Probabilistic Inference Networks.

about the rank of a document. The conditional probabilities may feel a bit counter-intuitive since the PIN is directed from the source to the target, whereas the conditional probabilities are of the form $P(\text{source}|\text{target})$. This analogy points us at the issue to decide whether the inference is $d \rightarrow q$ or $q \rightarrow d$.

For a document, the terms are target events, and for the query, the terms are source events. Document d_1 implies/contains three term events: t_1, t_2, t_3. This leads to $2^3 = 8$ min-terms, where a min-term is a conjunction of positive and negative term events (e.g., $t_1 \wedge t_2 \wedge \bar{t_2}$ is a min-term). Therefore, the computation of a PIN is of exponential complexity ($O(2^n)$, where n is the number of source events for a given node).

The overall idea of a PIN is to compute the conditional probability of any selected target node. The computation is based on the decomposition for a set of disjoint and exhaustive events. Let X be an exhaustive set of disjoint events.

$$P(q|d) = \sum_{x \in X} P(q|x) \cdot P(x|d) \qquad (2.128)$$

The min-terms are the disjoint events.

$$X = \{(t_1, t_2, t_3), (t_1, t_2, \bar{t_3}), \ldots\} \qquad (2.129)$$

The min-terms correspond to the Boolean conjunctions of the source events that point to the target.

The probability flow in a PIN can be described via a matrix; this matrix is referred to as the *link* or *transition* matrix. The *link* matrix L contains the transition probabilities $P(\text{target}|x, \text{source})$, where x is a min-term of the nodes that connect the target node to the source node. Usually, $P(\text{target}|x, \text{source}) = P(\text{target}|x)$ is assumed, and this assumption is referred to as the *linked independence assumption*. Using the link matrix, we obtain the following expressions:

$$L := \begin{bmatrix} P(q|x_1) & \cdots & P(q|x_n) \\ P(\bar{q}|x_1) & \cdots & P(\bar{q}|x_n) \end{bmatrix} \tag{2.130}$$

$$\begin{pmatrix} P(q|d) \\ P(\bar{q}|d) \end{pmatrix} = L \cdot \begin{pmatrix} P(x_1|d) \\ \vdots \\ P(x_n|d) \end{pmatrix} \tag{2.131}$$

For illustrating the link matrix, a matrix for three terms is shown next.

$$L^{\text{Transposed}} = \begin{bmatrix} P(q|t_1, t_2, t_3) & P(\bar{q}|t_1, t_2, t_3) \\ P(q|t_1, t_2, \bar{t}_3) & P(\bar{q}|t_1, t_2, \bar{t}_3) \\ P(q|t_1, \bar{t}_2, t_3) & P(\bar{q}|t_1, \bar{t}_2, t_3) \\ P(q|t_1, \bar{t}_2, \bar{t}_3) & P(\bar{q}|t_1, \bar{t}_2, \bar{t}_3) \\ P(q|\bar{t}_1, t_2, t_3) & P(\bar{q}|\bar{t}_1, t_2, t_3) \\ P(q|\bar{t}_1, t_2, \bar{t}_3) & P(\bar{q}|\bar{t}_1, t_2, \bar{t}_3) \\ P(q|\bar{t}_1, \bar{t}_2, t_3) & P(\bar{q}|\bar{t}_1, \bar{t}_2, t_3) \\ P(q|\bar{t}_1, \bar{t}_2, \bar{t}_3) & P(\bar{q}|\bar{t}_1, \bar{t}_2, \bar{t}_3) \end{bmatrix} \tag{2.132}$$

There are some special link matrices. The matrices L_{or} and L_{and} reflect the Boolean combination of the linkage between a source and a target.

$$L_{\text{or}} = \begin{bmatrix} 1 & 1 & 1 & 1 & 1 & 1 & 1 & 0 \\ 0 & 0 & 0 & 0 & 0 & 0 & 0 & 1 \end{bmatrix} \tag{2.133}$$

$$L_{\text{and}} = \begin{bmatrix} 1 & 0 & 0 & 0 & 0 & 0 & 0 & 0 \\ 0 & 1 & 1 & 1 & 1 & 1 & 1 & 1 \end{bmatrix} \tag{2.134}$$

It is evident that the link matrices for the Boolean cases correspond to a particular distribution of the probabilities $P(\text{target}|x)$. The multiplication of the link matrix with the probabilities of the sources yields the target probabilities. This is illustrated in the next equation of the "3-term" example.

$$\begin{pmatrix} P(q|d) \\ P(\bar{q}|d) \end{pmatrix} = L \cdot \begin{pmatrix} P(t_1, t_2, t_3|d) \\ P(t_1, t_2, \bar{t}_3|d) \\ P(t_1, \bar{t}_2, t_3|d) \\ P(t_1, \bar{t}_2, \bar{t}_3|d) \\ P(\bar{t}_1, t_2, t_3|d) \\ P(\bar{t}_1, t_2, \bar{t}_3|d) \\ P(\bar{t}_1, \bar{t}_2, t_3|d) \\ P(\bar{t}_1, \bar{t}_2, \bar{t}_3|d) \end{pmatrix} \tag{2.135}$$

Often, a PIN will be under-specified, i.e., not all min-term probabilities but only the single-event probabilities, e.g., $P(t|d)$ and $P(q|t)$ will be available.

2.7.1 THE TURTLE/CROFT LINK MATRIX

Croft and Turtle [1992], Turtle and Croft [1992] proposes a special setting of the link matrix. Let $w_t := P(q|t)$ be the query term probabilities. Then, estimate the link matrix elements $P(q|x)$, where x is a Boolean combination of terms, as follows.

$$L_{\text{Turtle/Croft}} = \begin{bmatrix} 1 & \frac{w_1+w_2}{w_0} & \frac{w_1+w_3}{w_0} & \frac{w_1}{w_0} & \frac{w_2+w_3}{w_0} & \frac{w_2}{w_0} & \frac{w_3}{w_0} & 0 \\ 0 & \frac{w_3}{w_0} & \frac{w_2}{w_0} & \frac{w_2+w_3}{w_0} & \frac{w_1}{w_0} & \frac{w_1+w_3}{w_0} & \frac{w_1+w_2}{w_0} & 1 \end{bmatrix} \tag{2.136}$$

The multiplication of the first row with the min-term probabilities yields the following:

$$P(q|d) =$$
$$\frac{w_1 + w_2 + w_3}{w_0} \cdot P(t_1, t_2, t_3|d) +$$
$$\frac{w_1 + w_2}{w_0} \cdot P(t_1, t_2, \bar{t_3}|d) + \frac{w_1 + w_3}{w_0} \cdot P(t_1, \bar{t_2}, t_3|d) + \frac{w_2 + w_3}{w_0} \cdot P(\bar{t_1}, t_2, t_3|d) +$$
$$\frac{w_1}{w_0} \cdot P(t_1, \bar{t_2}, \bar{t_3}|d) + \frac{w_2}{w_0} \cdot P(\bar{t_1}, t_2, \bar{t_3}|d) + \frac{w_3}{w_0} \cdot P(\bar{t_1}, \bar{t_2}, t_3|d)$$

The special setting of L leads to a formation of weights and probabilities that reduces to a closed form of linear complexity. The intermediate step is illustrated in the following equation (we use $t_i = P(t_i|d)$ for shortening the expressions).

$$w_1 t_1 + w_2 t_2 + w_3 t_3 =$$
$$\begin{array}{ll} w_1 t_1 t_2 t_3 + w_2 t_1 t_2 t_3 + w_3 t_1 t_2 t_3 + & \#w_1 + w_2 + w_3 \\ w_1 t_1 t_2 - w_1 t_1 t_2 t_3 + w_2 t_1 t_2 - w_2 t_1 t_2 t_3 + & \#w_1 + w_2 \\ w_1 t_1 t_3 - w_1 t_1 t_2 t_3 + w_3 t_1 t_3 - w_3 t_1 t_2 t_3 + & \#w_1 + w_3 \\ w_2 t_2 t_3 - w_2 t_1 t_2 t_3 + w_3 t_2 t_3 - w_3 t_1 t_2 t_3 + & \#w_2 + w_3 \\ w_1 t_1 - w_1 t_1 t_2 - w_1 t_1 t_3 + w_1 t_1 t_2 t_3 + & \#w_1 \\ w_2 t_2 - w_2 t_1 t_2 - w_2 t_2 t_3 + w_2 t_1 t_2 t_3 + & \#w_2 \\ w_3 t_3 - w_3 t_1 t_3 - w_3 t_2 t_3 + w_3 t_1 t_2 t_3 & \#w_3 \end{array}$$

Due to the Boolean combination of weights, all expressions with more than one term true cancel out. Thus, the probability $P(q|d)$ becomes:

$$P(q|d) = \frac{w_1}{w_0} \cdot P(t_1|d) + \frac{w_2}{w_0} \cdot P(t_2|d) + \frac{w_3}{w_0} \cdot P(t_3|d) \tag{2.137}$$

The term weight w_i corresponds to the conditional query probability $P(q|t_i)$.

$$w_i := P(q|t_i) \tag{2.138}$$

2.7.2 TERM WEIGHT AND RSV

The PIN-based term weight can be formally defined as follows.

Definition 2.49 PIN-based term weight w_{PIN}.

$$w_{\text{PIN}}(t, d, q, c) := \frac{1}{\sum_{t'} P(q|t', c)} \cdot P(q|t, c) \cdot P(t|d, c) \tag{2.139}$$

The PIN-based RSV is defined as the sum of PIN-based term weights.

Definition 2.50 PIN-based retrieval status value RSV_{PIN}.

$$\text{RSV}_{\text{PIN}}(d, q, c) := \sum_t w_{\text{PIN}}(t, d, q, c) \tag{2.140}$$

Inserting w_{PIN} yields the RSV in decomposed form.

$$\text{RSV}_{\text{PIN}}(d, q, c) = \frac{1}{\sum_t P(q|t, c)} \cdot \sum_{t \in d \cap q} P(q|t, c) \cdot P(t|d, c) \tag{2.141}$$

It is evident that $P(q|t, c)$ could be replaced by $\text{pidf}(t, c)$ because both values are high for rare terms. We look at this relationship between PIN's and TF-IDF in Section 3.9.6 (p. 104), TF-IDF and PIN's.

Example 2.51 PIN RSV computation Let the following term probabilities be given:

t_i	$P(t_i|d)$	$P(q|t_i)$
sailing	2/3	1/10,000
boats	1/2	1/1,000

Terms are independent events. $P(t|d)$ is proportional to the within-document term frequency, and $P(q|t)$ is proportional to the IDF. The RSV is:

$$\text{RSV}_{\text{PIN}}(d, q, c) = \frac{1}{1/10,000 + 1/1,000} \cdot (1/10,000 \cdot 2/3 + 1/1,000 \cdot 1/2) =$$

$$= \frac{1}{11/10,000} \cdot (2/30,000 + 1/2,000) = \frac{10,000}{11} \cdot (2 + 15)/30,000 =$$

$$= \frac{1}{11} \cdot (2 + 15)/3 = 17/33 \approx 0.51$$

2.7.3 SUMMARY

We have discussed the foundations of PIN's. We have reconsidered the special link matrix, $L_{\text{Turtle/Croft}}$, described in Croft and Turtle [1992], Turtle and Croft [1992], which leads to an RSV with linear complexity. Essentially, the RSV is the sum of the term weights $w_{\text{PIN}}(t, d, q, c) = \frac{P(q|t)}{\sum_{t'} P(q|t')} \cdot P(t|d)$. Herein, the probability $P(q|t)$ is proportional to the IDF, and the probability $P(t|d)$ is proportional to the within-document term frequency. This indicates the relationship between TF-IDF and PIN's; *see also* Section 3.9.6 (p. 104), TF-IDF and PIN's.

2.8 DIVERGENCE-BASED MODELS AND DFR

To approach the role of divergence-based models, we consider first a general example, and relate this to IR (terms and documents).

Example 2.52 Divergence.   Let P_{uk} be the probability function for the weather in the UK, and let P_{london} be the probability function for the weather in London. Let $X = \{\text{sunny, cloudy, rainy}, \ldots\}$ be the set of events.

The fraction $P_{\text{uk}}(\text{sunny})/P_{\text{london}}(\text{sunny})$ measures the difference between the two probabilities.

The weighted sum of the logarithm of the fractions of probabilities is known as KL-divergence:

$$D_{\text{KL}}\left(P_{\text{uk}} || P_{\text{london}}\right) = \sum_{x \in X} P_{\text{uk}}(x) \cdot \log \frac{P_{\text{uk}}(x)}{P_{\text{london}}(x)}$$

It can be viewed as the expectation value of the random variable for the logarithm of the fractions of the two probabilities. Also, KL-divergence is the difference between cross entropy, $H_{\text{cross}}(P_{\text{uk}}, P_{\text{london}})$ and entropy, $H(P_{\text{uk}})$; *see also* Section 3.11.6 (p. 111), Information Theory: KL-Divergence.

The probabilities can be estimated in different ways. One possibility is to observe the events over days. Let $n_{\text{Days}}(\text{sunny, uk})$ be the number of sunny days in the UK, and let $N_{\text{Days}}(\text{uk})$ be the total number of days. Then, $P_{\text{Days}}(\text{sunny}|\text{uk}) := n_{\text{Days}}(\text{sunny, uk})/N_{\text{Days}}(\text{uk})$ is the respective probability.

Another option could be to count the trips to the UK where one experienced at least one sunny day: $P_{\text{Trips}}(\text{sunny}|\text{uk}) := n_{\text{Trips}}(\text{sunny, uk})/N_{\text{Trips}}(\text{uk})$.

Regarding the analogy to IR, counting *sunny days* corresponds to counting *term occurrences*, and counting *trips* corresponds to counting *documents*; *see also* Section 2.4.2 (p. 36), Poisson Analogy: Sunny Days and Term Occurrences.

2.8.1 DFR: DIVERGENCE FROM RANDOMNESS

The underlying idea of DFR is as follows:[2]

---

[2]Quote from http://ir.dcs.gla.ac.uk/terrier/doc/dfr_description.html, 2006.

The more the divergence of the within-document term frequency (tf_d) from its frequency within the collection (tf_c), meaning the more divergent from randomness the term is, the more the information carried by the term in the document.

$$w_{\text{DFR-1},M}(t, d, \text{collection}) \propto -\log P_M(t \in d\,|\text{collection})$$

M stands for the type of model of the DFR employed to compute the probability.

We can translate this as follows: for a term occurring in a random pattern, $P_M(t \in d\,|c)$ is maximal, i.e., the DFR weight is minimal. On the other hand, $P_M(t \in d\,|c)$ is smaller than the maximal probability, if term t occurs in a non-random pattern. Whereas a randomly distributed term occurs in very few documents more than once, we find for terms in IR test collections that they occur in more documents more frequently than a model of randomness tells; *see also* Section 2.4 (p. 35), Poisson Model.

In addition to the probability $P(t \in d\,|c)$, there is the probability $P(\mathrm{tf}_d|c)$, the probability of the term frequency. Gianni Amati views the latter, $P(\mathrm{tf}_d|c)$, as the new DFR—the second-generation DFR.

$$w_{\text{DFR-2},M}(t, d, \text{collection}) \propto -\log P_M(\mathrm{tf}_d|\text{collection})$$

The original formulation, i.e., the first-generation DFR with $P(t \in d\,|c)$, can be expressed as the cumulative of the probabilities of the term frequency:

$$P(t \in d\,|\text{collection}) = P(\mathrm{tf}_d > 0|\text{collection}) = 1 - P(\mathrm{tf}_d = 0|\text{collection})$$

It is also helpful to apply the following notation:

$$P(t \in d\,|\text{collection}) = P(k_t > 0|d, \text{collection})$$

In this formulation, k_t is the frequency of term t, and it becomes explicit that the document event d is part of the conditional. Thus DFR-1 corresponds to the probability of the condition $k_t > 0$, and DFR-2 corresponds to the condition $k_t = \mathrm{tf}_d$.

Amati and van Rijsbergen [2002] introduced DFR, and important is that in addition to the two different conditions on tf_d there are two ways of computing the *informative content* of a term. The first is based on the negative logarithm of the frequency probability, and the second is the complement (Popper's formulation of informative content).

$$
\begin{aligned}
\mathrm{inf1}(t, d, c) &:= -\log P_1(\text{condition on } k_t|d, c) & (2.142)\\
\mathrm{inf2}(t, d, c) &:= 1 - P_2(\text{condition on } k_t|d, c) & (2.143)
\end{aligned}
$$

Both measures express that the informative content is high if the frequency probability is small (the term is rare).

The combination of the measures is at the core of DFR. Equation 1 from Amati and van Rijsbergen [2002] is:

$$w_{\text{DFR}}(t, d, c) = \mathrm{inf2}(t, d, c) \cdot \mathrm{inf1}(t, d, c) \qquad (2.144)$$

This equation is open for the two cases, $k_t > 0$ or $k_t = \text{tf}_d$, and two different models of randomness can be chosen for the two information measures. In addition, the condition can be adapted to $k_t = \text{tfn}_d$, where tfn_d is a normalized value. The normalization is a function of tf_d, the document length dl, and any other parameter such as the average document length avgdl.

In summary, DFR models are "made up" of three components (see Table I in Amati and van Rijsbergen [2002]):

1. Basic Models: Poisson (P); Approximation of the binomial models with the divergence (D); Geometric (G); Bose-Einstein; Mixture of Poisson and IDF; and others

2. First normalization: Laplace (L), Bernoulli (B)

3. Second (length) normalization:

   Hypothesis 1: Uniform term frequency distribution: tf_d/dl. Then, the normalized term frequency is $\text{tfn}_d = \text{tf}_d/(\text{dl}/\text{avgdl})$. This is because of the integral over the density function:

   $$\int_{\text{dl}}^{\text{dl}+\text{avgdl}} \text{tf}_d/\text{dl} \; dx = \text{tf}_d/\text{dl} \cdot \text{avgdl}$$

   Hypothesis 2: Term frequency density is a decreasing function: $\text{tf}_d/\text{length}$. Then, the following integral gives the normalized term frequency:

   $$\int_{\text{dl}}^{\text{dl}+\text{avgdl}} \text{tf}_d/x \; dx = \text{tf}_d \cdot \ln\left(1 + \frac{\text{avgdl}}{\text{dl}}\right)$$

Given this systematics, for example, the DFR model PL1 is a combination of Poisson (basic model), Laplace (first normalization), and hypothesis 1 (normalization with respect to the document length).

2.8.2   DFR: SAMPLING OVER DOCUMENTS AND LOCATIONS

Though the underlying idea of DFR seems intuitive, it is difficult to fully understand the effect of the formulae related to DFR[3]. To highlight some of the issues, we review the example given in Baeza-Yates and Ribeiro-Neto [2011], page 114.

Example 2.53   DFR, binomial probability.

"To illustrate, consider a collection with $N_D = 1,000$ documents and a term k_t [Baeza-Yates and Ribeiro-Neto [2011] use k_t to refer to a term; we use in this book t for the

---

[3]I would like to thank Gianni Amati, Ricardo Baeza-Yates, and Berthier Ribeiro-Neto for discussing the formulation of DFR.

term, and k_t for the frequency] that occurs $n_t = 10$ times in the collection. Then, the probability of observing $k_t = 4$ occurrences of term k_t [t] in a document is given by

$$P(k_t|c) = \binom{n_t}{k_t} \cdot p^{k_t} \cdot (1-p)^{(n_t-k_t)} = \binom{10}{4} \cdot \left(\frac{1}{1,000}\right)^4 \cdot \left(1-\left(\frac{1}{1,000}\right)\right)^{(10-4)}$$

which is a standard binomial distribution. In general, let $p = 1/N$ be the probability of observing a term in a document, where N is the total number of documents."

We first reconsider the binomial probability. The single event probability, $p_d = P(d|c) = 1/N_D(c) = 1/1,000$, is the probability of *document* d. The number of trials, $n_t = \text{tf}_c = 10$, is the number of times term t occurs in collection c.

$P_{\text{binomial},\text{tf}_c,p_d}(k_d)$ is the probability of a sequence
with $k_d = 4$ occurrences of document d in $n = \text{tf}_c = 10$ trials;
a trial corresponds to drawing a ball (document) from the urn (*Documents* in collection c).

Expressed as a conditional probability, we may write $P(k_d|t,c) = P_{\text{binomial},\text{tf}_c,P(d|c)}(k_d)$, and this underlines that the probability of the frequency k_d of the document d depends on tf_c, the number of occurrences of term t.

However, when estimating the probability of observing k_t occurrences of term t in a particular document, then we need to sample over term occurrences (locations at which terms occur).

Therefore, let $p_t = P_L(t|c) = 1/1,000$ be the single event probability, i.e., term t occurs in 0.1% of the *Locations*. For example, $P_L(t|c) = \text{tf}_c/N_L(c) = 100/10^5$, where $\text{tf}_c = n_L(t,c) = 100$ is the number of *Locations* at which term t occurs in collection c, and $N_L(c) = 10^5$ is the number of *Locations* (length of the collection). The number of trials is equal to the document length: $n_d = \text{dl}$.

$P_{\text{binomial},\text{dl},P_L(t|c)}(k_t)$ is the probability of a sequence
with $k_t = 4$ occurrences of term t in $n = \text{dl} = 10$ trials;
a trial corresponds to drawing a ball (location) from the urn (*Locations* in collection c).

We can imagine the urn to contain a ball per location, and each ball is labelled with the term that occurs at the location. In this formulation of the binomial, the number of trials is the document length, $n = \text{dl}$, rather than the collection-wide term frequency, $n = \text{tf}_c$.

2.8.3 DFR: BINOMIAL TRANSFORMATION STEP

Finally, we investigate how to relate the two binomial probabilities. For the first formulation, the average $\lambda = n \cdot p$ is as follows:

$$\lambda(t,c) = n_t \cdot P(d|c) = \text{tf}_c \cdot \frac{1}{N_D(c)} \tag{2.145}$$

This is the average occurrence of a term among all documents.

On the other hand, the expected frequency for document d is:

$$\lambda(t, d, c) = \text{dl} \cdot P_L(t|c) \tag{2.146}$$

How are the averages $\lambda(t, c)$ and $\lambda(t, d, c)$ related?

The following equation highlights that the averages are equal for the case $\text{dl} = \text{avgdl}$.

$$\lambda(t, d, c) = \text{dl} \cdot P_L(t|c) = \text{dl} \cdot \frac{\text{tf}_c / N_D(c)}{N_L(c)/N_D(c)} = \text{dl} \cdot \frac{\lambda(t, c)}{\text{avgdl}(c)} \tag{2.147}$$

The equation is based on dividing the numerator and denominator of $P_L(t|c)$ by $N_D(c)$. This leads to the right expression showing $\lambda(t, c)$ and $\text{avgdl}(c)$.

For $\text{dl} = \text{avgdl}(c)$, i.e., for a document of average length, the averages are equal, i.e., $\lambda(t, d, c) = \lambda(t, c)$. Therefore, the binomial and Poisson probabilities are equal. The following two equations, one for the binomial probability, and one for the Poisson probability, formalize this equality.

$$P_{\text{binomial}, n=\text{tf}_c, p_d=1/N_D(c)}(k_d) = P_{\text{binomial}, n=\text{avgdl}, p_t=\text{tf}_c/N_L(c)}(k_t) \tag{2.148}$$

$$P_{\text{Poisson}, \lambda=\text{tf}_c/N_D(c)}(k_d) = P_{\text{Poisson}, \lambda=\text{avgdl} \cdot \text{tf}_c/N_L(c)}(k_t) \tag{2.149}$$

The probability that the document d occurs k_d times in tf_c trials is equal to the probability that the term t occurs k_t times in avgdl trials. The formulation of the Poisson probability underlines that for the special case of a document of average length, the Poisson parameter is $\lambda(t, c) = \text{tf}_c/N_D(c)$.

This excursus regarding the binomial probability $P_{n,p}(k_t|c)$ helps to understand the DFR RSV and term weight.

2.8.4   DFR AND KL-DIVERGENCE

Taking DFR word-by-word, DFR is based on measuring the divergence between observed probability and model (randomness) probability. For DFR first-generation, the term probability is $P(k_t > 0|d, c)$. Accordingly, the KL divergence is:

$$D_{\text{KL}}(P_{\text{obs}}||P_{\text{random}}) = \sum_t P_{\text{obs}}(k_t > 0|d, c) \cdot \log \frac{P_{\text{obs}}(k_t > 0|d, c)}{P_{\text{random}}(k_t > 0|d, c)} \tag{2.150}$$

Here, the condition "$k_t > 0$" is equivalent to the event "$t \in d$."

For DFR second-generation, the term probability is $P(k_t|d, c)$. Here, the condition "$k_t = \text{tf}_d$" is equivalent to the event "tf_d."

$$D_{\text{KL}}(P_{\text{obs}}||P_{\text{random}}) = \sum_t P_{\text{obs}}(k_t|d, c) \cdot \log \frac{P_{\text{obs}}(k_t|d, c)}{P_{\text{random}}(k_t|d, c)} \tag{2.151}$$

KL-divergence is the difference between cross entropy and entropy; *see also* Section 3.11.6 (p. 111), Information Theory: KL Divergence. This can be applied to motivate a divergence-based score; Section 2.8.10 (p. 73), KL-Divergence Retrieval Model. Also, the difference between divergences, can be applied to explain LM, Section 3.11.8 (p. 112), and TF-IDF, Section 3.11.9 (p. 112).

2.8.5   POISSON AS A MODEL OF RANDOMNESS: $P(k_t > 0|d, c)$: DFR-1

If we employed the Poisson probability as a model of randomness, then, for $P(k_t > 0|d, c)$, we obtain:

$$w_{\text{DFR-1}}(t, d, c) \propto -\log\left(1 - P(k_t = 0|d, c)\right) = -\log\left(1 - e^{-\lambda(t,d,c)}\right) \tag{2.152}$$

The next transformation step is based on the Euler convergence (limit definition): *see also* Equation 2.39 (p. 21):

$$e^{-\lambda} = \lim_{n \to \infty} \left(1 - \frac{\lambda}{n}\right)^n$$

Using the convergence, we obtain:

$$w_{\text{DFR-1}}(t, d, c) \propto -\log\left(1 - \left(1 - \frac{\lambda(t, d, c)}{n}\right)^n\right) \tag{2.153}$$

The next transformation inserts $n = \text{dl}$ and, respectively, $\lambda(t, d, c) = \text{dl} \cdot P_L(t|c)$. This is because for a document, the sample size is $n = \text{dl}$.

$$w_{\text{DFR-1}}(t, d, c) \propto -\log\left(1 - (1 - P_L(t|c))^{\text{dl}}\right) \tag{2.154}$$

This equation shows that the DFR term weight is inverse proportional to the probability that term t occurs at least once in $n = \text{dl}$ trials.

2.8.6   POISSON AS A MODEL OF RANDOMNESS: $P(k_t = \text{tf}_d|d, c)$: DFR-2

Alternatively, we apply the logarithm to the Poisson probability $P(\text{tf}_d|c)$ rather than to $P(t \in d|c)$.

$$w_{\text{DFR-2}}(t, d, c) \propto -\log P(\text{tf}_d|d, c) = -\log\left(\frac{\lambda(t, d, c)^{\text{tf}_d}}{(\text{tf}_d)!} \cdot e^{-\lambda(t,d,c)}\right) \tag{2.155}$$

In the next step, we apply the natural logarithm to decompose the expression.

$$-\ln P(\text{tf}_d|d, c) = \ln((\text{tf}_d)!) - \text{tf}_d \cdot \ln(\lambda(t, d, c)) + \lambda(t, d, c) \tag{2.156}$$

To facilitate the expression, we use from now $k := \text{tf}_d$ and $\lambda := \lambda(t, d, c)$ (saving subscripts and parameters).

Next, Stirling's formula is applied for $\ln(k!)$:

$$\ln(k!) = k \cdot \ln(k) - k + 1/2 \cdot \ln(2 \cdot \pi \cdot k) \tag{2.157}$$

(We apply the basic formula; the more exact formula involves $1/(12 \cdot k)$). In the next equation, we insert Stirling's formula.

$$- \ln P(k|d,c) = k \cdot \ln(k) - k + 1/2 \cdot \ln(2 \cdot \pi \cdot k) - k \cdot \ln(\lambda) + \lambda \tag{2.158}$$

Some transformation steps group the expression as follows:

$$- \ln P(k|d,c) = k \cdot \ln \frac{k}{\lambda} + (\lambda - k) + 1/2 \cdot \ln(2 \cdot \pi \cdot k) \tag{2.159}$$

Next, we insert the average term frequency, $\lambda(t,d,c) = \mathrm{dl} \cdot P_L(t|c)$, to be expected in a document of length dl; *see also* Section 2.4 (p. 35), Poisson Model.

$$- \ln P(\mathrm{tf}_d|d,c) = \mathrm{tf}_d \cdot \ln \frac{\mathrm{tf}_d}{\mathrm{dl} \cdot P_L(t|c)} + (\mathrm{dl} \cdot P_L(t|c) - \mathrm{tf}_d) + 1/2 \cdot \ln(2 \cdot \pi \cdot \mathrm{tf}_d) \tag{2.160}$$

Finally, we apply the Poisson bridge (Section 3.7 (p. 93), Poisson Bridge) to replace the Location-based term probability $P_L(t|c)$ by an expression containing the Document-based term probability $P_D(t|c)$. This shows that a part of the DFR term weight contains an expression related to TF-IDF:

$$\mathrm{tf}_d \cdot - \ln(\mathrm{dl} \cdot P_L(t|c)) = \mathrm{tf}_d \cdot - \ln\left(\mathrm{dl} \cdot \frac{\mathrm{avgtf}(t,c)}{\mathrm{avgdl}(c)} \cdot P_D(t|c)\right) \tag{2.161}$$

Herein, not only the traditional IDF, $\mathrm{IDF}(t,c) = -\ln P_D(t|c)$, is explicit. Similar to the Poisson model, the burstiness of a term and a document length pivotization are explicit as well: $\mathrm{burstiness}(t,c) \propto \mathrm{avgtf}(t,c)$ and $\mathrm{pivdl}(c) = \mathrm{dl}/\mathrm{avgdl}(c)$; *see also* Section 3.9.2 (p. 98), TF-IDF and Poisson.

2.8.7   DFR: ELITE DOCUMENTS

The probabilities can be computed for a subset of the collection, for example, the elite documents selected for ranking the retrieved documents: $P(\mathrm{tf}_d > 0|\text{set of elite documents})$ and $P(\mathrm{tf}_d|\text{set of elite documents})$. For ranking different documents with respect to one query, the set of documents retrieved for the query (in a disjunctive interpretation) is a reasonable elite set. For a probabilistic ranking model, care has to be taken that the combination of probabilities estimated from different elite sets does not lead to a heuristic model.

2.8.8   DFR: EXAMPLE

To illustrate DFR further, we look at a synthetic example; *see also* Section 2.4.3 (p. 37), Poisson Example: Toy Data.

Example 2.54   DFR.   Let t be a term, and let c be a collection. Let the term occur in $\mathrm{tf}_c = n_L(t,c) = 200$ locations, and in $\mathrm{df}(t,c) = n_D(t,c) = 100$ documents. The average (expected) term frequency is $\text{avgtf}(t, c) = 200/100 = 2$; this is the average over the documents in which the term occurs.

Let $N_D(c) = 1{,}000$ be the total number of documents. The term occurs in 10% of the documents: $P_D(t|c) = 100/1{,}000$. The average (expected) term frequency is $\lambda(t, c) = 200/1{,}000 = 2/10$; this is the average over *all* documents.

The following table shows a row per term frequency $k_t = 0, \ldots, 6$. The column headed n_D is the number of *Documents* that contain k_t occurrences of t, i.e., $n_D(t, c, k_t)$. The column headed n_L is the number of *Locations* at which the term occurs: $n_L = k_t \cdot n_D$. The columns to the right show the observed and Poisson probabilities.

k_t	n_D	n_L	$P_{\text{obs,all}}(k_t)$	$P_{\text{Poisson,all},\lambda=0.02}(k_t)$	$P_{\text{obs,elite}}(k_t)$	$P_{\text{Poisson,elite},\lambda=2}(k_t)$
0	900	0	0.900	0.819	0.00	0.135
1	58	58	0.058	0.164	0.58	0.271
2	19	38	0.019	0.016	0.19	0.271
3	0	0	0.000	0.001	0.00	0.180
4	12	48	0.012	0.000	0.12	0.090
5	10	50	0.010	0.000	0.10	0.036
6	1	6	0.001	0.000	0.01	0.012
	1,000	200		$\lambda = 0.20$		$\lambda = \text{avgtf} = 2$

$P_{\text{obs,all}}(k_t)$ is the observed probability over all documents. $P_{\text{Poisson,all},\lambda}(k_t)$ is the Poisson probability, where $\lambda(t, c) = n_L(t, c)/N_D(c) = 0.20$ is the Poisson parameter. The table illustrates how the observed probability is different from the Poisson probability. $P_{\text{Poisson}}(1)$ is greater than $P_{\text{obs}}(1)$, whereas for $k_t > 1$, the observed probabilities are greater than the Poisson probabilities. There is more mass in the tail of the observed distribution than the Poisson distribution assumes (thin-tail distribution).

Moreover, the columns to the right illustrate the usage of the elite documents instead of all documents. Here, the single event probability is based on the locations of elite documents only.

2.8.9   TERM WEIGHTS AND RSV'S

We show the definitions of various DFR term weights. The general definition is as follows.

Definition 2.55   DFR term weight w_{DFR}.

$$w_{\text{DFR},M}(t, d, c) := -\log P_M(\text{condition on } k_t|c) \tag{2.162}$$

Next, we show some definitions for DFR-1, where the condition is $k_t > 0$, which is equivalent to $t \in d$. This is followed by definitions for DFR-2, where the condition is $k_t = \text{tf}_d$.

Definition 2.56   DFR-1 term weight $w_{\text{DFR-1}}$.

$$w_{\text{DFR-1},M}(t, d, c) := -\log P_M(t \in d|c) \tag{2.163}$$

Definition 2.57 DFR-1 term weight $w_{\text{DFR-1,binomial}}$.

$$w_{\text{DFR-1,binomial}}(t, d, c) := -\log\left[1 - (1 - 1/N_D(c))^{\text{tf}_c}\right] \tag{2.164}$$

As discussed in Section 2.8.3 (p. 66), Transformation Step, the genuine formulation should be based on the term probability $P_L(t|c) = \text{tf}_c/N_L(c)$ and on $n = \text{dl}$ trials. For a document of average document length, $\text{dl} = \text{avgdl}$, we obtain:

$$(1 - 1/N_D(c))^{\text{tf}_c} = (1 - \text{tf}_c/N_L(c))^{\text{avgdl}} \tag{2.165}$$

The truth of this equation is evident in the following rewriting:

$$(1 - 1/N_D(c))^{\text{tf}_c \cdot N_D(c)/N_D(c)} = (1 - \text{tf}_c/N_L(c))^{N_L(c)/N_D(c)} \tag{2.166}$$

Because of the Euler convergence (limit definition of the exponent function), $e^{-\lambda} = \lim_{N\to\infty}(1 - \lambda/N)^N$, see also Equation 2.39 (p. 21), we obtain:

$$\left(e^{-1}\right)^{\text{tf}_c/N_D(c)} = \left(e^{-\text{tf}_c}\right)^{1/N_D(c)} = e^{-\text{tf}_c/N_D(c)} \tag{2.167}$$

This transformations coincides with the definition of the Poisson-based DFR-1 term weight following next.

Definition 2.58 DFR-1 term weight $w_{\text{DFR-1,Poisson}}$. Let $\lambda(t, d, c) = \text{dl} \cdot \text{tf}_c/N_L(c)$ be the average occurrence of term t in document d.

$$w_{\text{DFR-1,Poisson}}(t, d, c) := -\log\left[1 - e^{-\lambda(t,d,c)}\right] \tag{2.168}$$

For a document of average length, this is:

$$e^{-\text{avgdl}\cdot\text{tf}_c/N_L(c)} = e^{-\text{tf}_c/N_D(c)} \tag{2.169}$$

This is the same expression as discussed in equation 2.167 for the binomial case.

Next, we consider the DFR-2 weights.

Definition 2.59 DFR-2 term weight $w_{\text{DFR-2}}$.

$$w_{\text{DFR-2},M}(t, d, c) := -\log P_M(\text{tf}_d|c) \tag{2.170}$$

Definition 2.60   DFR-2 term weight $w_{\text{DFR-2,binomial}}$.

$$w_{\text{DFR-2,binomial}}(t,d,c) := -\log\left[\binom{\text{tf}_c}{\text{tf}_d}\cdot\left(\frac{1}{N_D(c)}\right)^{\text{tf}_d}\cdot\left(1-\left(\frac{1}{N_D(c)}\right)\right)^{(\text{tf}_c-\text{tf}_d)}\right] \quad (2.171)$$

For the transformation step between $P_{\text{binomial},n=\text{tf}_c,p=1/N_D(c)}(k_d)$ and $P_{\text{binomial},n=\text{dl},p=\text{tf}_c/N_L(c)}(k_t)$, see Section 2.8.3 (p. 66), Transformation Step.

Definition 2.61   DFR-2 term weight $w_{\text{DFR-2,Poisson}}$.

$$w_{\text{DFR-2,Poisson}}(t,d,c) := -\log\left[\frac{\lambda(t,d,c)^{\text{tf}_d}}{\text{tf}_d!}\cdot e^{-\lambda(t,d,c)}\right] \quad (2.172)$$

The DFR RSV is defined as the sum of DFR term weights.

Definition 2.62   DFR retrieval status value RSV_{DFR}.

$$\text{RSV}_{\text{DFR},M}(d,q,c) := \sum_{t\in d\cap q} w_{\text{DFR},M}(t,d,c) \quad (2.173)$$

Inserting w_{DFR} yields the RSV in decomposed form. For the binomial probability in DFR-2, it is:

$$\text{RSV}_{\text{DFR-2,binomial}}(d,q,c) =$$
$$-\sum_{t\in d\cap q}\left[\log\binom{\text{tf}_c}{\text{tf}_d} + \text{tf}_d\cdot\log\frac{1}{N_D(c)} + (\text{tf}_c-\text{tf}_d)\cdot\log\left(1-\frac{1}{N_D(c)}\right)\right] \quad (2.174)$$

For the Poisson probability, it is:

$$\text{RSV}_{\text{DFR-2,Poisson}}(d,q,c) = -\sum_{t\in d\cap q}\left[\text{tf}_d\cdot\ln\frac{\text{tf}_c}{N_D(c)} - \ln((\text{tf}_d)!) - \frac{\text{tf}_c}{N_D(c)}\right] \quad (2.175)$$

see also Section 2.8.6 (p. 68), Poisson as Model of Randomness.

2.8.10 KL-DIVERGENCE RETRIEVAL MODEL

In Zhai [2009], page 55, the KL-divergence and a ranking score are related as follows.

$$\text{score}(d, q) = -D_{\text{KL}}\left(P_q \| P_d\right) \tag{2.176}$$

The motivation is that negative divergence is a similarity measure. KL-divergence is the difference between cross entropy and entropy; *see also* Section 3.11 (p. 108), Information Theory.

$$\text{score}(d, q) = -\left[H_{\text{cross}}(P_q, P_d) - H(P_q)\right] \tag{2.177}$$

Then, the score isis ranking-equivalent to the negative cross entropy, since the entropy of the query does not affect the ranking. The next steps relate cross entropy to the query likelihood:

$$
\begin{aligned}
\text{score}(d, q) \quad &\overset{\text{rank}}{=} \quad \sum_t P(t|q) \cdot \log P(t|d) \\
&= \quad \sum_t \frac{\text{tf}_q}{\text{ql}} \cdot \log P(t|d) \\
&\overset{\text{rank}}{=} \quad \sum_t \text{tf}_q \cdot \log P(t|d) \\
&= \quad \log P(q|d)
\end{aligned}
$$

This justifies the view that LM is a divergence-based model. We extend this discussion in chapter 3, where we show that LM can be seen to be proportional to the difference between query clarity and the divergence between document and query. In a similar way, TF-IDF can be seen to be proportional to the difference between "document clarity" and the divergence between query and document; *see also* Section 3.11.8 (p. 112), Difference between Divergences: LM; Section 3.11.9 (p. 112), Difference between Divergences: TF-IDF.

2.8.11 SUMMARY

We have discussed the foundations of divergence-based models and DFR.

Divergence between random variables (probability distributions) is a concept that many students perceive as relatively complex. I heard students speaking of "mathematical sophistication." This section on divergence aimed at demystifying divergence and DFR. In particular, we discussed the transformation step that relates the DFR model and the binomial probability, namely the probability that a term t occurs k_t in a document of length dl, given its single event probability $P_L(t|c) = \text{tf}_c / N_L(c)$. We discussed that for a document of average length, the DFR model corresponds to this binomial probability.

2.9   RELEVANCE-BASED MODELS

In this section we look at the main models to incorporate relevance information. Thereby we discuss the resemblance between the models.

2.9.1 ROCCHIO'S RELEVANCE FEEDBACK MODEL

Rocchio [1971], "Relevance Feedback in Information Retrieval," is the must-have reference and background for what a relevance feedback model aims at. There are two formulations that aggregate term weights:

$$\text{weight}(t, q) = \text{weight}'(t, q) + \frac{1}{|R|} \cdot \sum_{d \in R} \vec{d} - \frac{1}{|\bar{R}|} \cdot \sum_{d \in \bar{R}} \vec{d} \qquad (2.178)$$

$$\text{weight}(t, q) = \alpha \cdot \text{weight}'(t, q) + \beta \cdot \sum_{d \in R} \vec{d} - \gamma \cdot \sum_{d \in \bar{R}} \vec{d} \qquad (2.179)$$

In the second formulation, the parameters α, β, and γ allow for adjusting the impact of genuine query, relevant documents, and non-relevant documents, whereas in the first formulation, the impact is proportional to the cardinality of the sets of relevant and non-relevant documents.

2.9.2 THE PRF

The log-based formulation of the probabilistic odds of relevance is:

$$\log \frac{P(r|d, q)}{P(\bar{r}|d, q)} = \log\left(P(r|d, q)\right) - \log\left(P(\bar{r}|d, q)\right) \qquad (2.180)$$

After the transformation steps we considered in Section 2.2 (p. 23), PRF, term weight is:

$$w_{\text{PRF}}(t, r, \bar{r}) = \log \frac{P(t|r) \cdot P(\bar{t}|\bar{r})}{P(t|\bar{r}) \cdot P(\bar{t}|r)} = \log\left(P(t|r)/P(\bar{t}|r)\right) - \log\left(P(t|\bar{r})/P(\bar{t}|\bar{r})\right) \qquad (2.181)$$

The term probabilities are estimated in the usual way. For example: $P(t|r) = n_D(t, r)/N_D(r)$. This estimate can be expressed more general, namely as a sampling over the documents in the set D_r of relevant documents:

$$P(t|r) = \sum_{d \in D_r} P(t|d) \cdot P(d|r) \qquad (2.182)$$

This is the total probability for the set D_r where the documents are considered as disjoint events. With the prior $P(d|r) = 1/N_D(r)$, and $P(t|d) = 1$ if $t \in d$, and $P(t|d) = 0$ otherwise, the total probability is equal to the estimate $n_D(t, r)/N_D(r)$.

The formulation of the term weight underlines the resemblance between the Rocchio formula and the PRF. Both formulae rely on the idea to gather evidence from relevant documents and add this to the term weight, while subtracting the evidence regarding term occurrences in non-relevant documents. Relevance-based language models elaborate on the approach to sample over documents.

2.9.3 LAVRENKO'S RELEVANCE-BASED LANGUAGE MODELS

Lavrenko and Croft [2001], "Relevance-based Language Models," proposes an LM-based approach to estimate $P(t|r)$. The idea is that $P(t|r) = P(t|q)$ for missing relevance information.

There are two main methods for estimating $P(t|q)$: method 1 is based on "sampling (total probability) followed by a conditional independence assumption," and method 2, referred to as "conditional sampling", is based on "a conditional independence assumption followed by sampling (total probability)."

The paper views q as a vector, whereas in this book, we denote it as a sequence. The paper precisely positions that this "Relevance-based LM" is a "query expansion technique."

> We argue that $P(t|\vec{q})$ is a good approximation in the absence of training data: $P(t|r) \approx P(t|\vec{q})$. [The original papers uses $\vec{q} = q_1, \ldots, q_n$.]

> The main contribution of this work is a formal probabilistic approach to estimate $P(t|r)$, which has been done in a heuristic fashion by previous researchers. ...

> From a traditional IR perspective, our method is a massive query expansion technique.
> ...

> From an LM point of view, our method provides an elegant way of estimating a LM when we have no training examples except a very short (two to three word) description.

Because of $P(t, q) = P(t|q) \cdot P(q)$, and since $P(q)$ is a constant, the model is formulated for $P(t, q)$. For the formal description of the models let M be a sample of documents (this could be the top-k documents initially retrieved).

Method 1: Step 1a: Estimate $P(t, q)$ via the total probability over sample M:

$$P(t, q) = \sum_{m \in M} P(t, q|m) \cdot P(m)$$

Each m is a "language model," and in this context, documents could be viewed as models. Note the resemblance between this sampling and the sampling shown for PRF, in equation 2.182.

For example, given 10 documents, and the prior $P(m) = 1/10$ for each model (document). This means that each occurrence of t in document m will increase the probability $P(t, q)$.

Step 1b: Estimate $P(t, q|m)$ as the product of term and query probability. Make a conditional independence assumption, namely $P(q|t, m) = P(q|m)$.

$$P(t, q|m) = P(t|m) \cdot P(q|t, m) = P(t|m) \cdot P(q|m)$$

This assumption means that the query is viewed to be independent of the term under investigation. Moreover, apply a conditional independence assumption for the query terms:

$$P(t, q|m) = P(t|m) \cdot \prod_{t' \in q} P(t'|m)$$

This means that for $P(t, q|m) > 0$, there must be $P(t|m) > 0$ and $\forall t' : P(t'|m) > 0$.

Method 2:   Step 2a: Estimate $P(q|t)$ as the product of query term probabilities.

$$P(t, q) = P(t) \cdot P(q|t) = P(t) \cdot \prod_{t' \in q} P(t'|t)$$

Step 2b: Estimate $P(t'|t)$ via the total probability over sample M:

$$P(t'|t) = \sum_{m \in M} P(t'|m) \cdot P(m|t)$$

In this estimate, the so-called linked-independence assumption $P(t'|t, m) = P(t'|m)$ has been applied.

Both methods are elegant ways to estimate $P(t|r)$ for the case of missing relevance, and, if relevance data is available, then the relevant documents enhance the sample set M.

2.10   PRECISION AND RECALL

2.10.1   PRECISION AND RECALL: CONDITIONAL PROBABILITIES

Precision and recall are not what one would refer to as a "retrieval model." We include the evaluation measures into this chapter on retrieval models since both, retrieval and evaluation, are based on conditional probabilities.

Given a set of retrieved documents, and a set of relevant documents, precision is the portion of retrieved documents that are relevant, and recall is the portion of relevant documents that were retrieved.

Definition 2.63   Precision and recall: Conditional probabilities.   Precision is the conditional probability of the event "relevant" given the event "retrieved". Analogously, recall is the conditional probability of the event "retrieved" given the event "relevant". The definition and application of Bayes's theorem yields:

$$\text{precision}(q) \quad := \quad P(\text{relevant}|\text{retrieved}, q) = \frac{P(\text{retrieved, relevant}|q)}{P(\text{retrieved}|q)} \qquad (2.183)$$

$$\text{recall}(q) \quad := \quad P(\text{retrieved}|\text{relevant}, q) = \frac{P(\text{retrieved, relevant}|q)}{P(\text{relevant}|q)} \qquad (2.184)$$

2.10.2   AVERAGES: TOTAL PROBABILITIES

The total probability theorem can be used to express average precision and other measures such as discounted cumulative gain (DCG). There are two averages: 1. The average precision per query, which is the average over recall points. DCG can be viewed as a weighted average with a decaying weight for lower ranks. 2. The mean of the average precisions, which is the average over queries.

For the purpose of making the case, we look at the mean of the average precisions. Let Q be a set of queries.

$$\text{mean-avg-precision}(Q) := P_Q(\text{relevant}|\text{retrieved}) = \sum_{q \in Q} P(\text{relevant}|\text{retrieved}, q) \cdot P(q) \quad (2.185)$$

The query probability is usually the uniform prior, i.e., $P(q) = 1/|Q|$, but it could be used to reflect query aspects (e.g., difficulty, usefulness).

We have discussed the foundations of precision and recall. One of the main aspects was to revisit that precision and recall share the roots of IR models: probabilities. From this point of view, methods from IR models can be applied to evaluation, and the other way round, methods from evaluation may impact on IR models. This aspect will be discussed in the research outlook, end of this book.

2.11 SUMMARY

We have discussed the main strands of IR models: TF-IDF, PRF, BIR, Poisson, BM25, LM, PIN's and DFR. Figure 2.10 shows a concise overview summarizing the RSV's and term weights.

The joint display of the RSV's and term weights aims at indicating some of the symmetries and relationships between models. We have already outlined in this chapter on "Foundations" that all the models have probabilistic roots. The VSM (vector-space "model") has not been listed as a "model," since it is a framework in which any model can be expressed (see Section 3.3 (p. 83), VSM). Also, PIN's and DFR can be viewed as frameworks, i.e., models of a higher level than TF-IDF and LM.

The pure forms of TF-IDF and LM do not involve statistics over relevant documents. TF-IDF is based on $P(d|q)/P(d)$, and LM is based on $P(q|d)/P(q)$, which indicates that both models measure the same, namely $P(d, q)/(P(d) \cdot P(q))$, the dependence between d and q.

The PRF is the conceptual framework to incorporate relevance. BIR, Poisson, and BM25 are considered as the main instantiations of the PRF, whereby the Poisson model is less known than BIR and BM25. These models are based on the "document likelihood," $P(d|q)$. Naturally, the question is: what about the "query likelihood," $P(q|d)$? Is LM also an instantiation of the PRF? This question was one of the motivations to investigate and formalize the relationships between IR models.

TF-IDF
section 2.1
page 10

$$\mathrm{RSV}_{\text{TF-IDF}}(d,q,c) := \sum_t w_{\text{TF-IDF}}(t,d,q,c)$$

$$w_{\text{TF-IDF}}(t,d,q,c) := \mathrm{TF}(t,d) \cdot \mathrm{TF}(t,q) \cdot \mathrm{IDF}(t,c)$$

BIR
section 2.3
page 30

$$\mathrm{RSV}_{\text{BIR}}(d,q,r,\bar{r}) := \sum_{t \in d \cap q} w_{\text{BIR}}(t,r,\bar{r})$$

$$w_{\text{BIR}}(t,r,\bar{r}) := \log\left(\frac{P_D(t|r)}{P_D(t|\bar{r})} \cdot \frac{P_D(\bar{t}|\bar{r})}{P_D(\bar{t}|r)}\right), \qquad w_{\text{BIR,F1}}(t,r,c) := \log\frac{P_D(t|r)}{P_D(t|c)}$$

Poisson
section 2.4
page 36

$$\mathrm{RSV}_{\text{Poisson}}(d,q,r,\bar{r}) := \left[\sum_{t \in d \cap q} w_{\text{Poisson}}(t,d,q,r,\bar{r})\right] + \text{len\_norm}_{\text{Poisson}}$$

$$w_{\text{Poisson}}(t,d,q,r,\bar{r}) := \mathrm{TF}(t,d) \cdot \log\frac{\lambda(t,d,r)}{\lambda(t,d,\bar{r})} \qquad \left(= \mathrm{TF}(t,d) \cdot \log\frac{P_L(t|r)}{P_L(t|\bar{r})}\right)$$

BM25
section 2.5
page 46

$$\mathrm{RSV}_{\text{BM25},k_1,b,k_2,k_3}(d,q,r,\bar{r},c) := \left[\sum_{t \in d \cap q} w_{\text{BM25},k_1,b,k_3}(t,d,q,r,\bar{r})\right] + \text{len\_norm}_{\text{BM2}}$$

$$w_{\text{BM25},k_1,b,k_3}(t,d,q,r,\bar{r}) := \sum_{t \in d \cap q} \mathrm{TF}_{\text{BM25},k_1,b}(t,d) \cdot \mathrm{TF}_{\text{BM25},k_3}(t,q) \cdot w_{\text{RSJ}}(t,r$$

$$w_{\text{RSJ}} \text{ is a smooth variant of } w_{\text{BIR}}$$

LM
section 2.6
page 50

$$\mathrm{RSV}_{\text{JM-LM},\delta}(d,q,c) := \sum_{t \in d \cap q} w_{\text{JM-LM},\delta}(t,d,q,c)$$

$$w_{\text{JM-LM},\delta}(t,d,q,c) := \mathrm{TF}(t,q) \cdot \log\left(1 + \frac{\delta}{1-\delta} \cdot \frac{P(t|d)}{P(t|c)}\right)$$

$$\mathrm{RSV}_{\text{Dirich-LM},\mu}(d,q,c) := \sum_{t \in q} w_{\text{Dirich-LM},\mu}(t,d,q,c)$$

$$w_{\text{Dirich-LM},\mu}(t,d,q,c) := \mathrm{TF}(t,q) \cdot \log\left(\frac{\mu}{\mu+|d|} + \frac{|d|}{|d|+\mu} \cdot \frac{P(t|d)}{P(t|c)}\right)$$

PIN's
section 2.7
page 59

$$\mathrm{RSV}_{\text{PIN}}(d,q,c) := \sum_t w_{\text{PIN}}(t,d,q,c)$$

$$w_{\text{PIN}}(t,d,q,c) := \frac{1}{\sum_{t'} P(q|t',c)} \cdot P(q|t,c) \cdot P(t|d,c)$$

DFR
section 2.8.1
page 65

$$\mathrm{RSV}_{\text{DFR},M}(d,q,c) := \sum_{t \in d \cap q} w_{\text{DFR},M}(t,d,c)$$

$$w_{\text{DFR-1},M}(t,d,c) := -\log P_M(t \in d|c)$$

$$w_{\text{DFR-1,binomial}}(t,d,c) := -\log\left[1 - (1 - 1/N_D(c))^{\text{tf}_c}\right]$$

$$w_{\text{DFR-1,Poisson}}(t,d,c) := -\log\left[1 - e^{-\lambda(t,d,c)}\right]$$

$$w_{\text{DFR-2},M}(t,d,c) := -\log P_M(\text{tf}_d|c)$$

$$w_{\text{DFR-2,binomial}}(t,d,c) := -\log\left[\binom{\text{tf}_c}{\text{tf}_d} \cdot \left(\frac{1}{N_D(c)}\right)^{\text{tf}_d} \cdot \left(1 - \left(\frac{1}{N_D(c)}\right)\right)^{(\text{tf}_c - \text{tf}_d)}\right]$$

$$w_{\text{DFR-2,Poisson}}(t,d,c) := -\log\left[\frac{\lambda(t,d,c)^{\text{tf}_d}}{\text{tf}_d!} \cdot e^{-\lambda(t,d,c)}\right]$$

Figure 2.10: Retrieval Models: Overview.

CHAPTER 3

Relationships Between IR Models

The following list shows the structure of this chapter (the electronic version provides hyperlinks):

Section 3.1: PRF: Probabilistic Relevance Framework: Some of this section repeats what has been introduced in Section 2.2 (p. 23), PRF.

Section 3.2: Logical IR: $P(d \to q)$

Section 3.3: VSM: Vector-Space Model

Section 3.4: GVSM: Generalised Vector-Space Model

Section 3.5: A General Matrix Framework

Section 3.6: A Parallel Derivation of IR Models

Section 3.7: The Poisson Bridge

Section 3.8: Query Term Probability Assumptions

Section 3.9: TF-IDF and other models

Section 3.10: More Relationships: BM25 and LM, LM and PIN's

Section 3.11: Information Theory (with a focus on divergence)

Section 3.12: Summary (Relationship Overview in Figure 3.7)

The first eight sections discuss frameworks and formulae that help to relate IR models. Then, Section 3.9 pairs TF-IDF with most of the models discussed in chapter 2. Section 3.10 points at more relationships: BM25 and LM, LM and PIN's. This is finally followed by Section 3.11 which briefly reviews the main concepts of information theory. We include the concepts for two reasons. Firstly, they form the foundation of divergence-based models. Secondly, there is a divergence-based formulation of both, TF-IDF and LM.

3.1   PRF: THE PROBABILITY OF RELEVANCE FRAMEWORK

The probability of relevance framework has been introduced in Section 2.2 (p. 23), PRF. Some of the aspects will be repeated in the following. In the context of relationships, we briefly review the PRF, while highlighting the issues arising from viewing the document and query events as either a sequence of terms, a binary vector, or a frequency vector. This prepares the case to relate the PRF to TF-IDF and LM.

The starting point of the PRF is Bayes's theorem to estimate the relevance probability $P(r|d, q)$.

$$P(r|d, q) = \frac{P(r) \cdot P(d, q|r)}{P(d, q)} \tag{3.1}$$

The joint probability $P(d, q|r)$ can be decomposed in two ways:

$$\begin{align} P(d, q|r) &= P(q|r) \cdot P(d|q, r) \tag{3.2} \\ &= P(d|r) \cdot P(q|d, r) \tag{3.3} \end{align}$$

In equation 3.2, d depends on q, whereas in equation 3.3, q depends on d. $P(d|q)$ can be viewed as a foundation of TF-IDF, and $P(q|d)$ is the foundation of LM. Therefore, for LM, Lafferty and Zhai [2003] investigated how to relate $P(q|d, r)$ to $P(q|d)$; *see also* Equation 2.51 (p. 24), $P(d|q, r)$; Equation 2.52 (p. 24), $P(q|d, r)$.

The probabilities $P(d|q, r)$ and $P(q|d, r)$ are estimated as products of term probabilities. For an event h (hypothesis h) and event e (evidence e), the decomposition is:

$$P(h|e) = \prod_{t \text{ IN } h} P(t|e) = \prod_{t \in h} P(t|e)^{n(t,h)} \tag{3.4}$$

In this decomposition, the notation "t IN h" views the event h as a sequence of event occurrences; each t may occur multiple times. The notation "$t \in h$" views the event h as a set, and for each t, $n(t, h)$ is the number of occurrences of t in h.

Accordingly, the probabilities $P(d|q, r)$ and $P(q|d, r)$ can be decomposed as follows:

$$\begin{align} P(d|q, r) &= \prod_{t \text{ IN } d} P(t|q, r) \tag{3.5} \\ P(q|d, r) &= \prod_{t \text{ IN } q} P(t|d, r) \tag{3.6} \end{align}$$

Note the usage of t IN d, i.e., we have not yet aggregated the multiple occurrences the events. In fact, we have not specified yet what type of event t is.

For example, d could be a sequence of terms (i.e., the event space is $\{t_1, \ldots, t_n\}$), or d could be a sequence of 0/1 events (i.e., the event space is $\{0, 1\}$), or d could be a sequence of integers (i.e., the event space is $\{0, 1, 2, \ldots\}$).

For a sequence of terms, let $n(t,q)$ denote the number of times t occurs in query q. Then the independence assumption can be re-written as follows:

$$P(q|d,r) = P(t_1,\ldots,t_m|d,r) = \prod_{t \in q} P(t|d,r)^{n(t,q)} \qquad (3.7)$$

On the other hand, for the document, it is common to use a binary feature vector or a frequency vector:

$$P(d|q,r) = P(x_1,\ldots,x_n|q,r) = \prod_t P(x_t|q,r) \qquad (3.8)$$

$$P(d|q,r) = P(f_1,\ldots,f_n|q,r) = \prod_t P(f_t|q,r) \qquad (3.9)$$

Retrieval (ranking) is usually based on the probabilistic odds $P(r|d,q)/P(\bar{r}|d,q)$.

probabilistic odds: $$O(r|d,q) = \frac{P(r|d,q)}{P(\bar{r}|d,q)} \qquad (3.10)$$

For documents that are more likely to be relevant than not relevant, $P(r|d,q) > P(\bar{r}|d,q)$, i.e., $O(r|d,q) > 1$.

3.1.1   ESTIMATION OF TERM PROBABILITIES

Central to the PRF is the estimation of term probabilities. We outline in this section the issues regarding the event space used to estimate the probabilities. A more detailed discussion is in Section 3.6 (p. 92), Parallel Derivation.

The estimation of term probabilities can be based on

1. document frequencies,

2. location (term) frequencies, or

3. average frequencies.

Let u be a collection, and let D_u be the set of Documents associated with the collection (for relevant documents, $u = r$, and for non-relevant documents, $u = \bar{r}$).

Let $n_D(t,u)$ be the number of *Documents* in which term t occurs in u, and let $n_L(t,u)$ be the number of *Locations* at which term t occurs in u. Then, the document-frequency-based estimation is:

$$P(t|u) = P_D(t|u) = \frac{n_D(t,u)}{N_D(u)} \qquad (3.11)$$

This *Document-based* term probability is typically applied in the BIR model.

Alternatively, the location-frequency-based estimation is:

$$P(t|u) = P_L(t|u) = \frac{n_L(t,u)}{N_L(u)} \tag{3.12}$$

This *Location-based* term probability is typically applied in LM.

The third estimation is based on the average term frequency. There are two averages:

1. $\lambda_{\text{elite}}(t,u) := n_L(t,u)/n_D(t,u) = \text{tf}_u/\text{df}(t,u)$: the average frequency over the documents in which term t occurs; we denote the elite-based average as $\text{avgtf}(t,u) := \lambda_{\text{elite}}(t,u)$;

2. $\lambda_{\text{all}}(t,u) := n_L(t,u)/N_D(u) = \text{tf}_u/N_D(u)$: the average frequency over *all* the documents; $\lambda(t,u) := \lambda_{\text{all}}(t,u)$.

This leads to the third alternative for associating a probability with a term:

$$P(k_t|u) = P_{\text{Poisson},\lambda}(k_t|u) = \frac{\lambda(t,u)^{k_t}}{k_t!} \cdot e^{-\lambda(t,u)} \tag{3.13}$$

The three alternatives can be summarized as follows:

$$P(d) := \begin{cases} \begin{array}{lll} \text{probability} & \text{event space} & \\ \hline P(1,0,0,1,0,\ldots) & \{0,1\} & \text{binary} \\ P(t_1,t_4,t_1,\ldots) & \{t_1,t_2,\ldots\} & \text{terms} \\ P(2,0,0,1,0,\ldots) & \{0,1,2,\ldots\} & \text{frequencies} \end{array} \end{cases} \tag{3.14}$$

The first representation views the event d as a *binary* feature vector, the second as a sequence of *terms*, and the third as a *frequency* vector; *see also* Section 3.6 (p. 92), Parallel Derivation of Retrieval Models.

3.2 $P(d \rightarrow q)$: THE PROBABILITY THAT d IMPLIES q

van Rijsbergen [1986] proposed the framework of logical retrieval. The overall idea of $P(d \rightarrow q)$ is to define a logical implication that mirrors the notion of relevance. Then, the relevance event is replaced by the implication event. Mathematically, this is:

$$P(r|d,q) \propto P(d \rightarrow q) \tag{3.15}$$

The probability of relevance is viewed to be proportional to the probability of the implication.

Then, the task reduces (or expands, that depends on the view point and research) to estimating $P(d \rightarrow q)$. One approach is as follows:

$$P(d \rightarrow q) \propto P(q|d) \tag{3.16}$$

The probability of the implication is viewed to be proportional to the conditional probability.

When considering d and q as conjunctions of terms, then $d \to q$ measures exhaustiveness of d. For example, the implication $t_1 \wedge t_2 \to t_1$ is true, that is for each exhaustive document (document that contains ALL query terms), $P(q|d) = P(d \to q) = 1$. The less exhaustive a document is, the less $P(d \to q)$. On the contrary, $P(q \to d)$ measures the specificity of d.

Logical IR inspired various lines of research. By interpreting the implication in different ways, various retrieval models can be explained; Wong and Yao [1995]. The possible world semantics underlying probabilistic logics is a powerful framework to describe the "kinematics" of probabilities, i.e., the transfer of probability mass from some possible worlds to other possible worlds; Crestani and van Rijsbergen [1995], "Probability Kinematics in IR;" Crestani and Van Rijsbergen [1995], "IR by Logical Imaging." This endeavour is closely related to the discussion regarding "thin-tail" distributions in Section 2.4 (p. 35), Poisson and Section 2.8.1 (p. 63), DFR. Moreover, in addition to using logical IR as a framework for IR models, and as a means to adapt probabilistic reasoning, the logical implication $d \to q$ also inspired work on semantic retrieval, Meghini et al. [1993], Nie [1992], Roelleke and Fuhr [1996], since logic is an ideal candidate to model semantics and relationships.

3.3   THE VECTOR-SPACE "MODEL" (VSM)

This book does not list the VSM as a retrieval "model." Since retrieval models can be expressed in vector/matrix algebra, we view the VSM as a *framework* to describe, relate, and implement retrieval models.

Regarding the VSM being a *model*, the VSM views documents and queries as vectors, and it defines an RSV based on the cosine of the angle between the vectors. The cosine of the angle $\angle(\vec{d}, \vec{q})$ is as follows:

$$\cos(\angle(\vec{d}, \vec{q})) := \frac{\vec{d} \cdot \vec{q}}{\sqrt{\vec{d}^2} \cdot \sqrt{\vec{q}^2}} \qquad (3.17)$$

The query vector $\vec{q}$ is constant for a set of documents. Therefore, the query length $\sqrt{\vec{q}^2}$ does not affect the ranking. Then, $\text{RSV}_{\text{VSM}}(d, q)$ of the document-query pair (d, q) is defined as follows:

Definition 3.1   VSM retrieval status value RSV_{VSM}.

$$\text{RSV}_{\text{VSM}}(d, q) := \cos(\angle(\vec{d}, \vec{q})) \cdot \sqrt{\vec{q}^2} = \frac{\vec{d} \cdot \vec{q}}{\sqrt{\vec{d}^2}} \qquad (3.18)$$

The vector-space framework can be viewed as an alternative to the probabilistic relational algebra.

An engine that provides vector algebra operations can be used to implement many retrieval models (Cornacchia and de Vries [2007], Roelleke et al. [2006]).

Critical for the performance of the VSM is the choice of the vector-space and the setting of the vector components. A common approach is to consider a space of term vectors $\vec{t}_i$. This is reflected in the following example where we use a space of three terms of which the query contains t_1 and t_2:

$$\vec{q} = \begin{pmatrix} w_{q,1} \\ w_{q,2} \\ w_{q,3} \end{pmatrix} = \begin{pmatrix} 1 \\ 1 \\ 0 \end{pmatrix} = 1 \cdot \vec{t_1} + 1 \cdot \vec{t_2} + 0 \cdot \vec{t_3} \tag{3.19}$$

We use $w_{q,i}$ for referring to the i-th component of vector $\vec{q}$. Further, let two documents d_1 and d_2 be given:

$$\vec{d_1} = \begin{pmatrix} w_{d_1,1} \\ w_{d_1,2} \\ w_{d_1,3} \end{pmatrix} = \begin{pmatrix} 0 \\ 4 \\ 1 \end{pmatrix}$$

$$\vec{d_2} = \begin{pmatrix} w_{d_2,1} \\ w_{d_2,2} \\ w_{d_2,3} \end{pmatrix} = \begin{pmatrix} 1 \\ 0 \\ 2 \end{pmatrix}$$

Here, the vector components show that t_2 and t_3 represent d_1 where t_2 is a better representative than t_3. For d_2, t_3 is the best representative.

In the VSM, the normalization is with respect to the length of the vector.

$$\sqrt{\vec{d}^2} = \sqrt{w_{d,1}^2 + \dots + w_{d,n}^2} \tag{3.20}$$

This normalization leads to vectors of length 1.0.

$$1.0 = \left(\frac{\vec{d}}{\sqrt{\vec{d}^2}} \right)^2 \tag{3.21}$$

This is the so-called Euclidean norm, also referred to as the L_2 norm, $|\vec{d}|_{L_2} = \sqrt{\sum_i w_{d,i}^2}$, as opposed to the L_1 norm, which is $|\vec{d}|_{L_1} = \sum_i w_{d,i}$.

The scalar product of document and query is:

$$\vec{d}^T \cdot \vec{q} = \sum_i w_{d,i} \cdot w_{q,i} \tag{3.22}$$

A common approach is to set the document and query components as TF-IDF weights. In the VSM, TF-IDF weights are used for both, document and query. The following RSV uses within-document and within-query frequencies, and multiplies them with idf. The normalization is wrt the document. Let $\text{tf}_d \cdot \text{idf}(t, c)$ be the document vector components, and let $\text{tf}_q \cdot \text{idf}(t, c)$ be the query vector components.

$$\text{RSV}_{\text{VSM}}(d, q) = \frac{1}{\sqrt{\vec{d}^2}} \cdot \sum_t \text{tf}_d \cdot \text{tf}_q \cdot (\text{idf}(t, c))^2 \tag{3.23}$$

3.3.1 VSM AND PROBABILITIES

The VSM can be used in a convenient way to model probabilities; this approach has been utilized in Wong and Yao [1995] in the context of modeling $P(d \to q)$. Let $t_1, \ldots, t_n$ be disjoint and exhaustive events, i.e., $P(t_i \wedge t_j) = 0$ and $\sum_t P(t) = 1$. Then, the theorem of the total probability yields for the probabilities $P(q|d)$ and $P(d|q)$:

$$P(q|d) = \sum_t P(q|t) \cdot P(t|d) \tag{3.24}$$

$$P(d|q) = \sum_t P(d|t) \cdot P(t|q) \tag{3.25}$$

For $P(q|d)$, the interpretation of the query vector and the document vector is:

$$\vec{q} = \begin{pmatrix} P(q|t_1) \\ \vdots \\ P(q|t_n) \end{pmatrix} \qquad \vec{d} = \begin{pmatrix} P(t_1|d) \\ \vdots \\ P(t_n|d) \end{pmatrix} \tag{3.26}$$

Then, the vector product is equal to a probability, i.e., $P(q|d) = \vec{q} \cdot \vec{d}$.

3.4 THE GENERALISED VECTOR-SPACE MODEL (GVSM)

One of the main motivations to include the GVSM into this book is the following relationship between the total probability and the GVSM:

$$P(q|d) = \sum_t P(q|t) \cdot P(t|d) = \frac{1}{P(d)} \cdot \sum_t P(q|t) \cdot P(d|t) \cdot P(t) = \vec{d}^T \cdot G \cdot \vec{q} \tag{3.27}$$

The vector $\vec{d}$ reflects $P(d|t)$, and the matrix G contains the term probabilities $P(t)$ on the main diagonal, and the vector $\vec{q}$ reflects $P(q|t)$.

Before we continue the discussion of this relationship, we define RSV_{GVSM} and review the main motivation for the GVSM. The matrix components g_{ij} associate the component of dimension $\vec{t}_i$ with the component of dimension $\vec{t}_j$. The RSV_{GVSM} is defined as follows:

Definition 3.2 GVSM retrieval status value RSV_{GVSM}.

$$\text{RSV}_{\text{GVSM}}(d, q, G) := \vec{d}^T \cdot G \cdot \vec{q} \tag{3.28}$$

For keeping the formalism light, we omit here the normalization. For $G = I$ (I is the identity matrix, i.e., $g_{ii} = 1$, upper and lower triangle is zero), the generalized product is equal to the scalar product.

$$\vec{d}^T \cdot I \cdot \vec{q} = \vec{d}^T \cdot \vec{q} = w_{d,1} \cdot w_{q,1} + \ldots + w_{d,n} \cdot w_{q,n} \tag{3.29}$$

Next, consider an example where $g_{21} = 1$, i.e., the product $w_{d,2} \cdot w_{q,1}$ affects the RSV.

$$G = \begin{bmatrix} 1 & 0 & 0 \\ 1 & 1 & 0 \\ 0 & 0 & 1 \end{bmatrix}$$

This matrix G leads to the following RSV:

$$\mathrm{RSV}_{\mathrm{GSVM}}(d, q, G) = (w_{d,1} + w_{d,2}) \cdot w_{q,1} + w_{d,2} \cdot w_{q,2} + w_{d,3} \cdot w_{q,3} \qquad (3.30)$$

The GVSM is useful for matching semantically related terms. For example, let $t_1 =$ "classification" and $t_2 =$ "categorization" be two dimensions of the vector-space. Then, for the example matrix G above, a query for "classification" ($w_{q,1} = 1$) retrieves a document containing "categorization" ($w_{d,2} = 1$), even though $w_{q,2} = 0$, i.e., "categorization" does not occur in the query, and $w_{d,1} = 0$, i.e., "classification" does not occur in the document. This facility of the GVSM makes it the foundation of "LSA: latent semantic analysis," Deerwester et al. [1990], Dumais et al. [1988], Dupret [2003], also referred to as LSI, "latent semantic indexing." Hofmann [1999] describes the probabilistic variant, probabilistic latent semantic indexing (PLSI).

3.4.1   GVSM AND PROBABILITIES

The GVSM has an interesting relationship with the total probability. With $\vec{d}$ and $\vec{q}$ having components $P(d|t)$ and $P(q|t)$, we can define the matrix G to contain $P(t)$ on the main diagonal, with upper and lower triangle containing zeros. This leads to:

$$P(d, q) = \begin{pmatrix} P(d|t_1) \ldots P(d|t_n) \end{pmatrix} \cdot \begin{pmatrix} P(t_1) & & 0 \\ & \ddots & \\ 0 & & P(t_n) \end{pmatrix} \cdot \begin{pmatrix} P(q|t_1) \\ \vdots \\ P(d|t_n) \end{pmatrix} \qquad (3.31)$$

This representation raises the question of what is the meaning of the triangle elements. The triangle elements can be interpreted as conditional probabilities such as $P(t_i|t_j)$. Thus, the GVSM points a way to relate terms that, in the basic formulation of the total probability theorem, are disjoint events. The values in the upper and lower triangle reflect the dependence between terms, i.e., the terms overlap. The overlap is zero for disjoint terms.

The next equation shows the effect for a matrix where t_1 and t_2 are not disjoint, i.e., the terms "interfere." For non-disjoint terms, the matrix elements are: $g_{1,2} = P(t_2|t_1) \neq 0$ and $g_{2,1} = P(t_1|t_2) \neq 0$.

$$\mathrm{RSV}_{\mathrm{GSVM}}(d, q, G) = \qquad (3.32)$$
$$P(d|t_1) \cdot P(t_1) \cdot P(q|t_1) + P(d|t_2) \cdot P(t_2|t_1) \cdot P(q|t_1) +$$
$$P(d|t_2) \cdot P(t_2) \cdot P(q|t_2) + P(d|t_1) \cdot P(t_1|t_2) \cdot P(q|t_2) +$$
$$P(d|t_3) \cdot P(t_3) \cdot P(q|t_3)$$

With $g_{1,2}$ and $g_{2,1}$ set in this way, the query term probability $P(q|t_1)$ is multiplied by $P(t_1) \cdot P(d|t_1)$ and $P(t_2|t_1) \cdot P(d|t_2)$. With respect to the "classification=categorization" example, this is:

$$P(d|t_2) \quad \cdot \quad P(t_2|t_1) \quad \cdot \quad P(q|t_1)$$
$$P(d|\text{categorization}) \quad \cdot \quad P(\text{categorization}|\text{classification}) \quad \cdot \quad P(q|\text{classification})$$

This explains the role of G as a matrix of probabilities.

Next, we look at the GVSM slightly differently. We view G as the product of two matrices: $G_d^T \cdot G_q$. With the usual rules of vector-matrix algebra, we obtain the following scalar product:

$$\vec{d}^T \cdot G \cdot \vec{q} = \vec{d}^T \cdot (G_d^T \cdot G_q) \cdot \vec{q} = (G_d \cdot \vec{d})^T \cdot (G_q \cdot \vec{q}) \tag{3.33}$$

This equation illustrates that the GVSM leads to a formulation where the matrix-times-vector products yield a transformation of the vectors $\vec{d}$ and $\vec{q}$ into another space in which the scalar product $\vec{d_s} \cdot \vec{q_s}$ is equal to the generalized product $\vec{d} \cdot G \cdot \vec{q}$.

$$\vec{d_s}^T \cdot \vec{q_s} = (G_d \cdot \vec{d})^T \cdot (G_q \cdot \vec{q}) \tag{3.34}$$

With respect to the matrix G for modeling the total probability, this leads to the following matrices:

$$G_d = \begin{bmatrix} \sqrt{P(t_1)} & 0 & 0 \\ 0 & \sqrt{P(t_2)} & 0 \\ 0 & 0 & \sqrt{P(t_3)} \end{bmatrix} \qquad G_q = \begin{bmatrix} \sqrt{P(t_1)} & 0 & 0 \\ 0 & \sqrt{P(t_2)} & 0 \\ 0 & 0 & \sqrt{P(t_3)} \end{bmatrix}$$

The product of the matrices is:

$$G = G_d^T \cdot G_q = \begin{bmatrix} P(t_1) & 0 & 0 \\ 0 & P(t_2) & 0 \\ 0 & 0 & P(t_3) \end{bmatrix} \tag{3.35}$$

Particular to this formalization are the square roots of the probabilities. This relates the GVSM to the more general approaches that combine geometry and probabilities: Melucci [2008], Piwowarski et al. [2010], van Rijsbergen [2004].

In summary, the discussion of the VSM/GVSM framework pointed out that any retrieval model (e.g., TF-IDF, BM25, LM) can be expressed in a vector-like way. Geometric and probabilistic concepts can be combined, and the combination is based on choosing probabilities as vector/matrix components. The geometric operations (products of matrices and vectors) yield probabilities.

3.5   A GENERAL MATRIX FRAMEWORK

The original motivation of the general matrix framework, Roelleke et al. [2006], was to express several retrieval models and other concepts (e.g., structured document retrieval, evaluation measures) in a concise mathematical framework. Initially a secondary result was to establish a notation strictly based on the mathematical notion of matrices. From today's point of view, the notation gained a significant role. The matrix framework is the foundation of the notation, Section 1.3 (p. 3), employed for describing several retrieval models.

We revisit in this section the basics of the general matrix framework.

3.5.1   TERM-DOCUMENT MATRIX

Figure 3.1 shows a term-document matrix, a representation commonly used in IR.

TD_c		D_c					$n_D(t,c)$	$n_L(t,c)$
		doc1	doc2	doc3	doc4	doc5		
T_c	sailing	1	2	1	1	0	4	5
	boats	1	1	0	0	1	3	3
	east	0	0	1	0	0	1	1
	coast	0	0	1	0	0	1	1
	$n_T(d,c)$	2	2	3	1	1		
	$n_L(d,c)$	2	3	3	1	1		

Figure 3.1: Term-Document Matrix TD_c: Transpose of DT_c.

We refer to this matrix as TD_c since

1. the horizontal dimension corresponds to *Terms*,

2. the vertical dimension corresponds to *Documents*,

3. the dimensions span the space c (c is the collection).

From a formal point of view, the matrix represents the function $c : T_c \times D_c \to F$, where T_c is the set of *Terms* and D_c is the set of *Documents* in collection c. $F = \{0, 1, 2, \ldots\}$ is the set of frequencies. The function $c(t, d)$ corresponds to the matrix element, which is the *within-document term frequency*, and this leads to the following definition: $\text{tf}_d := c(t, d)$.

In a similar way, there are matrices per document and per query. For example, TL_d is the Term-Location matrix of document d. The function $d : T_d \times L_d \to \{0, 1\}$ returns the matrix element, where T_d is the set of *Terms* and L_d is the set of *Locations* in document d.

The notation $n_L(t, d) := c(t, d)$ makes explicit that the elements $c(t, d)$ of matrix TD_c correspond to the number of *Location* at which term t occurs in document d.

Then, for the matrices TD_c and TL_d, the dual notation to refer sums of matrix elements, is as follows. For the collection matrix TD_c, we obtain:

1. $n_T(d, c)$: number of *Terms* that occur in d of c

2. $n_D(t, c)$: number of *Documents* in which t occurs in c

In a dual way, for the document matrix TL_d, we obtain:

1. $n_T(l, d)$: number of *Terms* that occur at l in d

2. $n_L(t, d)$: number of *Locations* at which t occurs in d

The notation shown in figure 3.2 underlines how to derive a consistent notation based on the duality between TD_c and TL_d; *see also* Figure 1.2 (p. 5), Notation. According to this formal,

$n_D(t, c)$	number of *Documents* in which term t occurs in collection c	$\|\{d \mid d \in D_c \wedge c(t, d) > 0\}\|$
$n_L(t, c)$	number of *Locations* at which term t occurs in collection c	$\sum_{d \in D_c} c(t, d)$
$n_T(d, c)$	number of *Terms* in document d in collection c	$\|\{t \mid t \in T_c \wedge c(t, d) > 0\}\|$
$n_L(d, c)$	number of *Locations* in document d in collection c	$\sum_{t \in T_c} c(t, d)$
$N_D(c)$	number of *Documents* in collection c	$\|D_c\|$
$N_T(c)$	number of *Terms* in collection c	$\|T_c\|$
$N_L(c)$	number of *Locations* in collection c	$\sum_t n_L(t, c) (= \sum_d n_L(d, c))$
Frequencies		
$\mathrm{df}(t, c)$	document frequency of term t	$\mathrm{df}(t, c) := n_D(t, c)$
$\mathrm{tf}(d, c)$	term frequency of document d	$\mathrm{tf}(d, c) := n_T(d, c)$
$\mathrm{lf}(t, c)$	location frequency of term t	$\mathrm{lf}(t, c) := n_L(t, c)$
$\mathrm{lf}(d, c)$	location frequency of document d	$\mathrm{lf}(d, c) := n_L(d, c)$

Figure 3.2: Dual Notation based on Term-Document Matrix TD_c.

matrix-based approach to define counts, $\mathrm{tf}(d, c) := n_T(d, c)$ is the term frequency, i.e., the number of distinct terms in a document. This is consistent and dual to the document frequency, i.e., the number of distinct documents that contain a term. For maintaining a clear link to the traditional notation, we define $\mathrm{tf}_d := n_L(t, d)$ and $\mathrm{tf}_c := n_L(t, c)$. Also, $\mathrm{dl} := N_L(d) := n_L(d, c)$ is a consistent definition to refer to the document length of document d in collection c.

Retrieval parameters can be conveniently expressed in a mathematically consistent way. For example:

$$P_L(t|c) := \frac{n_L(t, c)}{N_L(c)} = \frac{\mathrm{tf}_c}{N_L(c)} \qquad P_L(d|c) := \frac{n_L(d, c)}{N_L(c)} = \frac{\mathrm{dl}}{N_L(c)}$$

$$P_L(t|d) := \frac{n_L(t, d)}{N_L(d)} = \frac{\mathrm{tf}_d}{\mathrm{dl}}$$

$$P_D(t|c) := \frac{n_D(t, c)}{N_D(c)} = \frac{\mathrm{df}(t, c)}{N_D(c)} \qquad P_T(d|c) := \frac{n_T(d, c)}{N_T(c)} = \frac{\mathrm{tf}(d, c)}{N_T(c)}$$

The notation supports the duality between inverse document frequency (high for rare/discriminative terms) and inverse term frequency (high for short/concise documents):

$$\text{idf}(t,c) := -\log P_D(t|c) \qquad \text{itf}(d,c) := -\log P_T(d|c)$$

Similar to the way a document-term matrix represents a collection, there are location-term matrices that represent the documents. Moreover, matrices are convenient for modeling links and structure. This leads to the following types of matrices:

DT_c	Document-Term matrix of collection c
ST_d	Section-Term matrix of document d
LT_d	Location-Term matrix of document d
PC_c	Parent-Child matrix of collection c
SD_c	Source-Destination (link) matrix of collection c

In a dual way to the counts for the DT_c, the counts for the other matrices follow. For example:

$n_D(t,c)$	number of Documents with term t in document d
$n_S(t,d)$	number of Sections with term t in document d
$n_L(t,d)$	number of Locations with term t in document d
$n_P(x,c)$	number of Parents with child x in collection c
$n_S(d,c)$	number of Sources with destination d in collection c

The matrix approach then leads to dual notions such as "inverse section frequency of a term" and "inverse source frequency of a destination." These are well-defined parameters that can be exploited for ranking retrieved items.

3.5.2   ON THE NOTATION ISSUE "TERM FREQUENCY"

This mathematical, matrix-based approach to IR makes explicit that for the two dimensions T and D, the term frequency is a feature of a document, and the document frequency is a feature of a term.

term frequency	document frequency
$\text{tf}(d,c) := n_T(d,c)$	$\text{df}(t,c) := n_D(t,c)$

The notion of "term frequency" in traditional IR leads to ambiguities. The "term frequency" used in IR, is actually the "location frequency of a term." This is the number of locations at which the term occurs. The following table underlines this notation issue.

		traditional notation
term frequency of d in c	$\text{tf}(d,c) := n_T(d,c)$	
document frequency of t in c	$\text{df}(t,c) := n_D(t,c)$	
location frequency of t in d	$\text{lf}(t,d) := n_L(t,d)$	$\text{tf}_d := n_L(t,d)$
location frequency of t in c	$\text{lf}(t,c) := n_L(t,c)$	$\text{tf}_c := n_L(t,c)$

The subscripts D, T, and L indicate the space; *see also* Section 1.3 (p. 3), Notation; Section 1.3.1 (p. 6), TF Notation Issue.

3.5.3   DOCUMENT-DOCUMENT MATRIX

Finally, we consider in this section matrices for modeling structure (link) information. For example, a relation covering the structure of the collection, as shown in the matrix CP_c (child-parent in collection c) in figure 3.3.

CP_c		doc1	doc2	P_c doc3	doc4	n_C(parent,c)	n_L(parent,c)
	doc1		1	2		2	3
C_c	doc2				1	1	1
	doc3					0	0
	doc4					0	0
n_P (child,c)	0	1	1	1			
n_L (child,c)	0	1	2	1			

Figure 3.3: Child-Parent Matrix CP_c: Transpose of PC_c.

Parameters (frequencies) such as n_C(parent, c) and n_P(child, c) are consistently defined based on the dimensions Child and Parent. For a tree structure, a child has one parent, and for a graph, we generalize toward source (parent) and destination (child), and a destination can be reached from several sources.

3.5.4   CO-OCCURRENCE MATRICES

For all matrices, similar operations can be defined. For example, the self-multiplications to model co-occurrence, co-references, and co-citations.

$$\text{document similarity (co-occurrence for terms): } DD_c \quad = \quad DT_c \cdot TD_c \qquad (3.36)$$
$$\text{term similarity (co-occurrence in documents): } TT_c \quad = \quad TD_c \cdot DT_c \qquad (3.37)$$

$$\text{parent similarity (co-reference): } PP_c \quad = \quad PC_c \cdot CP_c \qquad (3.38)$$
$$\text{child similarity (co-citation): } CC_c \quad = \quad CP_c \cdot PC_c \qquad (3.39)$$

The vision is that given a system that can handle large-scale matrix operations, techniques of IR can be implemented on such a common and unifying framework in a flexible and re-usable way, Cornacchia and de Vries [2007].

3.6   A PARALLEL DERIVATION OF PROBABILISTIC RETRIEVAL MODELS

Figure 3.4 shows the term probabilities and related parameters as they occur in BIR, Poisson, and LM.

model	BIR	Poisson	LM
event space	Presence of terms $x_t \in \{0,1\}$	Frequency of terms $k_t \in \{0,1,...,n\}$	Terms $t \in \{t_1,...,t_n\}$
term statistics	Documents/Documents $n_D(t,c)/N_D(c)$	Locations/Documents $\lambda(t,c) := n_L(t,c)/N_D(c)$	Locations/Locations $n_L(t,c)/N_L(c)$
probability	$$P_D(x_t|c) = \frac{n_D(x_t,c)}{N_D(c)}$$ probability that term t occurs in a document, given set D of Documents	$$P_\lambda(x_t|c) = \frac{\lambda^{k_t}}{k_t!} \cdot e^{-\lambda}$$ probability that term t occurs k_t times, given average occurrence $\lambda(t,c)$ $\lambda(t,c)$ is the average in a document of average length; the more general case is $\lambda(t,d,c) = \mathrm{dl} \cdot P_L(t|c)$	$$P_L(t|c) = \frac{n_L(t,c)}{N_L(c)}$$ probability that term t occurs in a location, given set L of Locations
urn model	one urn per term; one ball for each document balls show 0 or 1	one urn per term; one ball for each document balls show frequencies	one urn per collection; one ball for each term occurrence balls show terms

Figure 3.4: Parallel Derivation of Probabilistic Retrieval Models: Event Spaces.

This parallel consideration of event probabilities makes explicit the event spaces underlying the models. An event is either a binary feature, a frequency, or a term.

For BIR, the subscript D in $P_D(x_t|c)$ shows that the probability is based on counting "Documents," and the event notation x_t shows that the random variable is over binary term features, i.e., $x_t \in \{0, 1\}$. However, we will often use $P_D(t|c)$ and $P_D(\bar{t}|c)$ instead. Formally, the relationship between these two different expressions can be captured as follows:

$$P_D(t|c) := P_D(x_t = 1|c)$$
$$P_D(\bar{t}|c) := P_D(x_t = 0|c)$$

Also, it is sometimes easy to employ the following relationship between the binary event probability $P_D(x_t|c)$ and the term probability $P_D(t|c)$:

$$P_D(x_t|c) = P_D(t|c)^{x_t} \cdot P_D(\bar{t}|c)^{1-x_t}$$

This equation can be used in the context of the binomial probability. If $x_t = 1$, then $P_D(t|c)$ is the term probability; if $x_t = 0$, then it is $P_D(\bar{t}|c)$.

For Poisson, the subscript λ in $P_\lambda(k_t|c)$ shows that the probability is based on the average occurrence λ, and the event notation k_t shows that the random variable is over frequencies, i.e., $k_t \in \{0, 1, 2, \ldots\}$. The probability of a term frequency is the basis of DFR, Section 2.8.1 (p. 63), Divergence from Randomness.

For LM, the subscript L in $P_L(t|c)$ shows that the probability is based on counting "Locations," and the event notation t shows that the random variable is over terms, i.e., $t \in \{t_1, \ldots, t_n\}$.

This discussion shows that LM is based on "proper" term probabilities, whereas BIR and Poisson rely on probabilities of term features. Moreover, the parallel derivation of the models elicits the relationships between models given the relationships between event spaces.

3.7 THE POISSON BRIDGE:
$P_D(t|u) \cdot \text{avgtf}(t, u) = P_L(t|u) \cdot \text{avgdl}(u)$

In TF-IDF, the Document-based term probability $P_D(t|c)$ occurs, and in LM, the Location-based term probability $P_L(t|c)$ is the background probability. For investigating the relationships between models, the Poisson bridge is a helper to relate those two probabilities.

The bridge is based on the average frequency of the term, and since the average is the Poisson parameter, we refer to the relationship as "Poisson Bridge." Let $\lambda(t, u)$ be the average term frequency of term t over *all* documents in set u. Let $\text{avgtf}(t, u)$ be the average term frequency over elite documents (documents in which term t occurs). Let $\text{avgdl}(u)$ be the average document length. The Poisson bridge, Roelleke and Wang [2006], is defined as follows:

Definition 3.3 Poisson Bridge. Let u be the background (universal collection). For example, $u = c$ for the collection (set of all documents), or $u = r$ for the set of relevant documents, or $u = \bar{r}$ for the set of non-relevant documents.

$$\text{avgtf}(t, u) \cdot P_D(t|u) = \lambda(t, u) = \text{avgdl}(u) \cdot P_L(t|u) \tag{3.40}$$

To verify the equation, the decomposed form of the Poisson bridge is given next.

$$\frac{n_L(t, u)}{n_D(t, u)} \cdot \frac{n_D(t, u)}{N_D(u)} = \frac{n_L(t, u)}{N_D(u)} = \frac{N_L(u)}{N_D(u)} \cdot \frac{n_L(t, u)}{N_L(u)} \tag{3.41}$$

To illustrate the Poisson bridge, we look at an example.

For the term "africa" in TREC-2, the Poisson bridge is as follows.

Example 3.4 Poisson Bridge: "africa" in TREC-2   The basic statistics regarding number of documents, averages, and term occurrence are:

$$\begin{aligned}
N_D(\text{trec2}) &= 742,611 \\
\text{avgdl}(\text{trec2}) &\approx 350 \\
N_L(\text{trec2}) &\approx 25m \\
n_D(\text{africa, trec2}) &= 8,533 \\
n_L(\text{africa, trec2}) &= 19,681
\end{aligned}$$

The Poisson bridge is:

$$\frac{19,681}{8,533} \cdot \frac{8,533}{742,611} = \frac{19,681}{742,611} = \frac{25m}{742,611} \cdot \frac{19,681}{25m}$$

$$\text{avgtf}(t,c) \cdot P_D(t|c) = \quad \lambda(t,c) \quad = \text{avgdl}(c) \cdot P_L(t|c)$$

The Poisson bridge helps to insert the Document-based term probability, $P_D(t|c)$, into LM-based expressions, where the Location-based term probability, $P_L(t|c)$, is applied. Also, vice versa, the Location-based term probability can be inserted into TF-IDF, BIR, BM25, etc. These transformations isolate or make explicit parameters in retrieval models. Overall, this supports a theoretical/mathematical approach to relate IR models.

3.8 QUERY TERM PROBABILITY ASSUMPTIONS

3.8.1 QUERY TERM *MIXTURE* ASSUMPTION

This assumption is an extreme mixture assumption, assigning either the foreground (within-query) or the background (within-collection) probability.

Definition 3.5 Query term *mixture* assumption.

$$P(t|q,c) = \begin{cases} P(t|q) & \text{if } t \in q \\ P(t|c) & \text{if } t \notin q \end{cases} \tag{3.42}$$

see also Section 3.9.4 (p. 101), TF-IDF and LM.

3.8.2   QUERY TERM *BURSTINESS* ASSUMPTION

In the probabilistic derivation of IR models, we find expressions such as $P_L(t|q)/P_L(t|c)$. To relate such an expression to the document-based term probability, $P_D(t|c)$, we define the query term burstiness assumption.

Definition 3.6   Query term *burstiness* assumption.

$$P(t|q, c) = \frac{\text{avgtf}(t, c)}{\text{avgdl}(c)} \tag{3.43}$$

Because of the Poisson bridge, Section 3.7 (p. 93), the following equation holds:

$$P(t|q, c) = \frac{\text{avgtf}(t, c)}{\text{avgdl}(c)} = \frac{P_L(t|c)}{P_D(t|c)} \tag{3.44}$$

Example 3.7   Query term burstiness assumption.   Let the term t occur in 0.1 percent of the Documents, i.e., $P_D(t|c) = 1/1{,}000$. For $N_D(c) = 10^6$ documents, this means $\text{df}(t, c) = n_D(t, c) = 1{,}000$.

There are at least 1,000 term occurrences. Let the term occur in $\text{tf}_c = n_L(t, c) = 2{,}000$ Locations, i.e., the average term occurrence is $\text{avgtf}(t, c) = 2{,}000/1{,}000 = 2$.

Then, for $\text{avgdl}(c) = 1{,}000$, the Location-based collection-wide term probability is $P_L(t|c) = 2{,}000/10^9 = 2/10^6$.

For the within-query term probability, the assumption means:

$$P_L(t|q) = \frac{P_L(t|c)}{P_D(t|c)} = \frac{2/10^6}{1/1{,}000} = \frac{2}{1{,}000} = \frac{\text{avgtf}(t, c)}{\text{avgdl}(c)}$$

The within-query term probability, $P(t|q)$, is large if the term is bursty (high $\text{avgtf}(t, c)$). The rationale of the assumption is that the "virtual" query length is equal to the average document length, and the query term occurs with frequency $\text{tf}_q = \text{avgtf}(t, c)$ in the query. For real-world collections and the informative terms, the average term frequency is less than the average document length, $\text{avgtf}(t, c) < \text{avgdl}(c)$, and therefore, $P_L(t|c) < P_D(t|c)$.

This assumption means we can transform $\log \frac{P_L(t|q)}{P_L(t|c)}$ into $\log \frac{1}{P_D(t|c)}$. This can be used to relate the expression $P(d|q)/P(d)$ to TF-IDF; *see also* Section 3.9.4 (p. 101), TF-IDF and LM.

3.8.3 QUERY TERM *BIR* ASSUMPTION

Similar to the motivation for the query term burstiness assumption, we are looking for ways to relate $P(t|q)/P(t|c)$ to $(1 - P(t|c))/P(t|c)$, the latter being the expression familiar from Section 2.3 (p. 29), BIR.

Definition 3.8 Query term *BIR* assumption.

$$P(t|q,c) = \begin{cases} 1 - P(t|c) & \text{if } t \in q \\ P(t|c) & \text{if } t \notin q \end{cases} \tag{3.45}$$

This assumption means we can transform $\frac{P(t|q)}{P(t|c)}$ into $\frac{1-P(t|c)}{P(t|c)}$. For a rare term, $1 - P(t|c) \approx 1$, which is applied to establish the relationships between BIR and IDF.

Interesting in this context is the discussion whether $P(t|c)$ is Document-based or Location-based. For the Location-based estimate, we can apply the Poisson bridge: $P_L(t|c) = \frac{\text{avgtf}(t,c)}{\text{avgdl}(c)} \cdot P_D(t|c)$. This leads to $\frac{\text{avgdl}(c)/\text{avgtf}(t,c) - P_D(t|c)}{P_D(t|c)}$. This expression explicitly considers the burstiness of the terms.

3.9 TF-IDF

3.9.1 TF-IDF AND BIR

TF-IDF and BIR can be related by viewing the probability $P_D(t|c)$ as an approximation of the probability $P_D(t|\bar{r})$, which occurs in the BIR term weight. For TF-IDF, Definition 2.6 (p. 16), $\text{RSV}_{\text{TF-IDF}}$, and BIR, Definition 2.16 (p. 31), RSV_{BIR}, we have:

$$\text{RSV}_{\text{TF-IDF}}(d,q,c) = \sum_{t \in d \cap q} w_{\text{TF-IDF}}(t,d,q,c) \tag{3.46}$$

$$\text{RSV}_{\text{BIR}}(d,q,r,\bar{r}) = \sum_{t \in d \cap q} w_{\text{BIR}}(t,r,\bar{r}) \tag{3.47}$$

The respective term weights are:

$$w_{\text{TF-IDF}}(t,d,q,c) = \text{TF}(t,d) \cdot \text{TF}(t,q) \cdot \text{IDF}(t,c) = \frac{\text{tf}_d}{\text{tf}_d + K_d} \cdot \frac{\text{tf}_q}{\text{tf}_q + K_q} \cdot -\log P_D(t|c) \tag{3.48}$$

$$w_{\text{BIR}}(t,r,\bar{r}) := \log\left(\frac{P_D(t|r)}{P_D(t|\bar{r})} \cdot \frac{P_D(\bar{t}|\bar{r})}{P_D(\bar{t}|r)}\right) \tag{3.49}$$

Robertson [2004] views BIR as a theoretical justification of IDF, and in the following, we review this relationship.

Croft and Harper [1979] proposed for missing relevance, to assume that $P(t|r)/P(\bar{t}|r)$ is a constant.

$$C_r = \frac{P(t|r)}{1 - P(t|r)} \tag{3.50}$$

When inserting this into the BIR term weight, we obtain:

$$w_{\text{BIR},C_r}(t, r, \bar{r}) = \log(C_r) + \log \frac{1 - P(t|\bar{r})}{P(t|\bar{r})} \tag{3.51}$$

This equation underlines that in general the factor $\log C_r$ is part of the BIR term weight for missing relevance. For establishing the justification of IDF, let us assume $C_r = 1$. Then, we obtain:

$$w_{\text{BIR},C_r=1}(t, r, \bar{r}) = \log \frac{1 - P(t|\bar{r})}{P(t|\bar{r})} \tag{3.52}$$

The next step is to assume that the statistics in non-relevant, $\bar{r}$, can be approximated by the statistics in the collection, c. Then, we obtain the collection-based BIR term weight for missing relevance information ($D_r = \{\}$):

$$\text{IDF}_{\text{BIR}}(t, c) = \log \frac{1 - P_D(t|c)}{P_D(t|c)} = w_{\text{BIR}}(t, r, \bar{r} \equiv c) \quad [D_r = \{\}] \tag{3.53}$$

For $P(t|c) := P_D(t|c) = n_D(t, c)/N_D(c)$, this becomes:

$$\text{IDF}_{\text{BIR}}(t, c) = \log \frac{N_D(c) - n_D(t, c)}{n_D(t, c)} \quad \left(= \log \frac{N - n_t}{n_t} \right) \tag{3.54}$$

For $N >> n_t$, the following approximation can be applied:

$$\log \frac{N - n_t}{n_t} \approx \log \frac{N}{n_t} \tag{3.55}$$

This establishes the ground to view IDF as an approximation of the BIR term weight.

$$w_{\text{BIR}}(t, r, \bar{r} \equiv c) \approx \text{IDF}(t, c) \tag{3.56}$$

Another formulation of the relationship between TF-IDF and BIR is reported in de Vries and Roelleke [2005], where IDF is used to rewrite the BIR term weight. For the simplified (term presence-only) BIR term weight, this is:

$$w_{\text{BIR,presence-only}}(t, r, \bar{r}) = \text{IDF}(t, \bar{r}) - \text{IDF}(t, r) \tag{3.57}$$

The assumption $\text{IDF}(t, r) = 0$, i.e., a query term is assumed to occur in all relevant documents, leads to $w_{\text{BIR}}(t, c) = \text{IDF}(t, c)$.

When considering presence and absence, the relationship is:

$$w_{\text{BIR}}(t, r, \bar{r}) = \text{IDF}(t, \bar{r}) - \text{IDF}(t, r) + \text{IDF}(\bar{t}, r) - \text{IDF}(\bar{t}, \bar{r}) \tag{3.58}$$

This equation makes explicit that BIR can be viewed as a linear combination of IDF values.

In summary, the relationship between TF-IDF and BIR may be utilized to replace the IDF component in TF-IDF by an BIR-motivated weight:

$$\text{RSV}_{\text{TF-BIR}}(d, q, r, \bar{r}, c) := \sum_{t \in d \cap q} \text{TF}(t, d) \cdot \text{TF}(t, q) \cdot w_{\text{BIR}}(t, r, \bar{r}) \tag{3.59}$$

When using the RSJ term weight (smooth variant of the BIR term weight), then this becomes:

$$\text{RSV}_{\text{TF-RSJ}}(d, q, r, \bar{r}, c) := \sum_{t \in d \cap q} \text{TF}(t, d) \cdot \text{TF}(t, q) \cdot w_{\text{RSJ}}(t, r, \bar{r}) \tag{3.60}$$

This can be viewed as the foundation of BM25.

3.9.2   TF-IDF AND POISSON

The frequency-based formulation of the PRF applied the Poisson probability; *see also* Section 2.4 (p. 35), Poisson. This leads to an expression that explains TF-IDF.

The probability can be based on *all* of the documents, or on a subset (an elite set) of the documents. For example, the documents that contain at least one query term could be considered as the elite documents. Figure 3.5 shows the formulation of the parameters involved. Let u denote a set of documents. For example: $u = c$ for *all documents* or $u = r$ for *relevant documents*. The notation u_q refers to the elite documents (that contain at least one query term). Morever, avgdl(u) is the average documents over *all* documents in u, and avgdl(u_q) is the average over the *elite* documents.

The logarithm of the expected frequency $\lambda(t, d, u)$ leads to an expression where the IDF becomes explicit.

$$\log \lambda(t, d, u) = \log \left(\text{dl} \cdot P_L(t|u) \right) = \log \left(\frac{\text{dl}}{\text{avgdl}(u)} \cdot \text{avgtf}(t, u) \cdot P_D(t|u) \right) =$$

$$= \log \left(\frac{\text{dl}}{\text{avgdl}(u)} \right) + \log(\text{avgtf}(t, u)) - \text{IDF}(t, u)$$

In addition to the IDF, the expression contains a component reflecting length normalization, and a component reflecting burstiness.

length nor-
malization
The factor dl/avgdl equals one for a document of average length. Moreover, with respect to the PRF, the fraction of relevant and non-relevant documents means that dl cancels out. However, the factor avgdl(r)/avgdl($\bar{r}$) becomes explicit through this formulation.

all	elite
$\lambda(t,d,u) = \text{dl} \cdot P_L(t\vert u)$	$\lambda(t,d,u_q) = \text{dl} \cdot P_L(t\vert u_q)$
$\text{avgdl}(u) = \dfrac{N_L(u)}{N_D(u)}$	$\text{avgdl}(u_q) = \dfrac{N_L(u_q)}{N_D(u_q)}$ $u_q := \{d \vert \exists t \in q : t \in d\}$ $N_L(u_q) := \sum_{d \in u_q} \text{dl}$
$\text{dl} \neq \text{avgdl}(u)$ $\lambda(t,d,u) = \dfrac{\text{dl}}{\text{avgdl}(u)} \cdot \dfrac{n_L(t,u)}{N_D(u)}$	$\text{dl} \neq \text{avgdl}(u_q)$ $\lambda(t,d,u_q) = \dfrac{\text{dl}}{\text{avgdl}(u_q)} \cdot \dfrac{n_L(t,u_q)}{N_D(u_q)}$
$\text{dl} = \text{avgdl}(u)$ $\lambda(t,u) = \dfrac{n_L(t,u)}{N_D(u)} \qquad \left(= \dfrac{\text{tf}_u}{N_D(u)}\right)$	$\text{dl} = \text{avgdl}(u_q)$ $\lambda(t,u_q) = \dfrac{n_L(t,u_q)}{N_D(u_q)}$

Figure 3.5: Poisson Parameter λ for *all* and *elite* Documents.

burstiness

The logarithm of the average term frequency in elite documents measures burstiness:

$$\text{burstiness}(t,u) := \log \text{avgtf}(t,u) \tag{3.61}$$

A term is bursty if it occurs with a high term frequency in the documents in which it occurs. Using burstiness, IDF, and average document length, the Poisson term weight can be formulated as follows:

$$\begin{aligned} w_{\text{Poisson}}(t,d,q,r,\bar{r}) = \quad &\text{(3.62)} \\ \text{TF}(t,d) \cdot (\text{IDF}(t,\bar{r}) - \text{IDF}(t,r)) + \\ \text{TF}(t,d) \cdot (\text{burstiness}(t,r) - \text{burstiness}(t,\bar{r})) + \\ \text{TF}(t,d) \cdot \log \frac{\text{avgdl}(\bar{r})}{\text{avgdl}(r)} \end{aligned}$$

When grouping the expression by relevant and non-relevant, we obtain:

$$\begin{aligned} w_{\text{Poisson}}(t,d,q,r,\bar{r}) = \quad &\text{(3.63)} \\ \text{TF}(t,d) \cdot \big(\text{IDF}(t,\bar{r}) - \text{burstiness}(t,\bar{r}) + \log \text{avgdl}(\bar{r})\big) - \\ \text{TF}(t,d) \cdot \big(\text{IDF}(t,r) - \text{burstiness}(t,r) + \log \text{avgdl}(r)\big) \end{aligned}$$

The expressions underline the interplay between burstiness and IDF and average document length, between relevant and non-relevant. The term weight is high if the term is bursty and frequent in relevant documents, and solitude (not bursty) and rare in non-relevant documents.

With respect to the Poisson term weight, TF-IDF can be viewed as assuming $\text{IDF}(t,c) \approx \text{IDF}(t,\bar{r}) - \text{IDF}(t,r)$, i.e., the collection-based IDF is proportional to the difference between the IDF over non-relevant and over relevant documents. For good terms, the approximation $\text{IDF}(t, r) \approx 0$ feels reasonable, if we were to assume that good terms are frequent in relevant documents. Moreover, TF-IDF can be viewed as assuming that burstiness is the same in relevant and non-relevant documents. More precisely, TF-IDF can be viewed as a model that assumes that the combination of burstiness and average document length components does not affect the ranking.

3.9.3 TF-IDF AND BM25

When comparing the RSV's of TF-IDF and BM25, then it becomes evident that where TF-IDF uses $\text{IDF}(t, c)$, BM25 uses $w_{\text{RSJ}}(t, d, q, r, \bar{r})$. We find in the literature BM25 formulations that use IDF rather than the RSJ weight; *see also* Section 2.5 (p. 45), BM25. Also, the naive form of TF-IDF is based on TF_{total}, whereas BM25 uses TF_{BM25}. Changing the TF quantification leads to TF_{BM25}-IDF, which can be viewed as an approximation of BM25 for the case of missing relevance information.

The Laplace-like correction (smoothing) of the BIR term weight is the step to transform the BIR weight into the RSJ weight:

$$w_{\text{RSJ}}(t, r, c) \propto \text{IDF}_{\text{BIR}}(t, c) = \log \frac{N_D(c) - n_D(t, c) + 0.5}{n_D(t, c) + 0.5} \qquad (3.64)$$

see also Section 2.3.5 (p. 33), RSJ Term Weight.

The following table shows a side-by-side of a naive and a BM25-motivated TF-IDF.

"Naive" TF-IDF	BM25-motivated TF-IDF
$\text{TF}_{\text{total}}(t, d) \cdot \text{IDF}(t, c)$	$\text{TF}_{\text{BM25}}(t, d) \cdot w_{\text{RSJ}}(t, c)$
insert frequency-based parameters	
$n_L(t, d) \cdot -\log \dfrac{n_D(t, c)}{N_D(c)}$	$\dfrac{n_L(t, d)}{n_L(t, d) + K_d} \cdot -\log \dfrac{n_D(t, c) + 0.5}{N_D(c) - n_D(t, c) + 0.5}$
rewrite using a probability-based formulation	
$\text{dl} \cdot P_L(t\|d) \cdot -\log P_D(t\|c)$	$\dfrac{P_L(t\|d)}{P_L(t\|d) + K_d/\text{dl}} \cdot -\log \dfrac{P_D(t\|c) + \frac{0.5}{N_D(c)}}{1 - P_D(t\|c) + \frac{0.5}{N_D(c)}}$

In summary, this section draws a relationship between TF-IDF and BM25, this relationship being based on what has been discussed in Section 3.9.1 (p. 96), TF-IDF and BIR. For the case of missing relevance, IDF can be viewed as an approximation of the RSJ term weight. On the other hand, the RSJ term weight can be used instead of IDF. Regarding the TF, we discussed that TF_{total} corresponds to making an independence assumption, whereas TF_{BM25} captures the dependence of the multiple occurrences of the term; *see also* Section 2.1.7 (p. 17), Semi-subsumed Events Occurrences. The relationship between TF-IDF and BM25 gives ground to the notion "TF-RSJ," where the TF component is BM25-TF, and the IDF term weight is replaced by the RSJ term weight.

3.9.4 TF-IDF AND LM

Hiemstra [2000] showed a potential way to view LM as a probabilistic interpretation of TF-IDF. Essentially, the relationship is based on the observation that there is an inverse term probability involved in both TF-IDF and LM.

Moreover, Hiemstra [2000] and Kamps et al. [2004], "Length Normalization in XML Retrieval," show the following estimates for the term probabilities used in LM:

$$P(t|d) = \frac{\text{tf}(t,d)}{\sum_{t'} \text{tf}(t',d)} = \frac{\text{tf}_d}{\text{dl}} \tag{3.65}$$

$$P(t|c) = \frac{\text{df}(t,c)}{\sum_{t'} \text{df}(t',c)} = \frac{\text{df}(t,c)}{N_D(c)} \tag{3.66}$$

The Location-based within-document term probability, $P(t|d) := P_L(t|d)$, is the foreground probability, and the Document-based collection-wide term probability, $P(t|c) := P_D(t|c)$, is the background probability. The subscripts L and D indicate that the foreground is "Location-based" (the Locations at which terms occur are the balls in the urn) whereas the background is "Document-based" (the Documents in which terms occur are the balls in the urn). From an event space of view, the background probability should be "Location-based" as well.

$$P_L(t|c) = P(t|c) = \frac{\text{tf}(t,c)}{\sum_{t'} \text{tf}(t',c)} = \frac{\text{tf}_c}{N_L(c)} \tag{3.67}$$

The "Location-based" probability is more correct in the sense that then both, the within-document and the collection-wide probability are based on "Locations."

When following the argument in Section 1.3 (p. 3), Notation, regarding "term frequency" versus "location" frequency, the duality between the two term probabilities is evident.

$$P_L(t|d) = \frac{\text{lf}(t,d)}{\sum_{t'} \text{lf}(t',d)} = \frac{n_L(t,d)}{N_L(d)} = \frac{\text{tf}_d}{\text{dl}} \tag{3.68}$$

$$P_L(t|c) = \frac{\text{lf}(t,c)}{\sum_{t'} \text{lf}(t',c)} = \frac{n_L(t,c)}{N_L(c)} = \frac{\text{tf}_c}{\text{collection\_length}} \tag{3.69}$$

By assuming a document-based background model for LM, Hiemstra [2000], the side-by-side of simplified TF-IDF and LM term weights is as follows:

TF-IDF	LM
$\text{TF}(t,d) \cdot \log \dfrac{1}{P_D(t|c)}$	$\text{TF}(t,q) \cdot \log \left(1 + \dfrac{\delta}{1-\delta} \cdot \dfrac{P_L(t|d)}{P_D(t|c)}\right)$

Here, the inverse of $P_D(t|c)$ is present in the TF-IDF and LM term weights. Given that from a probabilistic, event-space-based, point of view, $P_L(t|c)$ should be used in the LM formulation, the question is how this affects the relationship between TF-IDF and LM. For discussing this question, we apply the Poisson bridge to replace $P_L(t|c)$ in the genuine LM formulation.

$$\text{TF}(t,q) \cdot \log \left(1 + \frac{\delta}{1-\delta} \cdot \frac{P_L(t|d)}{P_L(t|c)} \right) = \text{TF}(t,q) \cdot \log \left(1 + \frac{\delta}{1-\delta} \cdot \frac{P_L(t|d)}{\frac{\text{avgtf}(t,c)}{\text{avgdl}(c)} \cdot P_D(t|c)} \right)$$

Eventually we could construct from this expression a transformation to show a relationship between TF-IDF and LM.

When looking at this issue, it turned out that a more immediate relationship follows from the fact that TF-IDF can be derived from $P(d|q,c)$ and LM from $P(q|d,c)$. Both, TF-IDF and LM are proportional to the document-query independence measure.

$$\text{RSV}_{\text{TF-IDF}}(d,q,c) \propto \frac{P(d,q|c)}{P(d|c) \cdot P(q|c)} \tag{3.70}$$

$$\text{RSV}_{\text{LM}}(d,q,c) \propto \frac{P(d,q|c)}{P(d|c) \cdot P(q|c)} \tag{3.71}$$

Based on this view, TF-IDF and LM measure the same. Of course, they are not ranking equivalent; the different decompositions into term probabilities, and the assumptions applied, break the ranking equivalence.

TF-IDF estimates $P(d|q,c)$ from the product of term probabilities, $P(t|q,c)$, whereas LM estimates $P(q|d,c)$ from $P(t|d,c)$. For the term probabilities, different mixtures are applied. TF-IDF is based on the "extreme mixture," where $P(t|q,c) = P(t|q)$ for query terms and $P(t|q,c) = P(t|c)$ for non-query terms. LM applies the linear mixture $P(t|d,c) = \delta_d \cdot P(t|d) + (1-\delta_d) \cdot P(t|c)$ for all terms.

3.9.5 TF-IDF AND LM: SIDE-BY-SIDE

Figure 3.6 shows a side-by-side derivation of TF-IDF and LM.

TF-IDF, based on $P(d|q,c)/P(d|c)$, decomposes the document event, whereas LM, based on $P(q|d,c)/P(q|c)$, decomposes the query event. This shows that the two models share the same root:

$$\text{TF-IDF} \equiv \frac{P(d|q,c)}{P(d|c)} = \frac{P(d,q|c)}{P(d|c) \cdot P(q|c)} = \frac{P(q|d,c)}{P(q|c)} \equiv \text{LM} \tag{3.72}$$

Starting out with the same root, TF-IDF decomposes the document event, and LM decomposes the query event. TF-IDF can be viewed as applying an extreme mixture, whereas LM applies the linear mixture. TF-IDF normalizes by $P(d|c)$, and LM by $P(q|c)$.

TF-IDF	LM
$$P(d|q,c) = \prod_{t \in d} P(t|q,c)^{n(t,d)}$$	$$P(q|d,c) = \prod_{t \in q} P(t|d,c)^{n(t,q)}$$
$$\frac{P(d|q,c)}{P(d|c)} = \prod_{t \in d} \left(\frac{P(t|q,c)}{P(t|c)} \right)^{n(t,d)}$$	$$\frac{P(q|d,c)}{P(q|c)} = \prod_{t \in q} \left(\frac{P(t|d,c)}{P(t|c)} \right)^{n(t,q)}$$
Step 1: extreme mixture $$P(t|q,c) = \begin{cases} P(t|q) & t \in q \\ P(t|c) & t \notin q \end{cases}$$	linear mixture $$P(t|d,c) = \delta_d \cdot P(t|d) + (1-\delta_d) \cdot P(t|c)$$
$$\frac{P(d|q,c)}{P(d|c)} = \prod_{t \in d \cap q} \left(\frac{P(t|q)}{P(t|c)} \right)^{n(t,d)}$$	$$\frac{P(q|d,c)}{P(q|c)} = \prod_{t \in q} \left(\delta_d \cdot \frac{P(t|d)}{P(t|c)} + (1-\delta_d) \right)^{n(t,q)}$$

Step 2: apply logarithm; replace the total term frequencies $n(t,d)$ and $n(t,q)$ by TF quantification

$$\log \frac{P(d|q,c)}{P(d|c)} =$$ $$\sum_{t \in d \cap q} \text{TF}(t,d) \cdot \log \left(\frac{P(t|q)}{P(t|c)} \right)$$	$$\log \frac{P(q|d,c)}{P(q|c)} =$$ $$\sum_{t \in q} \text{TF}(t,q) \cdot \log \left(\delta_d \cdot \frac{P(t|d)}{P(t|c)} + (1-\delta_d) \right)$$

Step 3: query term probability assumption: insert mixture parameter and $P(t|d)$ estimate burstiness

$$P(t|q,c) = \frac{\text{avgtf}(t,c)}{\text{avgdl}(c)}$$	$$\delta_d = \frac{\text{dl}}{\text{dl}+\mu}; \quad P(t|d) = \frac{\text{tf}_d}{\text{dl}}$$
$$\log \frac{P(d|q,c)}{P(d|c)} =$$ $$\sum_{t \in d \cap q} \text{TF}(t,d) \cdot \log \left(\frac{1}{P_D(t|c)} \right)$$	$$\log \frac{P(q|d,c)}{P(q|c)} =$$ $$\sum_{t \in q} \text{TF}(t,q) \cdot \log \left(\frac{\text{tf}_d}{(\text{dl}+\mu) \cdot P(t|c)} + \frac{\mu}{\mu + \text{dl}} \right)$$
Step 4: $\text{IDF}(t,c) = -\log P_D(t|c)$	combine expressions
$$\log \frac{P(d|q,c)}{P(d|c)} =$$ $$\sum_{t \in d \cap q} \text{TF}(t,d) \cdot \text{IDF}(t,c)$$	$$\log \frac{P(q|d,c)}{P(q|c)} =$$ $$\sum_{t \in q} \text{TF}(t,q) \cdot \log \left(\frac{\text{tf}_d + \mu \cdot P(t|c)}{\text{dl} \cdot P(t|c) + \mu \cdot P(t|c)} \right)$$

Figure 3.6: TF-IDF and LM: Side-by-Side.

Step 1 in Figure 3.6 highlights the type of mixture assumption: extreme mixture assumption on the TF-IDF side, linear mixture assumption on the LM side (Dirichlet mixture, parameter $\delta_d = \text{dl}/(\text{dl} + \mu)$).

Step 2 applies the logarithm. Also, it replaces the total term occurrence counts, $n(t, d)$ and $n(t, q)$, by TF quantifications. The TF quantification reflects the dependence of the multiple occurrences of a term.

Step 3 on the TF-IDF side deals with the transformation from $P_L(t|q)/P_L(t|c)$ to $1/P_D(t|c)$. For this transformation, we apply the query term *burstiness* assumption:

$$P(t|q, c) = \frac{\text{avgtf}(t, c)}{\text{avgdl}(c)}$$

see also Section 3.8 (p. 94), Query Term Probability Assumptions. The assumption means that with respect to this mixture-based derivation based on the event space "set of terms," TF-IDF assumes that the query term probability is equal to the fraction of the elite-average term frequency, $\text{avgtf}(t, c)$, and the average document length, $\text{avgdl}(c)$. The elite-average term frequency is proportional to burstiness.

Step 3 on the LM side inserts the mixture parameter and the likelihood estimate $P(t|d) = \text{tf}_d/\text{dl}$.

Step 4 on the TF-IDF side inserts IDF. On the LM side, the final step combines the expressions.

Overall, this side-by-side derivation of TF-IDF and LM, based on the event space of "terms," underlines that TF-IDF and LM can be viewed as measuring the same, namely the document-query (in)dependence, $P(d, q|c)/(P(d|c) \cdot P(q|c))$.

3.9.6   TF-IDF AND PIN'S

For independent terms, in the PIN $d \to \{t_1, t_2, t_3\} \to q$, we derived the following equation:

$$P(q|d) = \sum_t \frac{P(q|t)}{\sum_{t'} P(q|t')} \cdot P(t|d) \tag{3.73}$$

see also Section 2.7 (p. 58), PIN's; Equation 2.137 (p. 61), $P(q|d)$.

For the computation of $P(q|t)$, imagine to add virtually a tuple "(t, q)" for each query term, to the collection. Then, for each term, $P(q|t) > 0$. For terms that do not occur in the collection, i.e., only do occur in the query, $P(q|t) = 1$.

$P(q|t)$ is greater for rare terms than for frequent terms, i.e., $P(q|t)$ is proportional to $\text{IDF}(t)$. Whereas $P(q|t)$ is based on all the term occurrences, $\text{IDF}(t) = -\log P_D(t)$ is based on the space of Documents.

For the computation of $P(t|d)$, if we choose the usual estimate, then this is $P(t|d) = \text{tf}_d/\text{dl} = \text{TF}_{\text{sum}}(t, d)$. We know for TF-IDF, that $\text{TF}_{\text{BM25}}(t, d)$ performs better. The estimate $P(t|d) = \text{TF}_{\text{BM25}}(t, d) = \text{tf}_d/(\text{tf}_d + K)$ can be interpreted in the Laplace sense (see Amati and van Rijsbergen [2002], Section 3.9.8 (p. 105), TF-IDF and DFR).

This justifies the following relationships:

$$P(t|d) \propto \mathrm{TF}(t, d) \tag{3.74}$$

$$P(q|t) \propto \mathrm{IDF}(t) \tag{3.75}$$

$$\sum_t \frac{P(q|t)}{\sum_{t'} P(q|t')} \cdot P(t|d) \propto \sum_t \frac{\mathrm{IDF}(t)}{\sum_{t'} \mathrm{IDF}(t')} \cdot \mathrm{TF}(t, d) \tag{3.76}$$

The PIN RSV is proportional to TF-IDF. See also Equation 2.141 (p. 62), $\mathrm{RSV_{PIN}}$, Equation 2.30 (p. 16), $\mathrm{RSV_{TF\text{-}IDF}}$.

3.9.7   TF-IDF AND DIVERGENCE

Section 2.8 (p. 63), Divergence-based Models, has already pointed at relationships between TF-IDF and divergence. In the following sections we look at two approaches: "TF-IDF and DFR: Risk-times-Gain," and "TF-IDF and DFR: A Gap-based Model." Moreover, a relationship between TF-IDF and divergence (in general) is captured under information theory, in Section 3.11.9 (p. 112), Difference between Divergences: TF-IDF.

3.9.8   TF-IDF AND DFR: RISK TIMES GAIN

Amati and van Rijsbergen [2002] introduces a particular usage of DFR to interpret TF-IDF. To make the step toward TF-IDF, there is the following definition of P_1. "P_1 is the probability that a given document contains tf_d tokens of the given term:"

$$P_1(\mathrm{tf}_d|c) := \left(\frac{\mathrm{df}(t, c)}{N_D(c)} \right)^{\mathrm{tf}_d} \tag{3.77}$$

This can be enhanced with any smoothing, for example:

$$P_1(\mathrm{tf}_d|c) := \left(\frac{\mathrm{df}(t, c) + 0.5}{N_D(c) + 1} \right)^{\mathrm{tf}_d} \tag{3.78}$$

Then, we obtain an explanation of TF-IDF:

$$\mathrm{inf1}(t, d, c) = -\log P_1(\mathrm{tf}_d|c) = \mathrm{tf}_d \cdot \mathrm{idf}(t, c) \tag{3.79}$$

Looking carefully at this formulation discloses that P_1 is the probability of a particular sequence of documents that all contain the respective term. The sequence contains tf_d documents.

The reason why this setting of P_1 is chosen is to establish a relationship between DFR and TF-IDF. The missing link, namely the normalization of the TF component, can be achieved by choosing inf2 accordingly.

$$\mathrm{inf2}(t, d, c) = 1 - P_2(\mathrm{tf}_d|c) = 1 - \frac{\mathrm{tf}_d}{\mathrm{tf}_d + 1} = \frac{1}{\mathrm{tf}_d + 1} \tag{3.80}$$

Here, $P_2(\text{tf}_d|c)$ models the aftereffect (Laplace law of succession).

With terminology regarding inf1, inf2, gain, risk, and loss, the formulation is as follows:

$$
\begin{aligned}
\text{inf1} &= \text{gain} + \text{loss} \\
w_{\text{DFR}} &= \text{gain} \\
w_{\text{DFR}} &= \text{inf1} - \text{loss} \\
\text{loss} &= P_2 \cdot \text{inf1} \\
\text{risk} &= \text{inf2} = 1 - P_2 = \frac{1}{\text{tf}_d + K} \\
w_{\text{DFR}} &= \text{risk} \cdot \text{inf1} \\
w_{\text{DFR}}(t, d, c) &= \frac{\text{tf}_d}{\text{tf}_d + 1} \cdot \text{idf}(t, c)
\end{aligned}
$$

This leads to a DFR-based formulation of TF-IDF with the BM25-TF quantification.

3.9.9 TF-IDF AND DFR: GAPS BETWEEN TERM OCCURRENCES

Clarifying the relationship between TF-IDF and DFR took more effort than expected, and I would like to thank Gianni Amati for the discussions and hours we have spent together on the what and how of DFR and TF-IDF.

I had been struggling with the risk-times-gain approach to arrive at the TF quantification $\text{tf}_d/(\text{tf}_d + K)$. Therefore, Gianni and I discussed repeatedly the roots of DFR. Currently, I prefer an interpretation that rests on the combination of two models: a model for computing the probability of a document that contains the term, and a model for computing the probability of the gap between two term occurrences.

For the first model, the probability to find $k_t > 0$ occurrences in a particular document d is proportional to finding a document that contains t.

$$
P(k_t > 0|d, c) \propto P(k_t > 0|c) \tag{3.81}
$$

In a more verbose way, the probabilities can be expressed as follows:

$$
P(k_t > 0 \text{ in document } d|c) \propto P(\text{exists a document that contains } t|c) \tag{3.82}
$$

Then, the maximum-likelihood estimate is the usual document-frequency-based term probability:

$$
P(k_t > 0|c) = P_D(t|c) = \frac{n_D(t, c)}{N_D(c)} \qquad \left(= \frac{\text{df}(t, c)}{N_D(c)} \right) \tag{3.83}
$$

We refer to this randomness model as M_{df}, since it is based on the document frequency of the term.

For the second randomness model, let term t occur tf_d times in document d. Then, $\lambda_{\text{gap}}(t, d) := \text{dl}/(\text{tf}_d + 1)$ is the average gap length. For example, for a document where $\text{dl} = 100$, and for a term with $\text{tf}_d = 3$, the average gap length is 25. This is independent of the positions of the term. Let the term occur at positions 10, 50, and 80. The average gap length is $(10 + 40 + 30 + 20)/(3 + 1)$. Assuming a Poisson distribution, $P_{\text{gap}}(0|t, d) = e^{-\lambda_{\text{gap}}(t,d)}$ is the probability that a gap of length zero occurs.

The greater the probability of $t \in d$, the greater the probability to find a gap of length zero, i.e., the greater the probability that two term occurrences are adjacent to each other. Therefore, $P(k_t > 0)$ is proportional to $P(\text{gap-length} = 0)$.

$$P(k_t > 0|d, c) \propto P(\text{gap-length} = 0|t, d) \qquad (3.84)$$

When choosing the gap probability as a randomness model M_{gap}, then we obtain:

$$-\ln P_{M_{\text{gap}}}(t \in d|c) = -\ln e^{-\text{dl}/(\text{tf}_d + 1)} = \frac{\text{dl}}{\text{tf}_d + 1} \qquad (3.85)$$

The combination of the two randomness models M_{gap} and M_{df} is as follows:

$$w_{\text{DFR,df+gap}}(t, d, c) = w_{\text{DFR},M_{\text{gap}}}(t, d, c) \cdot w_{\text{DFR},M_{\text{df}}}(t, d, c) = \left[\frac{\text{dl}}{\text{tf}_d + 1}\right] \cdot \left[-\log \frac{n_D(t, c)}{N_D(c)}\right]$$

The next steps applies the cross entropy, Section 3.11.5 (p. 110):

$$H_{\text{cross}}(P_{\text{obs}}(k_t > 0|d, c), P_{\text{DFR,df+gap}}(t|d, c)) = \sum_{t \in \{t_1, t_2, \dots\}} P_{\text{obs}}(k_t > 0|d, c) \cdot w_{\text{DFR,df+gap}}(t, d, c)$$

The observed probability is proportional to the within-document term probability.

$$P_{\text{obs}}(k_t > 0|d, c) \propto P(t|d) = \frac{\text{tf}_d}{\text{dl}}$$

Inserting this into the cross entropy yields:

$$H_{\text{cross}}(P(t|d), P_{\text{DFR,df+gap}}(t|d, c)) \propto \sum_{t \in \{t_1, t_2, \dots\}} \text{tf}_d/\text{dl} \cdot w_{\text{DFR,df+gap}}(t, d, c) \qquad (3.86)$$

Finally, inserting the DFR term weight and reducing the expression leads to:

$$H_{\text{cross}}(P(t|d), P_{\text{DFR,df+gap}}(t|d, c)) \propto \sum_{t \in \{t_1, t_2, \dots\}} \frac{\text{tf}_d}{\text{tf}_d + 1} \cdot \text{idf}(t, c) \qquad (3.87)$$

Thus, TF-IDF is shown to be proportional to the cross entropy between the within-document term probability $P(t|d) = \text{tf}_d/\text{dl}$ and the term probability $P_{\text{DFR,df+gap}}(t|d, c) = P_D(t|c)^{\text{dl}/(\text{tf}_d + 1)}$.

3.10   MORE RELATIONSHIPS: BM25 AND LM, LM AND PIN'S

Regarding BM25 and LM, Lavrenko and Croft [2001], "Relevance-based Language Models," provide the starting point, and Lafferty and Zhai [2003] proposes a relationship between the odds of relevance, $O(r|d,q)$ and $P(q|d)$. This relationship and the assumptions required to establish it, are controversial, Luk [2008]; *see also* Section 2.2 (p. 23), PRF. Given the complexity of the relationship between BM25 and LM, this relationship is not yet covered in this lecture series. The research outlook positions the models and indicates the type of relationship to be explored.

Regarding LM and PIN's, Metzler and Croft [2004], "Combining the language model and inference network approaches to retrieval" describes the relationship, following up on Croft and Turtle [1992], Turtle and Croft [1992] who laid out earlier the PIN case for IR. The case "LM and PIN's" is interesting because on one hand, there is the conjunctive decomposition of $P(q|d)$ as known for LM, and on the other hand, there is the disjunctive (weighted sum) decomposition of $P(q|d)$ that is related to TF-IDF; Section 3.9.6 (p. 104), TF-IDF and PIN's.

3.11   INFORMATION THEORY

We revisit in the following selected concepts of information theory that are relevant to IR. Thereby, we point at the relationships between divergence and IR models. In one overview, the concepts are:

Section 3.11.1 Entropy $H(X)$

Section 3.11.2 Joint Entropy $H(X, Y) := H_{\text{joint}}(X, Y)$

Section 3.11.3 Conditional Entropy $H(X||Y) = H(X, Y) - H(Y)$

Section 3.11.4 Mutual Information $\text{MI}(X, Y) = H(X) + H(Y) - H(X, Y)$

Section 3.11.5 Cross Entropy $H(X; Y) := H_{\text{cross}}(X, Y)$

Section 3.11.6 KL-Divergence $D_{\text{KL}}(X||Y) = H_{\text{cross}}(X, Y) - H(Y)$

Section 3.11.7 Query Clarity: $D_{\text{KL}}(P_q||P_c)$

Section 3.11.8 LM = clarity(query) – divergence(query || doc)

Section 3.11.9 TF-IDF = clarity(doc) – divergence(doc || query)

3.11.1 ENTROPY

When discussing relationships between IR models, then information theory and its most popular concept, entropy, have to be included, although the relationship between IR models and information theory is controversial; Robertson [2004].

Definition 3.9 Entropy. Let $X_P = \{t_1, \ldots, t_n\}$ be a set of events, where $P(t)$ is the probability of event t. With respect to IR, the set could be a vocabulary, i.e., a set of terms (words). We can also denote X as a probability distribution: $X = (P(t_1), \ldots, P(t_n))$.

$H(X)$ denotes the entropy of X.

$$H(X) := \sum_{t \in X} P(t) \cdot -\log P(t) \tag{3.88}$$

More precisely, the notation is $H(P_X)$ or $H(P(X))$, but often the probability function P is omitted.

This definition of entropy is sometimes referred to as "Shannon's theorem," though the theorem is that entropy is equal to the expected code length.

The resemblance between entropy and TF-IDF has inspired researchers to establish a relationship between TF-IDF and information theory, Aizawa [2003]. When discussing this with Stephen Robertson, he pointed out: "There is no connection between TF-IDF and entropy (Shannon). The primary goal of the entropy formula is to estimate the bandwidth required to transfer signals." Though there is no direct relationship immediately evident, entropy-related concepts (cross entropy, divergence) can be used to explain IR models; Zhai [2009]; *see also* Section 2.8.10 (p. 73), KL-Divergence Retrieval Model.

Next, we briefly review the interpretation of entropy, and introduce conditional entropy and KL-divergence. Entropy is used to determine the bandwidth required to transfer a stream of signals, where a signal corresponds to the occurrence of a token, and $P(t)$ is the probability of the token.

Example 3.10 Entropy. Given two streams $s_a = 1, 1, 1, 0$ and $s_b = 1, 1, 0, 0$. The entropy's are:

$$
\begin{aligned}
H_{s_a} &= 3/4 \cdot -\log_2(3/4) + 1/4 \cdot -\log_2(1/4) &= 3/4 \cdot (2 - \log_2 3) + 1/4 \cdot (2 - \log_2 1) < 1 \\
H_{s_b} &= 2/4 \cdot -\log_2(2/4) + 2/4 \cdot -\log_2(2/4) &= (2/4 \cdot (2 - \log_2 2)) \cdot 2 = 1
\end{aligned}
$$

$H_{s_b} > H_{s_a}$: in stream b the distribution of tokens is uniform; the entropy is maximal if the probabilities are uniform (equi-probable).

Entropy is the expectation value of the code length. The bandwidth required to transfer a stream is equal to the number of signals (length of stream) times the entropy (expected code length).

3.11.2 JOINT ENTROPY

Joint entropy is the entropy of the joint events of two random variables.

$$H(X, Y) := H_{\text{joint}}(X, Y) := \sum_{x,y} P(x, y) \cdot -\log P(x, y) \qquad (3.89)$$

3.11.3 CONDITIONAL ENTROPY

Conditional entropy is the difference between joint entropy and entropy.

$$H(X||Y) := H(X, Y) - H(Y) \qquad (3.90)$$

Conditional entropy, $H(X||Y)$, is not to be confused with KL-divergence, $D_{\text{KL}}(X||Y)$.

3.11.4 MUTUAL INFORMATION (MI)

MI measures the (in)dependence between two random variables.

$$\text{MI}(X, Y) := H(X) + H(Y) - H(X, Y) \qquad (3.91)$$

For independence, $\text{MI}(X, Y) = 0$; however, $\text{MI}(X, Y) = 0$ does not necessarily mean independence.

3.11.5 CROSS ENTROPY

Cross entropy is a generalization of entropy:

$$H(X; Y) := H_{\text{cross}}(X, Y) := \sum_{t} P_X(t) \cdot -\log P_Y(t) \qquad (3.92)$$

For $P_X = P_Y$, cross entropy is entropy. Cross entropy can be interpreted as the expected code length when transferring a stream of signals, where the tokens are distributed according to P_X, and the encoding is based on P_Y. Regarding the notation, $H_{\text{cross}}(P_X, P_Y)$, is equivalent to $H_{\text{cross}}(X, Y)$.

The following equation shows the relationship between cross entropy and joint entropy.

$$H_{\text{cross}}(P(X, Y), P(X, Y)) = H_{\text{joint}}(X, Y) \qquad (3.93)$$

The cross entropy between X and Y is greater than (or equal to) the entropy of Y:

$$H_{\text{cross}}(X, Y) \geq H(Y) \qquad (3.94)$$

Intuitively, this is the case since an encoding, based on P_Y, of a stream of signals in which tokens are distributed according to P_X, requires more bandwidth than an encoding based on P_Y.

Whereas the relationship between basic entropy and IR is not clear, cross entropy and IR immediately connect for the case of LM; *see also* Section 2.8.10 (p. 73), KL-Divergence Retrieval Model.

$$H_{\text{cross}}(P_q, P_d) = \sum_t P_q(t) \cdot -\log P_d(t) \tag{3.95}$$

see also Section 3.11.8 (p. 112), Difference between Divergences: LM.

3.11.6 KL-DIVERGENCE

KL-divergence is the difference between cross entropy and entropy.

$$D_{\text{KL}}(X||Y) := H_{\text{cross}}(X, Y) - H(X) \tag{3.96}$$

KL-divergence is positive, since cross entropy is greater than entropy.

The KL-divergence can be applied to express mutual information (MI):

$$\text{MI}(X, Y) = D_{\text{KL}}(P(X, Y)||P(X) \cdot P(Y)) \tag{3.97}$$

MI is the KL-divergence between the joint probability $P(X, Y)$ and the product $P(X) \cdot P(Y)$, i.e., the divergence between the joint probability and "independence."

The relationship between KL-divergence and conditional entropy is illustrated in the following sequence of equations:

$$
\begin{aligned}
H(X||Y) &= H(X, Y) - H(Y) \\
&= H(X, Y) - H(Y) + H(X) - H(X) \\
&= H(X) - [H(X) + H(Y) - H(X, Y)] \\
&= H(X) - \text{MI}(X, Y) \\
&= H(X) - D_{\text{KL}}(P(X, Y)||P(X) \cdot P(Y))
\end{aligned}
$$

Conditional entropy is the difference between joint entropy and entropy. By adding $0 = H(X) - H(X)$ to the equation, one can rewrite the right side using MI and KL-divergence, respectively.

Retrieval models can be shown to be related to the KL-divergence. See also Section 2.8.10 (p. 73), KL-Divergence Retrieval Model.

3.11.7 QUERY CLARITY: DIVERGENCE(QUERY || COLLECTION)

Query clarity is the divergence between the within-query term probability, $P_q(t) = P(t|q)$, and the collection-wide term probability, $P_c(t) = P(t|c)$.

$$D_{\text{KL}}(P_q||P_c) = \sum_t P_q(t) \cdot \log \frac{P_q(t)}{P_c(t)} \tag{3.98}$$

A query is clear if the term probabilities, $P(t|q)$ and $P(t|c)$, are different, i.e., if the term distribution in the query is different from the term distribution in the collection.

The concept of query clarity is related to "query selectivity." There are different ways to define query selectivity, and one of the common approaches is the sum of IDF values.

In a dual way to query clarity, one can define document clarity.

The difference between divergences leads to expressions that can be used to explain TF-IDF and LM.

3.11.8 LM = CLARITY(QUERY) − DIVERGENCE(QUERY ‖ DOC)

Consider the difference between two query "clarity's," $D_{KL}(P_q\|P_c)$ and $D_{KL}(P_q\|P_d)$.

$$D_{KL}\left(P_q\|P_c\right) - D_{KL}\left(P_q\|P_d\right) =$$
$$= \sum_t P_q(t) \cdot \log \frac{P_q(t)}{P_c(t)} - \sum_t P_q(t) \cdot \log \frac{P_q(t)}{P_d(t)} = \sum_t P_q(t) \cdot \log \frac{P_d(t)}{P_c(t)} \quad (3.99)$$

The first divergence measures the query "clarity:" a query is clear if it is divergent from the collection. The second divergence measures how divergent q is from d: a document is not relevant if the query is divergent from the document, or, in other words, a document is relevant if the query is not divergent from the document. The next equation inserts $P_q(t) = P(t|q)$, etc.

$$\sum_t P_q(t) \cdot \log \frac{P_d(t)}{P_c(t)} = \sum_t P(t|q) \cdot \log \frac{P(t|d)}{P(t|c)}$$

Finally, by inserting the usual mixture for $P(t|d)$, the difference between divergences can immediately be seen to be related to RSV_{LM}.

$$\sum_t P(t|q) \cdot \log \frac{P(t|d)}{P(t|c)} = \sum_{t\in q} \frac{tf_q}{ql} \cdot \log \frac{\lambda_d \cdot P(t|d) + (1-\lambda_d) \cdot P(t|c)}{P(t|c)}$$
$$\propto \sum_{t\in q} TF(t,q) \cdot \log \frac{\lambda_d \cdot P(t|d) + (1-\lambda_d) \cdot P(t|c)}{P(t|c)} \quad (3.100)$$

For $P(t|q)$, we applied $P(t|q) \propto TF(t,q)$; this is justified since ql does not affect the ranking. For $P(t|d)$, we used the linear mixture of foreground and background model.

3.11.9 TF-IDF = CLARITY(DOC) − DIVERGENCE(DOC ‖ QUERY)

In a dual way, by changing the roles of d and q, the difference between divergences can be related to $RSV_{TF\text{-}IDF}$. Consider the difference between $D_{KL}(P_d\|P_c)$ and $D_{KL}(P_d\|P_q)$.

$$D_{KL}\left(P_d\|P_c\right) - D_{KL}\left(P_d\|P_q\right) =$$
$$= \sum_t P_d(t) \cdot \log \frac{P_d(t)}{P_c(t)} - \sum_t P_d(t) \cdot \log \frac{P_d(t)}{P_q(t)} = \sum_t P_d(t) \cdot \log \frac{P_q(t)}{P_c(t)} \quad (3.101)$$

The next equation inserts $P_q(t) = P(t|q)$, etc.

$$\sum_t P_d(t) \cdot \log \frac{P_q(t)}{P_c(t)} = \sum_t P(t|d) \cdot \log \frac{P(t|q)}{P(t|c)}$$

In Section 3.8 (p. 94), Query Term Probability Assumptions, we discussed the following bursti-
ness assumption for the query term probability $P(t|q)$:

$$P(t|q,c) = \frac{\text{avgtf}(t,c)}{\text{avgdl}(c)}$$

By inserting this assumption, and by using the Poisson bridge, $P_L(t|c) = \text{avgtf}(t,c)/\text{avgdl}(c) \cdot P_D(t|c)$, the difference between divergences can be seen to be related to $\text{RSV}_{\text{TF-IDF}}$.

$$\sum_t P(t|d) \cdot \log \frac{P(t|q)}{P(t|c)} = \sum_{t \in q} \frac{\text{tf}_d}{\text{dl}} \cdot \log \frac{1}{P_D(t|c)}$$

$$\propto \sum_{t \in q} \text{TF}(t,d) \cdot \log \frac{1}{P_D(t|c)} \tag{3.102}$$

Alternatively, one could apply an extreme mixture: $P(t|q) = 1 - P(t|c)$ for query terms, and $P(t|q) = P(t|c)$ for non-query terms. This is followed by the transformation from $P(t|c)$ to the Document-based probability $P_D(t|c)$; *see also* Section 3.7 (p. 93), Poisson Bridge. The interesting aspect of this alternative is that we obtain the expression $(\text{avgdl}(c)/\text{avgtf}(t,c) - P_D(t|c))/P_D(t|c)$, where avgtf and avgdl are explicit; *see also* Section 3.8.3 (p. 96), Query term BIR assumption.

Overall, the difference between divergences is a concise framework to explain both, LM and TF-IDF.

3.12 SUMMARY

There are several frameworks that can be viewed as meta-models that house the more concrete models such as TF-IDF, BM25, and LM. We have looked at the main frameworks: probabilistic relevance framework (PRF), logical IR, VSM and its generalization, the GVSM. Model instances can be derived and/or expressed in these frameworks. The general matrix framework underlines this aspect.

Moreover, the parallel derivation of models clarifies the different event spaces of a "term probability" used in BIR, Poisson, and LM. Figure 3.7 shows an overview over the main relation-ships.

Firstly, there are the different event spaces: for BIR, $\{0,1\}$, for Poisson, the frequencies, $\{0,1,2,\ldots\}$, and for LM, the terms themselves, i.e., $\{t_1,t_2,\ldots\}$. We discussed how the event spaces can be related to each other.

Second, there are the BIR-based justification of IDF, and the IDF-based formulation of the BIR term weight.

Third, the Poisson term weight elicits the usual TF-IDF component, and in addition, shows how the parameters *burstiness* and average document length theoretically should complement the IDF component. Also, the version of the Poisson model for missing relevance is related to

Section 3.6 (p. 94), Parallel Derivation of IR Models:

BIR: $x_t \in \{0, 1\}$:

$$P(t|c) = P_D(x_t = 1|c) = \frac{n_D(t, c)}{N_D(c)}$$

Poisson: $k_t \in \{0, 1, 2, \ldots\}$:

$$P(t|c) = P_\lambda(k_t|c) = \frac{\lambda^{k_t}}{k_t!} \cdot e^{-\lambda}$$

LM: $t \in \{t_1, t_2, \ldots\}$:

$$P(t|c) = P_L(t|c) = \frac{n_L(t, c)}{N_L(c)}$$

Term probabilities and event spaces; see also Figure 3.4 (p. 94), Parallel Derivation of IR Models.

Section 3.9.1 (p. 98), Relationship between TF-IDF and BIR:

$$\text{IDF}_{\text{BIR}}(t, c) = \log \frac{1 - P_D(t|c)}{P_D(t|c)} = w_{\text{BIR}}(t, r, \bar{r} \equiv c) \quad [D_r = \{\}] \qquad \text{Equation 3.53 (p. 99), BIR-based IDF}$$

$$w_{\text{BIR}}(t, r, \bar{r}) = \text{IDF}(t, \bar{r}) - \text{IDF}(t, r) + \text{IDF}(\bar{t}, r) - \text{IDF}(\bar{t}, \bar{r}) \qquad \text{Equation 3.58 (p. 99), IDF-based BIR}$$

Section 3.9.2 (p. 100), Relationship between TF-IDF and Poisson:

$$w_{\text{Poisson}}(t, d, q, r, \bar{r}) =$$
$$\text{TF}(t, d) \cdot \left(\text{IDF}(t, \bar{r}) - \text{burstiness}(t, \bar{r}) + \log \text{avgdl}(\bar{r})\right) -$$
$$\text{TF}(t, d) \cdot \left(\text{IDF}(t, r) - \text{burstiness}(t, r) + \log \text{avgdl}(r)\right) \qquad \text{Equation 3.64 (p. 101), Poisson Term Weight}$$

Section 3.9.4 (p. 102), Relationship between TF-IDF and LM:

$$\text{TF-IDF} \equiv \frac{P(d|q, c)}{P(d|c)} = \frac{P(d, q|c)}{P(d|c) \cdot P(q|c)} = \frac{P(q|d, c)}{P(q|c)} \equiv \text{LM} \qquad \text{Equation 3.72 (p. 104), DQI Bridge}$$

see also Figure 3.6 (p. 115), TF-IDF and LM: Side-by-Side.

Section 3.9.9 (p. 106), Relationship between TF-IDF and DFR: Gaps:

$$M_{\text{gap}}: \quad P(k_t > 0|d, c) \quad \propto \quad P(\text{gap-length}(t) = 0|d) = e^{-\text{dl}/(\text{tf}_d + 1)}$$

$$M_{\text{df}}: \quad P(k_t > 0|d, c) \quad \propto \quad P(\text{exists a document that contains } t|c) = \frac{\text{df}(t, c)}{N_D(c)}$$

Differences between Divergences:

$$\text{RSV}_{\text{LM}}(d, q, c) \quad \propto \quad D_{\text{KL}}\left(P_q || P_c\right) - D_{\text{KL}}\left(P_q || P_d\right) \qquad \text{Equation 3.100 (p. 112), Divergence and LM}$$
$$\text{RSV}_{\text{TF-IDF}}(d, q, c) \quad \propto \quad D_{\text{KL}}\left(P_d || P_c\right) - D_{\text{KL}}\left(P_d || P_q\right) \qquad \text{Equation 3.102 (p. 113), Divergence and TF-IDF}$$

Figure 3.7: Relationships between Retrieval Models: Overview.

divergence-based retrieval, if we were to choose the Poisson probability as the model of randomness.

Fourth, there is the relationship between TF-IDF and LM: it can be shown that both models measure the document-query-(in)dependence (DQI). The DQI is a factor that occurs in mutual information (MI), i.e., the DQI is proportional to $\text{MI}(d, q)$.

Fifth, the relationship between TF-IDF and DFR can be based on a randomness model that computes the probability of the gap-length between two term occurrences.

Sixth, both, LM and TF-IDF can be shown to be related to the differences between divergences. This extends the view that LM is divergence-based; see also Section 2.8.10 (p. 73), KL-Divergence-Retrieval-Model.

CHAPTER 4

Summary & Research Outlook

4.1 SUMMARY

This book provides the mathematical core of the main strands of IR models: TF-IDF, PRF, BIR, BM25, LM, and DFR. Most of what is presented in this book is common knowledge to researchers familiar with IR models. Some of the more recent or less known insights shown in this book, are:

1. Section 2.1 (p. 9), TF-IDF:
   We structured the TF and IDF variants. We emphasized that the TF variants reflect a dependence assumption. For example, the logarithmic TF, Section 2.1.2 (p. 12), corresponds to assuming that the second term occurrence has an impact of $1/2$, the third occurrence $1/3$, and so forth (harmonic sum). The BM25-TF can be related to the harmonic sum of squares, i.e., the second term occurrence has an impact of $1/2^2$, the third occurrence $1/3^2$, and so forth.

   Section 2.1.7 (p. 17), Semi-subsumed Event Occurrences:
   We discussed that $n/((n + 1)/2)$, the mid-point between independence and subsumption, assigns a probabilistic semantics to the BM25-TF quantification, $\frac{\mathrm{tf}_d}{\mathrm{tf}_d + K_d}$.

2. Section 2.3 (p. 29), BIR:
   Section 2.3.6 (p. 33), 0.5 Smoothing in the RSJ Term Weight:
   We looked at Laplace-based and mixture-based arguments regarding the 0.5 in w_{RSJ}, the term weight employed in BM25.

3. Section 2.4 (p. 35), Poisson Model:
   The Poisson term weight, w_{Poisson}, contains the common IDF component, $-\log P_D(t|c)$, and makes explicit components such as "burstiness," $\mathrm{avgtf}(t, c)$, and "document length normalization," dl/avgdl.

4. Section 2.6 (p. 49), LM:
   There are various forms to denote the LM-based term weight. One form, referred to as LM2, section 2.6.6, is currently not common, but is useful for implementing LM, and also for relating LM to other retrieval models. For example, both the BM25-TF and LM2 are essentially ratios of probabilities, and this motivates the idea to explore ratio-based formulations of retrieval models.

5. Section 2.8 (p. 63), Divergence-based Models:
   Section 2.8.1 (p. 63), DFR:
   We discussed the DFR first generation, $P(t \in d | c)$, and the DFR second generation, $P(\text{tf}_d | c)$. Also, we investigated the meaning of the DFR RSV, which is based on a binomial probability of k_d occurrences of document d, and how this is related to k_t occurrences of term t. The Poisson model and DFR are related for the case where the Poisson model is formulated for missing relevance, and the Poisson probability is chosen as a model of randomness.

6. Section 2.10 (p. 76), Precision and Recall:
   Precision and Recall, and IR models share the same root: probabilities. This leads to some interesting dualities, pointing at pathways to transfer methods from IR models to evaluation, and vice versa.

7. Section 3.3 (p. 83), VSM:
   Section 3.4 (p. 85), GVSM:
   The vector-space "model" is a framework in which TF-IDF, BM25, and LM can be expressed. Already the VSM, but in particular the GVSM, are frameworks that can be used to combine geometric measures with concepts of probability theory.

8. Section 3.7 (p. 93), Poisson Bridge:
   This equation helps to relate Document-based and Location-based term probabilities. The Document-based term probability $P_D(t|c)$ occurs in TF-IDF, and the Location-based term probability $P_L(t|c)$ occurs in LM.

9. Section 3.9 (p. 96), Relationships: TF-IDF:
   Section 3.9.5 (p. 102), TF-IDF and LM: Side-by-Side:
   This derivation shows that TF-IDF and LM measure the same, namely the document-query-independence: $\text{DQI} := P(d,q)/(P(d) \cdot P(q))$. Besides establishing the relationship between TF-IDF and LM, the derivation also establishes probabilistic roots for TF-IDF.

   Section 3.9.9 (p. 106), TF-IDF and DFR: Gaps between Term Occurrences:
   In addition to the traditional explanation based on the combination of risk and gain, we have considered an explanation that is based on combining a document-frequency-based DFR model with a gap-based DFR model, where the latter is based on the probability of the gap size between two term occurrences.

10. Section 3.11.8 (p. 112), Divergence and LM:
    Section 3.11.9 (p. 112), Divergence and TF-IDF:
    TF-IDF and LM are shown to be proportional to differences between divergences. So far, only LM is viewed to be based on the KL-divergence (see Zhai [2009], page 55). We have looked at this aspect in Section 2.8.10 (p. 73), KL-Divergence Retrieval Model.

4.2 RESEARCH OUTLOOK

This book contributes a consolidation of IR models, and this consolidation discloses research issues and opportunities. Forecasting the roads ahead is speculative, but there is evidence that retrieval models and evaluation models have to evolve, and that model combinations improve performance. Also, dependence of events (term occurrences and user interactions), and the sequence of events, need to be reflected in a more sophisticated way. Moreover, the candidate result, retrieved by the basic models, needs to be post-processed for obtaining a satisfying result. Finally, similar to physics, a discipline that greatly advanced because of its close interplay with math, I believe that IR has to improve its interplay with math. This leads to the following items in the research outlook:

Section 4.2.1: Retrieval Models

Section 4.2.2: Evaluation Models

Section 4.2.3: A Unified Framework for Retrieval AND Evaluation

Section 4.2.4: Model Combinations and New Models (query performance prediction)

Section 4.2.5: Dependence-aware Models, Sequence-based Models, Order-aware Models

Section 4.2.6: Query-Log Models and other More-Evidence Models

Section 4.2.7: Phase-2 Models: Retrieval Result Condensation Models (diversity, novelty)

Section 4.2.8: Theoretical Framework to Predict Ranking Quality

Section 4.2.9: Math for IR

Section 4.2.10: Abstraction for IR

4.2.1 RETRIEVAL MODELS

Figure 4.1 shows a lattice of relevance and likelihood.

Relevance is "present" or "missing," and the likelihood is "document" likelihood or "query" likelihood. In this lattice, we can position the models TF-IDF, LM, and BM25.

This lattice emphasizes that TF-IDF and LM measure the same, namely the document-query (in)dependence (DQI).

$$\text{TF-IDF} \equiv \frac{P(d|q)}{P(d)} = \frac{P(d,q)}{P(d) \cdot P(q)} = \frac{P(q|d)}{P(q)} \equiv \text{LM}$$

The discussion that aims to classify the models to be either discriminative (TF-IDF, which document is implied by the query, $q \rightarrow d$) or generative (LM, which document implies/generates the query, $d \rightarrow q$), is then led by the decomposition of either document or query event. TF-IDF

	likelihood	
	$P(d\|q)/P(d)$	$P(q\|d)/P(q)$
relevance information	Traditional PRF/BM25 $$\frac{P(d\|q,r)}{P(d\|q,\bar{r})} \overset{\text{rank}}{=} \frac{P(d\|q,r)}{P(d\|q,\bar{r})} \cdot \frac{P(q\|r)}{P(q\|\bar{r})}$$ $\text{RSV}_{\text{TF-IDF}}(d,q,\bar{r}) - \text{RSV}_{\text{TF-IDF}}(d,q,r)$	LM-based PRF/BM25 $$\frac{P(q\|d,r)}{P(q\|d,\bar{r})} \cdot \frac{P(d\|r)}{P(d\|\bar{r})}$$ $\text{RSV}_{\text{LM}}(d,q,\bar{r}) - \text{RSV}_{\text{LM}}(d,q,r)$
NO relevance information	TF-IDF $$\frac{P(d\|q,c)}{P(d\|c)}$$	LM $$P(q\|d,c) \overset{\text{rank}}{=} \frac{P(q\|d,c)}{P(q\|c)}$$

Figure 4.1: Model Lattice.

decomposes the document event, whereas LM decomposes the query event. This complements the view of logical IR, Nie [1992], van Rijsbergen [1986], Wong and Yao [1995], where retrieval scores are viewed to be a semantics of $P(d \rightarrow q)$.

Moreover, the lattice underlines that PRF/BM25, traditionally based on the document likelihood, $P(d|q,r)$, can be viewed as the general form of TF-IDF, or, in other words, TF-IDF is a special form of BM25. When using IDF in place of the RSJ term weight, then BM25 can be formulated as the difference between $\text{RSV}_{\text{TF-IDF}}(d, q, \bar{r})$ and $\text{RSV}_{\text{TF-IDF}}(d, q, r)$. In a similar way, an LM-based "BM25" is the difference between the respective LM-based RSV's. LM and PRF are on different levels, and regarding the discussion that LM is proportional to the probabilistic odds, the lattice emphasizes that, similar to the way TF-IDF and traditional BM25 are related, there is an LM-based "PRF/BM25," i.e., a consequent decomposition of the odds of relevance based on $P(q|d,r)$, where the query event is decomposed. In traditional BM25, the RSJ term weight is based on a binary event space. For the LM-based BM25, the term weight is based on the space of terms.

4.2.2   EVALUATION MODELS

This book is about retrieval models, and Section 2.10 (p. 76), Precision & Recall, established that probability theory is the common ancestor of both, retrieval models and evaluation models. Precision and recall are conditional probabilities, and the mean average precision can be expressed via the total probability theorem.

Taking this probabilistic view on evaluation, the idea is to devise a unified model that is an abstraction of retrieval AND evaluation.

4.2.3 A UNIFIED FRAMEWORK FOR RETRIEVAL AND EVALUATION

The idea to devise unified models is a continuous research topic, and for IR, its foundation may be Robertson et al. [1982], "The Unified Probabilistic Model for IR." Also, Stephen Robertson presented in his keynote at the SIGIR 2004 Theory Workshop "A new unified probabilistic model".

The unified model we discuss here in the research outlook rests on the idea of exploring a duality between retrieval and evaluation. The duality is based on the following two probabilities: $P(\text{relevant}|d, q)$ and $P(\text{useful}|\text{retrieved}, \text{relevant})$. Figure 4.2 shows the way the duality between retrieval and evaluation unfolds.

Retrieval	TF-IDF	LM
with event "rel" probabilistic odds Bayesian classifier	$\dfrac{P(d\,\|q, \text{rel})}{P(d\,\|q, \neg\text{rel})} \cdot \dfrac{P(q\,\|\,\text{rel})}{P(q\,\|\neg\text{rel})}$	$\dfrac{P(q\,\|d, \text{rel})}{P(q\,\|d, \neg\text{rel})} \cdot \dfrac{P(d\,\|\,\text{rel})}{P(d\,\|\neg\text{rel})}$
without event "rel" conditional / prior dependence measure	$\dfrac{P(d\,\|q)}{P(d)} = \dfrac{P(d,q)}{P(d) \cdot P(q)}$	$\dfrac{P(q\,\|d)}{P(q)} = \dfrac{P(q,d)}{P(q) \cdot P(d)}$
basic implication	$P(d\,\|q)$	$P(q\,\|d)$
Evaluation	Precision	Recall
with event "useful" probabilistic odds Bayesian classifier	$\dfrac{P(\text{rel}\|\text{retr}, \text{useful})}{P(\text{rel}\|\text{retr}, \neg\text{useful})} \cdot \dfrac{P(\text{retr}\|\text{useful})}{P(\text{retr}\|\neg\text{useful})}$	$\dfrac{P(\text{retr}\|\text{rel}, \text{useful})}{P(\text{retr}\|\text{rel}, \neg\text{useful})} \cdot \dfrac{P(\text{rel}\|\text{useful})}{P(\text{rel}\|\neg\,\text{useful})}$
withouth event "useful" conditional / prior dependence measure	$\dfrac{P(\text{rel}\|\text{retr})}{P(\text{rel})} = \dfrac{P(\text{rel}, \text{retr})}{P(\text{rel}) \cdot P(\text{retr})}$	$\dfrac{P(\text{retr}\|\text{rel})}{P(\text{retr})} = \dfrac{P(\text{retr}, \text{rel})}{P(\text{retr}) \cdot P(\text{rel})}$
basic implication	$P(\text{rel}\|\text{retr})$	$P(\text{retr}\|\text{rel})$

Figure 4.2: Unified Model Lattice: Retrieval and Evaluation.

The unified model has five parameters, as the following pseudo-code illustrates:

```
define UnifiedModel(Task, Hypothesis, Model1, Event1, Model2, Event2) {
# $Task & $Model1                        & $Model2
```

```
#        & P($Event1 | $Event2, $Hypothesis) & P($Event2 | $Event1, $Hypothesis)
}

main () {
  UnifiedModel("Retrieval",  rel,    "TF-IDF",    d,   "LM",    q);
  UnifiedModel("Evaluation", useful, "Precision", rel, "Recall", retr);
}
```

Note that this arrangement is not supposed to indicate that TF-IDF is precision-oriented and LM is recall-oriented. The message of the arrangement is that in this template we realize that what is familiar for IR models can be transferred to evaluation, and the other way round, what is familiar for evaluation, can be transferred to IR models.

We know for retrieval models that the coverage of the dependencies of the multiple occurrences of a term, expressed as the TF quantification, is important. We know that a concept of "discriminativeness" is essential. How do event frequencies and discriminativeness transfer to evaluation models?

Whereas on the retrieval side, the probabilistic odds are the most recognized approach to IR, on the evaluation side, the basic implications dominate. This naturally leads to the question of how to evolve evaluation measures, taking advantage of what is known for retrieval models.

The F1-measure combines the two sides of evaluation, where F1 is the harmonic mean of precision and recall. How does this combination transfer to IR models?

In a direct comparison, retrieval and evaluation read as follows:

The $\boxed{\text{document}}$ is $\boxed{\text{relevant}}$ for the $\boxed{\text{query}}$ if
the probability $P(\text{relevant}|d, q)$ is greater than $P(\neg\text{relevant}|d, q)$.

The $\boxed{\text{retrieved documents}}$ are $\boxed{\text{useful}}$ for the $\boxed{\text{relevant documents}}$ if
the probability $P(\text{useful}|\text{retr}, \text{rel})$ is greater than $P(\neg\text{useful}|\text{retr}, \text{rel})$.

In summary, the relationships between retrieval and evaluation can be exploited to transfer concept from evaluation to retrieval, and vice versa.

4.2.4   MODEL COMBINATIONS AND "NEW" MODELS

Investigations into model combinations show pathways to improving retrieval quality. One promising approach is query performance prediction (QPP, select model and parameters based on query features), Hauff et al. [2010], Shtok et al. [2010]. This will lead to "new" models, but it is currently an open question how predictors will find their way into widely accepted standards of retrieval models. What will become the standard TF-IDF-QPP and LM-QPP?

Other candidates for pathways to new models are divergence-based models, or, in the wider context, moving from "probabilistic models" toward "information-theoretic" models. DFR is an information-theoretic model, however, there is the view that the other models embody components of DFR, and can be explained as being divergence-based.

Whether QPP or DFR or other, one of the overall questions is where to search for new models. Chengxiang Zhai described the question at ICTIR 2011 like this:

> We can either search near to the models we know, or we search in far away land, search in completely new areas.

"Near to the models we know" means to search in the quadrangle TF-IDF, LM, TF-IDF-BM25, and LM-BM25. Considering relevance, user profiles (personalization) and query features (performance prediction) is still near to what we know.

"Search far away" means to go beyond what we usually do. Maybe this means to go back to the basics, back to the good old vector-space model, where the Euclidean norm and other normalization in combination with the state-of-the-art knowledge about event dependencies, likelihoods, and event spaces may lead to improvements. Already van Rijsbergen [2004] points at this combination of probabilistic and geometric methods that may lead to "new" models.

Though around since the early 00s, divergence-based models still feel at the beginning in the sense that they are still perceived as being complex. This book has highlighted some of the issues regarding DFR, discussed the relationships between DFR and the binomial probability, and between divergence and the more intuitive models such as TF-IDF, BM25, and LM. It is interesting that currently we work in a vicinity where IR models are closer to "probability theory" than to "information theory." I believe that the road to new models means first to establish new math, for example, new mathematical concepts to capture aspects such as the dependence of event occurrences, or new math that merges probability theory and information theory.

4.2.5   DEPENDENCE-AWARE MODELS

A simple test such as a web search with query "information retrieval" versus "retrieval information" shows: the order (sequence) of words does matter. The algorithm (let the query term probability depend on the position, or apply a phrase-based matching to complement the single-term match) is the secret of the engineers. From an IR model perspective, the standard formulations of "bag-of-word" IR models do not consider the order of terms in the sequences that represent queries and documents.

Even when agreeing that the TF component models a form of dependence assumption, the order of terms is not reflected. Dependence comes in different contexts and forms. Hou et al. [2011], "High-Order Word Dependence Mining," showed that the modeling of triplets, that is dependencies of order 3, is conducive for IR. Zhai et al. [2003], "Beyond Independent Relevance," pointed at the dependence in subtopic retrieval, and the dependence between the hits in a retrieval result. Wu and Roelleke [2009] proposed semi-subsumption as a notion to describe the dependence inherently modeled by the BM25-TF.

Overall, the standard "bag-of-word" formulations need to evolve to standards that capture dependence, sequences (order) and proximity (back to the roots of IR). The problem here is not so much to find "a model," the problem seems to be to find a formulation, that is to find concepts that are easy to grasp, and lead to a widely known standard.

4.2.6   "QUERY-LOG" AND OTHER MORE-EVIDENCE MODELS

The field "learning to rank," Li [2011], shows that given more evidence than the similarity of terms, retrieval quality can be improved. Mixing topical scores with other scores such as popularity-based scores (web pages, page-rank, Brin and Page [1998b]) is well known to enhance retrieval performance. In addition to exploiting evidence about the collection of documents, it is conducive to exploit evidence about collections of queries, as, for example, demonstrated by Deng et al. [2009], where a notion "IQF: inverse query frequency" has been proposed, and this confirms the benefits of taking advantage of dualities and relationships between models.

This book focused on the consolidation of *topical* models. Future research into foundations of IR models could lead to standard formulations that mix the main types and sources of evidence. Regarding types of evidence, state-of-the-art search systems mix topical evidence and structural evidence (bibliographic coupling, co-citations, in-links and out-links, partitioning of documents). Regarding source of evidence, the collection of documents, the collection of queries, the user profile, and domain-specific background knowledge (e.g., a list of synonyms or a more refined taxonomy) are common sources when devising a ranking function. The research challenge is to shape standards of formal models that capture the different types and sources of evidence.

4.2.7   PHASE-2 MODELS: RETRIEVAL RESULT CONDENSATION MODELS

Today's retrieval systems are based on several retrieval phases. The main two phases are:

1. Retrieve the result candidates where the ranking is based on content, structure, and relationships. Also, parameters such as user profile (location, age, gender, history) can be included for a customer-specific ranking.

2. Condense the result. This phase takes a holistic view at the retrieval result, exploiting the relationships between the retrieved items.

Phase-2, the condensation of the result, aims at making the result satisfactory, diverse, personal, profitable, attractive, etc. This phase means to promote some of the result candidates and demote others. Whereas TF-IDF, BM25, and LM are widely known "standards" for the first phase, the models used for the second phase are specific.

Topics such as diversification and result clustering (aggregation) are ubiquitous and it can be expected that similar to the way TF-IDF and friends are established standards, we will see standards for result post-processing becoming as widely known as the basic IR models. Kurland et al. [2011], "A Unified Framework for Post-Retrieval Query-Performance Prediction," is one of the attempts pointing the way toward the unification and consolidation of this field.

4.2.8   A THEORETICAL FRAMEWORK TO PREDICT RANKING QUALITY

Before the laws of force and gravity were formulated, researchers lifted and bounced many objects of different kinds and measured speed and effect. Again and again.

Whereas in the physical world, there are models to compute expected speed and impact of an accelerating object, it is not clear whether we can find a formal framework that tells for a retrieval model the expected quality. I appreciate the comment of IR experts and colleagues saying: "This is nonsense." Definitely, it is challenging. The axiomatic framework, Fang and Zhai [2005], is a milestone in devising a theoretical framework in which to express what must hold for a retrieval function for it to be reasonable. Relatively remote to IR but relevant in this context is work on formalizing properties of knowledge and belief; Fagin and Halpern [1994]. This type of theoretical work tells us how to formalize properties and concepts that are difficult to capture formally.

4.2.9   MIR: MATH FOR IR

Physics always has inspired and rewritten math, and many mathematical concepts only came into existence because physicians required an abstraction to describe problems and phenomenas.

One of the main endeavours of this book is to base the consolidation of IR models on a non-ambiguous and concise mathematical world. The journey was more complicated than expected, and crystalising and stabilising the mathematical ingredients have required in-depth studies of mathematical groundwork. One of the conclusions is: we need more math for IR.

In probability theory, we usually meet the traditional assumptions: independent, disjoint, and subsumed events. To move some of the achievements of IR into other application domains, research is required that generates and establishes new, IR-driven math, to transfer what is learned from IR models into the mathematical world of probability theory.

TF-IDF, a compact, mathematical expression, has been a popular retrieval model for more than 40 years, and BM25 and LM are catching up. Is there a new intuitive formula, a new mathematical concept, that will lead to a new retrieval model?

4.2.10   AIR: ABSTRACTION FOR IR

Math for IR is only one form of abstraction. Other, more concrete forms of abstraction are programming languages, software environments, data models, and knowledge representation. Cornacchia et al. [2008], Fuhr [1995], Meghini et al. [1993], Roelleke et al. [2008] and related publications point at possibilities to employ mathematical frameworks and probabilistic variants of logic's (descriptive languages) for modeling IR models and tasks. Whereas Lucene-based implementations of search systems become popular, and the traditional term-document (key-value) index is still the dominating "data model" for IR, and the gap between database solutions and IR systems is still wide, there is a demand for technology that on one hand is lighter weight than traditional "elephant" DB technology, and on the other hand reliably delivers levels of abstraction that make building and maintaining application-specific IR systems more efficient.

This book provides a mathematical basis and a detailed consolidation of models, and this is the footwork required for establishing higher abstraction for IR.

Bibliography

Aizawa, A. (2003). An information-theoretic perspective of tf-idf measures. *Information Processing and Management*, 39:45–65. DOI: 10.1016/S0306-4573(02)00021-3. 109

Aly, R. and Demeester, T. (2011). Towards a better understanding of the relationship between probabilistic models in IR. In *ICTIR, Bertinoro, Italy*, volume 6931, pages 164–175. DOI: 10.1007/978-3-642-23318-0_16. 3

Amati, G. (2009). BM25. In Liu, L. and Özsu, M. T., editors, *Encyclopedia of Database Systems*, pages 257–260. Springer US. 34

Amati, G. and van Rijsbergen, C. J. (2002). Probabilistic models of information retrieval based on measuring the divergence from randomness. *ACM Transaction on Information Systems (TOIS)*, 20(4):357–389. DOI: 10.1145/582415.582416. 2, 64, 65, 104, 105

Azzopardi, L. and Roelleke, T. (2007). Explicitly considering relevance within the language modelling framework. In *Proceedings of the 1st International Conference on Theory of Information Retrieval (ICTIR 07) - Studies in Theory of Information Retrieval*. 25, 58

Baeza-Yates, R. A. and Ribeiro-Neto, B. A. (2011). *Modern Information Retrieval - the concepts and technology behind search, Second edition*. Pearson Education Ltd., Harlow, England. 3, 65

Belew, R. K. (2000). *Finding out about*. Cambridge University Press. 3

Bookstein, A. (1980). Fuzzy requests: An approach to weighted Boolean searches. *Journal of the American Society for Information Science*, 31:240–247. DOI: 10.1002/asi.4630310403. 1

Brin, S. and Page, L. (1998a). The anatomy of a large-scale hypertextual web search engine. *Computer Networks*, 30(1-7):107–117. DOI: 10.1016/j.comnet.2012.10.007.

Brin, S. and Page, L. (1998b). The anatomy of a large-scale hypertextual web search engine. In *7th International WWW Conference, Brisbane, Australia*. DOI: 10.1016/j.comnet.2012.10.007. 124

Bronstein, I. N. (1987). *Taschenbuch der Mathematik*. Harri Deutsch, Thun, Frankfurt am Main. 21

Bruza, P. and Song, D. (2003). A comparison of various approaches for using probabilistic dependencies in language modeling. In DBLP:conf/sigir/2003 [2003], pages 419–420. 2

Church, K. and Gale, W. (1995). Inverse document frequency (idf): A measure of deviation from Poisson. In *Proceedings of the Third Workshop on Very Large Corpora*, pages 121–130. 16, 35

Cooper, W. (1991). Some inconsistencies and misnomers in probabilistic IR. In Bookstein, A., Chiaramella, Y., Salton, G., and Raghavan, V., editors, *Proceedings of the Fourteenth Annual International ACM SIGIR Conference on Research and Development in Information Retrieval*, pages 57–61, New York.

Cooper, W. S. (1988). Getting beyond Boole. *Information Processing and Management*, 24(3):243–248. DOI: 10.1016/0306-4573(88)90091-X.

Cooper, W. S. (1994). Triennial ACM SIGIR award presentation and paper: The formalism of probability theory in IR: A foundation for an encumbrance. In Croft and van Rijsbergen [1994], pages 242–248.

Cornacchia, R. and de Vries, A. P. (2007). A parameterised search system. In *ECIR*, pages 4–15. DOI: 10.1007/978-3-540-71496-5_4. 83, 91

Cornacchia, R., Héman, S., Zukowski, M., de Vries, A. P., and Boncz, P. A. (2008). Flexible and efficient IR using array databases. *VLDB J.*, 17(1). DOI: 10.1007/s00778-007-0071-0. 125

Crestani, F. and Van Rijsbergen, C. J. (1995). Information retrieval by logical imaging. *Journal of Documentation*, 51(1):3–17. DOI: 10.1108/eb026939. 83

Crestani, F. and van Rijsbergen, C. J. (1995). Probability kinematics in information retrieval. In Fox et al. [1995], pages 291–299. 83

Croft, B. and Lafferty, J., editors (2003). *Language Modeling for Information Retrieval*. Kluwer. DOI: 10.1007/978-94-017-0171-6. 49, 130

Croft, W. and Harper, D. (1979). Using probabilistic models of document retrieval without relevance information. *Journal of Documentation*, 35:285–295. DOI: 10.1108/eb026683. 1, 32, 96

Croft, W. and Turtle, H. (1992). Retrieval of complex objects. In Pirotte, A., Delobel, C., and Gottlob, G., editors, *Advances in Database Technology — EDBT'92*, pages 217–229, Berlin et al. Springer. 61, 63, 108

Croft, W. B. and van Rijsbergen, C. J., editors (1994). *Proceedings of the Seventeenth Annual International ACM SIGIR Conference on Research and Development in Information Retrieval*, London, et al. Springer-Verlag. 128, 132

DBLP:conf/sigir/2003 (2003). *SIGIR 2003: Proceedings of the 26th Annual International ACM SIGIR Conference on Research and Development in Information Retrieval, July 28 - August 1, 2003, Toronto, Canada*. ACM. 127

de Vries, A. and Roelleke, T. (2005). Relevance information: A loss of entropy but a gain for IDF? In *ACM SIGIR*, pages 282–289, Salvador, Brazil. DOI: 10.1145/1076034.1076084. 34, 97

Deerwester, S., Dumais, S., Furnas, G., Landauer, T., and Harshman, R. (1990). Indexing by latent semantic analysis. *Journal of the American Society for Information Science*, 41(6):391–407. DOI: 10.1002/(SICI)1097-4571(199009)41:6%3C391::AID-ASI1%3E3.0.CO;2-9. 86

Deng, H., King, I., and Lyu, M. R. (2009). Entropy-biased models for query representation on the click graph. In *Proceedings of the 32nd international ACM SIGIR conference on Research and development in information retrieval*, SIGIR '09, pages 339–346, New York, NY, USA. ACM. DOI: 10.1145/1571941.1572001. 124

Dumais, S. T., Furnas, G. W.and Landauer, T. K., and Deerwester, S. (1988). Using latent semantic analysis to improve information retrieval. pages 281–285. 86

Dupret, G. (2003). Latent concepts and the number orthogonal factors in latent semantic analysis. In *SIGIR*, pages 221–226. DOI: 10.1145/860435.860477. 86

Fagin, R. and Halpern, J. (1994). Reasoning about knowledge and probability. *Journal of the ACM*, 41(2):340–367. DOI: 10.1145/174652.174658. 125

Fang, H. and Zhai, C. (2005). An exploration of axiomatic approaches to information retrieval. In *SIGIR '05: Proceedings of the 28th annual international ACM SIGIR conference on Research and development in information retrieval*, pages 480–487, New York, NY, USA. ACM. DOI: 10.1145/1076034.1076116. 2, 125

Fox, E., Ingwersen, P., and Fidel, R., editors (1995). *Proceedings of the 18th Annual International ACM SIGIR Conference on Research and Development in Information Retrieval*, New York. ACM. 128, 129

Fuhr, N. (1989). Models for retrieval with probabilistic indexing. *Information Processing and Management*, 25(1):55–72. DOI: 10.1016/0306-4573(89)90091-5. 27, 28

Fuhr, N. (1992a). Integration of probabilistic fact and text retrieval. In Belkin, N., Ingwersen, P., and Pejtersen, M., editors, *Proceedings of the Fifteenth Annual International ACM SIGIR Conference on Research and Development in Information Retrieval*, pages 211–222, New York. 25

Fuhr, N. (1992b). Probabilistic models in information retrieval. *The Computer Journal*, 35(3):243–255. DOI: 10.1093/comjnl/35.3.243.

Fuhr, N. (1995). Probabilistic datalog - a logic for powerful retrieval methods. In Fox et al. [1995], pages 282–290. 125

Gordon, M. and Lenk, P. (1992). When is the probability ranking principle suboptimal? *Journal of the American Society for Information Science*, 43(1):1–14. DOI: 10.1002/(SICI)1097-4571(199201)43:1%3C1::AID-ASI1%3E3.0.CO;2-5. 27

Grossman, D. A. and Frieder, O. (2004). *Information Retrieval. Algorithms and Heuristics, 2nd ed.*, volume 15 of *The Information Retrieval Series*. Springer. 3

Hauff, C., Azzopardi, L., Hiemstra, D., and de Jong, F. (2010). Query performance prediction: Evaluation contrasted with effectiveness. In Gurrin, C., He, Y., Kazai, G., Kruschwitz, U., Little, S., Roelleke, T., Rüger, S. M., and van Rijsbergen, K., editors, *ECIR*, volume 5993 of *Lecture Notes in Computer Science*, pages 204–216. Springer. 122

He, B. and Ounis, I. (2005). Term frequency normalisation tuning for BM25 and DFR models. In *ECIR*, pages 200–214. DOI: 10.1007/978-3-540-31865-1_15.

Hiemstra, D. (2000). A probabilistic justification for using tf.idf term weighting in information retrieval. *International Journal on Digital Libraries*, 3(2):131–139. DOI: 10.1007/s007999900025. 2, 49, 54, 101

Hofmann, T. (1999). Probabilistic latent semantic indexing. In *SIGIR*, pages 50–57. ACM. DOI: 10.1145/312624.312649. 86

Hou, Y., He, L., Zhao, X., and Song, D. (2011). Pure high-order word dependence mining via information geometry. In *Advances in Information Retrieval Theory: Third International Conference, ICTIR, 2011, Bertinoro, Italy, September 12-14, 2011, Proceedings*, volume 6931, pages 64–76. Springer-Verlag New York Inc. DOI: 10.1007/978-3-642-23318-0_8. 2, 3, 123

Kamps, J., de Rijke, M., and Sigurbjörnsson, B. (2004). Length normalization in XML retrieval. In *Proceedings of the 27th annual international ACM SIGIR conference on research and development in information retrieval*, pages 80–87, New York, NY, USA. ACM Press. DOI: 10.1145/1008992.1009009. 101

Kleinberg, J. (1999). Authoritative sources in a hyperlinked environment. *Journal of ACM*, 46. DOI: 10.1145/324133.324140.

Kurland, O., Shtok, A., Carmel, D., and Hummel, S. (2011). A unified framework for post-retrieval query-performance prediction. In *ICTIR*, pages 15–26. DOI: 10.1007/978-3-642-23318-0_4. 124

Lafferty, J. and Zhai, C. (2003). *Probabilistic Relevance Models Based on Document and Query Generation*, chapter 1. In Croft and Lafferty [2003]. 1, 3, 25, 58, 80, 108

Lavrenko, V. and Croft, W. B. (2001). Relevance-based language models. In *SIGIR*, pages 120–127. ACM. 2, 25, 58, 75, 108

Li, H. (2011). *Learning to Rank for Information Retrieval and Natural Language Processing*. Synthesis Lectures on Human Language Technologies. Morgan & Claypool Publishers. DOI: 10.2200/S00348ED1V01Y201104HLT012. 47, 124

Luk, R. W. P. (2008). On event space and rank equivalence between probabilistic retrieval models. *Inf. Retr.*, 11(6):539–561. DOI: 10.1007/s10791-008-9062-z. 3, 25, 108

Manning, C. D., Raghavan, P., and Schuetze, H., editors (2008). *Introduction to Information Retrieval*. Cambridge University Press. DOI: 10.1017/CBO9780511809071. 3

Margulis, E. (1992). N-poisson document modelling. In Belkin, N., Ingwersen, P., and Pejtersen, M., editors, *Proceedings of the Fifteenth Annual International ACM SIGIR Conference on Research and Development in Information Retrieval*, pages 177–189, New York. 35

Maron, M. and Kuhns, J. (1960). On relevance, probabilistic indexing, and information retrieval. *Journal of the ACM*, 7:216–244. DOI: 10.1145/321033.321035. 1

Meghini, C., Sebastiani, F., Straccia, U., and Thanos, C. (1993). A model of information retrieval based on a terminological logic. In Korfhage, R., Rasmussen, E., and Willett, P., editors, *Proceedings of the Sixteenth Annual International ACM SIGIR Conference on Research and Development in Information Retrieval*, pages 298–308, New York. ACM. 83, 125

Melucci, M. (2008). A basis for information retrieval in context. *ACM Transactions on Information Systems (TOIS)*, 26(3). DOI: 10.1145/1361684.1361687. 87

Metzler, D. (2008). Generalized inverse document frequency. In Shanahan, J. G., Amer-Yahia, S., Manolescu, I., Zhang, Y., Evans, D. A., Kolcz, A., Choi, K.-S., and Chowdhury, A., editors, *CIKM*, pages 399–408. ACM. 16

Metzler, D. and Croft, W. B. (2004). Combining the language model and inference network approaches to retrieval. *Information Processing & Management*, 40(5):735–750. DOI: 10.1016/j.ipm.2004.05.001. 108

Nie, J. (1992). Towards a probabilistic modal logic for semantic-based information retrieval. In Belkin, N., Ingwersen, P., and Pejtersen, M., editors, *Proceedings of the Fifteenth Annual International ACM SIGIR Conference on Research and Development in Information Retrieval*, pages 140–151, New York. 83, 120

Piwowarski, B., Frommholz, I., Lalmas, M., and Van Rijsbergen, K. (2010). What can Quantum Theory Bring to Information Retrieval? In *Proc. 19th International Conference on Information and Knowledge Management*, pages 59–68. DOI: 10.1145/1871437.1871450. 87

Ponte, J. and Croft, W. (1998). A language modeling approach to information retrieval. In Croft, W. B., Moffat, A., van Rijsbergen, C. J., Wilkinson, R., and Zobel, J., editors, *Proceedings of the*

21st Annual International ACM SIGIR Conference on Research and Development in Information Retrieval, pages 275–281, New York. ACM. 1, 49

Robertson, S. (1977). The probability ranking principle in IR. *Journal of Documentation*, 33:294–304. DOI: 10.1108/eb026647. 26

Robertson, S. (2004). Understanding inverse document frequency: On theoretical arguments for idf. *Journal of Documentation*, 60:503–520. DOI: 10.1108/00220410410560582. 3, 96, 109

Robertson, S. (2005). On event spaces and probabilistic models in information retrieval. *Information Retrieval Journal*, 8(2):319–329. DOI: 10.1007/s10791-005-5665-9. 3

Robertson, S., Maron, M., and Cooper, W. (1982). The unified probabilistic model for ir. In Salton, G. and Schneider, H.-J., editors, *Research and Development in Information Retrieval*, pages 108–117, Berlin et al. Springer. DOI: 10.1007/BFb0036332. 121

Robertson, S., S. Walker, S. J., Hancock-Beaulieu, M., and Gatford, M. (1994). Okapi at TREC-3. In *Text REtrieval Conference*. 45

Robertson, S. and Sparck-Jones, K. (1976). Relevance weighting of search terms. *Journal of the American Society for Information Science*, 27:129–146. DOI: 10.1002/asi.4630270302. 1, 30

Robertson, S. E. and Walker, S. (1994). Some simple effective approximations to the 2-Poisson model for probabilistic weighted retrieval. In Croft and van Rijsbergen [1994], pages 232–241. 1, 35, 44, 45

Robertson, S. E., Walker, S., and Hancock-Beaulieu, M. (1995). Large test collection experiments on an operational interactive system: Okapi at TREC. *Information Processing and Management*, 31:345–360. DOI: 10.1016/0306-4573(94)00051-4. 1, 45

Robertson, S. E., Walker, S., and Hancock-Beaulieu, M. (1998). Okapi at trec-7: Automatic ad hoc, filtering, vlc and interactive. In *TREC*, pages 199–210. 45, 47

Robertson, S. E. and Zaragoza, H. (2009). The probabilistic relevance framework: Bm25 and beyond. *Foundations and Trends in Information Retrieval*, 3(4):333–389. DOI: 10.1561/1500000019. 3, 45

Rocchio, J. (1971). Relevance feedback in information retrieval. In Salton [1971]. 1, 74

Roelleke, T. (2003). A frequency-based and a Poisson-based probability of being informative. In *ACM SIGIR*, pages 227–234, Toronto, Canada. DOI: 10.1145/860435.860478. 20

Roelleke, T. and Fuhr, N. (1996). Retrieval of complex objects using a four-valued logic. In Frei, H.-P., Harmann, D., Schäuble, P., and Wilkinson, R., editors, *Proceedings of the 19th International ACM SIGIR Conference on Research and Development in Information Retrieval*, pages 206–214, New York. ACM. 83

Roelleke, T., Tsikrika, T., and Kazai, G. (2006). A general matrix framework for modelling information retrieval. *Journal on Information Processing & Management (IP&M), Special Issue on Theory in Information Retrieval*, 42(1). DOI: 10.1016/j.ipm.2004.11.006. 6, 83, 88

Roelleke, T. and Wang, J. (2006). A parallel derivation of probabilistic information retrieval models. In *ACM SIGIR*, pages 107–114, Seattle, USA. DOI: 10.1145/1148170.1148192. 2, 14, 93

Roelleke, T. and Wang, J. (2008). TF-IDF uncovered: A study of theories and probabilities. In *ACM SIGIR*, pages 435–442, Singapore. DOI: 10.1145/1390334.1390409. 3

Roelleke, T., Wu, H., Wang, J., and Azzam, H. (2008). Modelling retrieval models in a probabilistic relational algebra with a new operator: The relational Bayes. *VLDB Journal*, 17(1):5–37. DOI: 10.1007/s00778-007-0073-y. 125

Salton, G., editor (1971). *The SMART Retrieval System - Experiments in Automatic Document Processing*. Prentice Hall, Englewood, Cliffs, New Jersey. 1, 132

Salton, G., Fox, E., and Wu, H. (1983). Extended Boolean information retrieval. *Communications of the ACM*, 26:1022–1036. DOI: 10.1145/182.358466. 1

Salton, G., Wong, A., and Yang, C. (1975). A vector space model for automatic indexing. *Communications of the ACM*, 18:613–620. DOI: 10.1145/361219.361220. 1

Shtok, A., Kurland, O., and Carmel, D. (2010). Using statistical decision theory and relevance models for query-performance prediction. In Crestani, F., Marchand-Maillet, S., Chen, H.-H., Efthimiadis, E. N., and Savoy, J., editors, *SIGIR*, pages 259–266. ACM. 122

Singhal, A., Buckley, C., and Mitra, M. (1996). Pivoted document length normalisation. In Frei, H., Harmann, D., Schäuble, P., and Wilkinson, R., editors, *Proceedings of the 19th Annual International ACM SIGIR Conference on Research and Development in Information Retrieval*, pages 21–39, New York. ACM. 1

Sparck-Jones, K., Robertson, S., Hiemstra, D., and Zaragoza, H. (2003). Language modelling and relevance. *Language Modelling for Information Retrieval*, pages 57–70. DOI: 10.1007/978-94-017-0171-6_3. 2, 58

Sparck-Jones, K., Walker, S., and Robertson, S. E. (2000). A probabilistic model of information retrieval: development and comparative experiments: Part 1. *Information Processing and Management*, 26:779–808. DOI: 10.1016/S0306-4573(00)00015-7.

Turtle, H. and Croft, W. (1991). Efficient probabilistic inference for text retrieval. In *Proceedings RIAO 91*, pages 644–661, Paris, France.

Turtle, H. and Croft, W. (1992). A comparison of text retrieval models. *The Computer Journal*, 35. DOI: 10.1093/comjnl/35.3.279. 61, 63, 108

Turtle, H. and Croft, W. B. (1990). Inference networks for document retrieval. In Vidick, J.-L., editor, *Proceedings of the 13th International Conference on Research and Development in Information Retrieval*, pages 1–24, New York. ACM. 58

van Rijsbergen, C. J. (1979). *Information Retrieval*. Butterworths, London, 2. edition. http://www.dcs.glasgow.ac.uk/Keith/Preface.html. 3, 30

van Rijsbergen, C. J. (1986). A non-classical logic for information retrieval. *The Computer Journal*, 29(6):481–485. DOI: 10.1093/comjnl/29.6.481. 1, 82, 120

van Rijsbergen, C. J. (1989). Towards an information logic. In Belkin, N. and van Rijsbergen, C. J., editors, *Proceedings of the Twelfth Annual International ACM SIGIR Conference on Research and Development in Information Retrieval*, pages 77–86, New York.

van Rijsbergen, C. J. (2004). *The Geometry of Information Retrieval*. Cambridge University Press. DOI: 10.1017/CBO9780511543333. 3, 87, 123

Wong, S. and Yao, Y. (1995). On modeling information retrieval with probabilistic inference. *ACM Transactions on Information Systems*, 13(1):38–68. DOI: 10.1145/195705.195713. 1, 83, 85, 120

Wu, H. and Roelleke, T. (2009). Semi-subsumed events: A probabilistic semantics for the BM25 term frequency quantification. In *ICTIR (International Conference on Theory in Information Retrieval)*. Springer. DOI: 10.1007/978-3-642-04417-5_43. 17, 123

Xue, X., Jeon, J., and Croft, W. B. (2008). Retrieval models for question and answer archives. In Myaeng, S.-H., Oard, D. W., Sebastiani, F., Chua, T.-S., and Leong, M.-K., editors, *SIGIR*, pages 475–482. ACM. 50

Zaragoza, H., Hiemstra, D., Tipping, M. E., and Robertson, S. E. (2003). Bayesian extension to the language model for ad hoc information retrieval. In *ACM SIGIR*, pages 4–9, Toronto, Canada. DOI: 10.1145/860435.860439.

Zhai, C. (2009). *Statistical Language Models for Information Retrieval*. Morgan & Claypool Publishers. DOI: 10.2200/S00158ED1V01Y200811HLT001. xix, 3, 7, 73, 109, 118

Zhai, C. X., Cohen, W. W., and Lafferty, J. (2003). Beyond independent relevance: methods and evaluation metrics for subtopic retrieval. In *Proceedings of the 26th annual international ACM SIGIR conference on Research and development in informaion retrieval*, SIGIR '03, pages 10–17, New York, NY, USA. ACM. DOI: 10.1145/860435.860440. 123

Author's Biography

THOMAS ROELLEKE

Thomas Roelleke holds a Dr rer nat (Ph.D.) and a Diplom der Ingenieur-Informatik (MSc in Engineering & Computer Science) of the University of Dortmund.

After school education in Meschede, Germany, he attended the b.i.b., the Nixdorf Computer school for professions in informatics, in Paderborn. Nixdorf Computer awarded him a sales and management trainee program, after which he was appointed as product consultant in the Unix/DB/4GL marketing of Nixdorf Computer. He studied Diplom-Ingenieur-Informatik at the University of Dortmund (UniDo), and was later a lecturer/researcher at UniDo. His research focused on probabilistic reasoning and knowledge representations, hypermedia retrieval, and the integration of retrieval and database technologies. His lecturing included information/database systems, object-oriented design and programming, and software engineering. He obtained his Ph.D. in 1999 for the thesis titled "POOL: A probabilistic object-oriented logic for the representation and retrieval of complex objects—a model for hypermedia retrieval". Since 1999, he has been working as a strategic IT consultant, founder and director of small businesses, research fellow, and lecturer at the Queen Mary University of London (QMUL).

Research contributions include a probabilistic relational algebra (PRA), a probabilistic object-oriented logic (POOL), the relational Bayes, a matrix-based framework for IR, a parallel derivation of IR models, a probabilistic interpretation of the BM25-TF based on "semi-subsumed" event occurrences, and theoretical studies of retrieval models.

Thomas Roelleke lives in England, in a village in the middle between buzzy London and beautiful East Anglia.

Index

Printed in the United States
by Baker & Taylor Publisher Services